AMERICA'S MUSICAL LANDSCAPE

AMERICA'S MUSICAL LANDSCAPE

Second Edition

Jean Ferris

Associate Professor
Arizona State University

Madison, Wisconsin•Dubuque, Iowa•Indianapolis, Indiana
Melbourne, Australia•Oxford, England

Book Team

Editor *Kathleen Nietzke*
Developmental Editor *Deborah D. Reinbold*
Production Editor *Kennie Harris*
Designer *Kristyn A. Kalnes*
Art Editor/Art Processor *Kathleen M. Huinker*
Photo Editor *Judi L. David*
Permissions Editor *Vicki Krug*
Visuals/Design Developmental Consultant *Marilyn A. Phelps*
Visuals/Design Freelance Specialist *Mary L. Christianson*
Publishing Services Specialist *Sherry Padden*
Marketing Manager *Carla J. Aspelmeier*
Advertising Manager *Jodi Rymer*

Brown & Benchmark

A Division of Wm. C. Brown Communications, Inc.

Vice President and General Manager *Thomas E. Doran*
Editor in Chief *Edgar J. Laube*
Executive Managing Editor *Ed Bartell*
Executive Editor *Stan Stoga*
National Sales Manager *Eric Ziegler*
Director of CourseResource *Kathy Law Laube*
Director of CourseSystems *Chris Rogers*

Director of Marketing *Sue Simon*
Director of Production *Vickie Putman Caughron*
Imaging Group Manager *Chuck Carpenter*
Manager of Visuals and Design *Faye M. Schilling*
Design Manager *Jac Tilton*
Art Manager *Janice Roerig*
Permissions/Records Manager *Connie Allendorf*

Wm. C. Brown Communications, Inc.

Chairman Emeritus *Wm. C. Brown*
Chairman and Chief Executive Officer *Mark C. Falb*
President and Chief Operating Officer *G. Franklin Lewis*
Corporate Vice President, President of WCB Manufacturing *Roger Meyer*

Cover and part openers 1–9: *Road to Taos* by Mary Silverwood, 1991.
Pastel painting on black rag paper, 21″ × 29″.

Consulting Editor *Frederick W. Westphal*

Library of Congress Catalog Card Number: 92–70780

ISBN 0–697–12516–5
    0–697–16946–4 (textbook with cassettes)

Printed in the United States of America by Wm. C. Brown Communications, Inc.,
2460 Kerper Boulevard, Dubuque, IA 52001

10 9 8 7 6 5 4 3 2 1

To Chiara, Meghan, and Caitlyn,
who bring us joy,
and who already know the joy of music

CONTENTS

chapter 2
European Precursors of American Music   31

chapter 3
At the Time of the Settlers   39

PART 2
THE EIGHTEENTH CENTURY   53

chapter 4
The Age of Classicism   54

PART 5

AMERICAN MUSIC COMES OF AGE 133

PART 6

MUSICAL THEATER 163

PART 8

JAZZ   227

chapter 27
The Many Moods of Rock   283

postlude
Some New Sounds of Music   290

COLOR PLATES

LISTENING EXAMPLES

Listening Examples are recorded on a ninety-minute cassette that is available from the publisher.

Optional Listening Examples

Optional Listening Examples are printed in the Instructor's Manual and may be copied and distributed to students.

PREFACE

With the exception of certain scholars and enthusiasts, Americans have remained largely unaware of the treasure trove that comprises their rich musical heritage. Thus, the recent offerings of courses based upon the American music experience are welcome indeed, though one is inevitably disappointed at what must be left out of a one-semester course.

However, to accentuate the positive, we tackle here the happy task of introducing to non-music majors musical terms and (more significantly) concepts using selected examples of American music. These serve every bit as well as the European works commonly included in the traditional music appreciation class, while providing the added advantage of expanding the familiar repertoire to include American works. Every kind of music—popular and classical, instrumental and vocal, religious and secular, serious and frivolous, practical or for art's sake only—is included in the American experience and belongs in a survey of American music.

Throughout the text, I have related music to other arts, intending to help those more familiar with visual or literary concepts. Because non-musicians are often better able to grasp concepts of style and technique in terms of visual rather than aural experience, I believe that such comparison has pedagogical as well as aesthetic value. Thus, it is no coincidence that the compatibility of the arts is suggested in the title of this text. It is also exquisitely expressed in Asher B. Durand's painting *Kindred Spirits* (color plate 1), which portrays an American poet (William Cullen Bryant) and an American painter (Thomas Cole) sharing aesthetic appreciation and proud admiration for their country's natural splendours. The painting served as inspiration for and reinforcement of the concepts of this text, which considers all of the arts as kindred spirits and the American arts as supreme examples of human accomplishment. Further, music and the other arts are related throughout the text to the social context in which they were conceived.

The scope of the book has been limited in quantity and variety of material, with a one-semester course in mind. Most instructors will probably find they cannot include everything within that time, but the text may be adapted to allow teachers of varied preference and inclination to choose what to include and what to omit. The addition of a chapter on Native American musics fills a long-standing and regrettable void, and the fact that it was written by an authority in the field, Dr. J. Richard Haefer, assures its integrity. Of course, we barely scratch the surface of a rich and unique music experience, but is that not the purpose of a survey course?

Another particularly significant enhancement in the second edition is an accompanying ninety-minute cassette, which includes all of the Listening Examples printed in the text. Guides for additional examples, referred to in the text as Optional Listening Examples, are printed in the Instructor's Manual and may be copied and distributed to students, greatly increasing the flexibility of the text. Those pieces that are less readily accessible in the usual music library have been included on the cassette, while recordings of the longer, major works mentioned in the Instructor's Manual should be generally available to those who wish to use them. The difficult decision not to include representative rock examples was reached in the interest of making the best use of space on the tape, and in consideration of the fact that instructors are likely to differ widely in their choice of which modern popular pieces to present. Further, such examples are widely available. For those who prefer a structured list of representative examples, several rock texts now on the market include extensive discographies.

The organization of the text is uncomplicated and straightforward, beginning with an introductory outline of essential terms and basic music concepts that may be assigned for reading at the beginning of the term or recommended for reference throughout the course. Subsequent chapters generally follow a chronological scheme that serves well through the nineteenth century. However, the unprecedented variety and complexity of twentieth-century music render consideration by genre more expedient after 1900.

My gratitude to those who assisted in developing the first edition remains undimmed, and I wish to name again Dr. Wallace Rave, who contributed to that edition's section on jazz, and Dr. Robert D. Reynolds, who participated generously in the preparation of my first textbook and who has provided inspiration and support ever since. Many thanks to Dr. J. Richard Haefer for the authoritative chapter he contributed to this edition. The editors and the complete book team at Brown and Benchmark have been endlessly helpful and delightful to work with, and for editors Deborah Reinbold and Kennie Harris, I have heartfelt affection as well as professional admiration. I am grateful, too, to the following prepublication reviewers, whose suggestions immeasurably enhanced the text: Lee Ann Anderson, Hiram College; Patricia Gray, Rhodes College; Mara Parker, California State University–Stanislaus; and Charles J. Scanzello, Kutztown University.

INTRODUCTION

Although most of us have little or no formal training in music, we find that music enhances many of our social, religious, and work-related experiences. We dine, dance, drive, work, and study to music. Music regulates the rhythms of exercising, marching, and dancing. It soothes or excites our emotions and provides entertainment and intellectual stimulation.

The more we understand about musical forms and the elements that constitute the materials of music, the better we are prepared to enjoy music of all kinds. Recognition of the historical context in which music was conceived also enhances appreciation. An awareness of the relationships between music and the other arts of a given period adds a further dimension to our understanding and pleasure.

In the spirit of shared appreciation expressed in color plate 1, we shall explore the accomplishments of American artists in every field, but especially in the realm of music. It is my personal wish that your delight in listening to music will increase immeasurably as you explore the many and varied aspects of America's musical landscape.

THE ELEMENTS
OF MUSICAL SOUND

Prelude

Musicians generally recognize five basic **elements of music:** rhythm, meter, melody, harmony, and timbre. (Meter is sometimes considered a quality of rhythm, but here we shall treat it as an element in its own right.) These are the fundamental materials of which music is composed.

As we listen to music, one of the elements—a memorable melody, a compelling rhythm, or the unusual sound of an exotic musical instrument— may particularly attract our attention at a given time. More often, though, we are affected by the *combination* of two or more of the elements of music, without considering the significance of each one. (In somewhat the same way, we may savor a delicious casserole without methodically analyzing the names and proportions of each ingredient.)

In any case, an understanding of the elements of music enhances our listening ability and enables us to discuss a musical composition in some detail. An increased awareness of what we hear also significantly increases our capacity to enjoy all kinds of music.

Rhythm has to do with time relationships in music. Because music always consists of some arrangement of long and short sounds and silences, music always has rhythm, and rhythm is the most basic of the elements.

RHYTHM

The system of music notation used in the Western world indicates the *proportional* length of each sound and silence. That is, written music dictates the duration of each sound or silence only in relation to other sounds and silences in the piece. Musical sounds are written as **notes,** and notated silences are called **rests.**

Rhythmic values are expressed in the familiar terminology of fractions (table P1.1). Thus, the value of a *half note* is half that of a *whole note*. But the specific duration of a half note depends upon the *tempo*, or rate of speed, at which the music is performed.

Notating Music

	TABLE P1.1				
	Rhythmic Notation				

TABLE P1.1

Rhythmic Notation

This table assumes the quarter note equals one beat. Any other note may equal one beat instead, and the other note values then change proportionately.

Notated Symbol	Name	Rest	Number of Beats per Note	Number of Notes Equal to 4 Beats
o	whole note	—	4	1
♩	half note	—	2	2
♩	quarter note	𝄾	1	4
♪	eighth note	𝄾	$\frac{1}{2}$	8
♪	sixteenth note	𝄾	$\frac{1}{4}$	16

Tempo

Tempo, which means time in Italian, is one of many Italian words that have been adopted into a virtually universal music language. During the sixteenth and seventeenth centuries, Italy was the center of music activity, and musicians traveled from all over the Western world to study there. Before returning to their own countries, they absorbed the techniques and much of the terminology of their Italian masters, which they then shared with their own students and patrons at home.

Since that time, many Italian music terms have been used all over the world. However, as nationalistic tendencies strengthened, beginning in the mid-nineteenth century, some composers preferred to use their native languages to indicate the tempo, as well as other expressive characteristics, of their compositions.

Concert audiences quickly become familiar with the common tempo terms—in Italian or in other languages—for they are regularly used in printed concert programs today. Table P1.2 includes the most common Italian words for tempos.

A more precise method of indicating tempo is with the **metronome,** a mechanical instrument that may be set to sound regular beats within a wide range of fast and slow tempos. Some metronomes provide a visual as well as an audible expression of the beat (fig. P1.1). The metronome indicates how many times a particular note, or its equivalent, should occur in one minute. For example, ♩ = **60** means that *one quarter note* (or *two eighth notes,* or any equivalent) will occur at the rate of sixty times a minute.

TABLE P1.2
Common Tempo Indications

largo	slow; "broad"
adagio	slow; "at ease"
andante	moderately slow; "walking" tempo
moderato	moderate
allegro	fast; cheerful
presto	very fast
vivace	lively
molto	very (*allegro molto* = very fast)
non troppo	not too much (*allegro non troppo* = not too fast)
con brio	with spirit

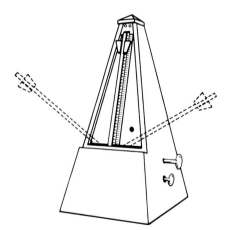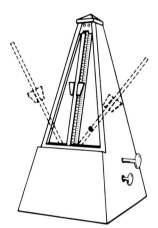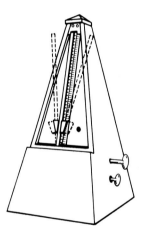

Placing the weight at the top of the arm marks a slow beat.

Lowering the weight increases the tempo to moderate . . .

. . . or fast.

Figure P1.1

A metronome.

METER

Just as the words in a sentence may contain any number of accented and unaccented syllables, musical sounds may occur without specific rhythmic organization. If, however, musical sounds are arranged in rhythmic *patterns,* similar to those of poetry as opposed to prose, we say the music is **metered.**

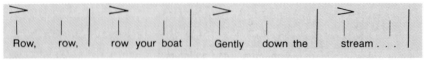

Duple meter

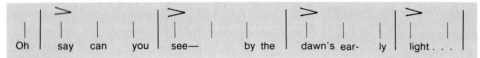

Triple meter

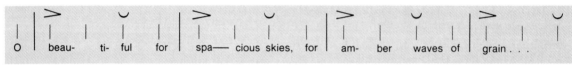

Quadruple meter

Figure P1.2

Common meters, showing accents.

Measures

Meter organizes rhythm into units called **measures,** each containing a particular number of pulses or **beats.** The common meters are *duple* (two beats per measure), *triple* (three beats per measure), and *quadruple* (four beats per measure).

In Western practice, the first beat of each measure is normally **accented.** If there are four or more beats per measure, there is at least one secondary accent as well. For example, in quadruple meter (fig. P1.2), the secondary accent falls on the third beat.

MELODY

Musical sounds are called **tones** and are caused by something vibrating at a particular **frequency,** or rate of speed. Tones are said to be "high" or "low" in **pitch,** depending upon the rate of vibration of the medium producing the sound. The faster a string on a violin or the column of air in a trumpet is vibrating, the higher the level of pitch. Much as a sentence is a meaningful succession of words, a **melody** is a meaningful succession of tones of various levels of pitch.

Tones have *letter* names, **A** through **G.** The **interval,** or distance between tones, is named according to the *number* of tones it includes. For example, from **A** to **B** is a *second,* from **A** to **C,** a *third,* and so on. The most basic interval is the *eighth,* or **octave,** in which the higher of the two tones vibrates at exactly twice the rate of the lower tone.

The two tones of an octave share the same letter name, and they sound nearly alike, because the simple relationship of their frequencies (the ratio 2:1) causes little tension between them. All keys on a keyboard that bear

The short strings on the harp produce higher pitches than the long strings because the short strings vibrate more rapidly. (H. Armstrong Roberts, Inc.)

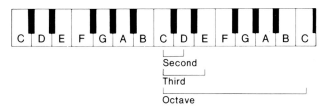

Figure P1.3

A piano keyboard, indicating intervals of a second, a third, and an octave.

the same letter name *look* the same as well, for they occupy the same position relative to other keys. For example, if we start at the left of the keyboard and move up, we see that the last white key before the third of the three black keys is always an **A** (fig. P1.3). Similarly, **D** is always the white note between the two black notes on a keyboard.

Figure P1.4

The major and minor scales. (*a*) The pattern of whole (W) and half (H) steps that constitutes a *major* scale. (*b*) The pattern of whole and half steps that constitutes a *minor* scale.

(a)

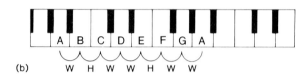

(b)

Scales

Melodies are based upon stepwise rising or descending patterns of pitches within the range of an octave; these patterns are called **scales.** By the seventeenth century, two particular seven-note scales had been accepted as those that best served European composers of concert music. These, the **major** and the **minor** scales, continue to be prevalent in Western music today.

Major and Minor Scales

The major and minor scales, also sometimes called the **diatonic** scales, each include two **half steps** (the closest distance between two keys on a keyboard) and five **whole steps** (the equivalent of two half steps). However, the music based upon each of them differs in effect because of the different *order* in which the half and whole steps occur (fig. P1.4). For instance, from the second to the third step of the major scale is a *whole* step, but from the second to the third step of the minor scale is a *half* step—producing an entirely different effect.

The white notes of the octave from **C** to **C** on the keyboard correspond to the pattern of the *major* scale. By following the same ascending or descending pattern of half and whole steps, we may begin on *any* tone and produce a major scale.

The white notes of the octave from **A** to **A** correspond to the pattern of the *minor* scale. By following that pattern of half and whole steps, we may begin on any tone and produce a minor scale.

If you can play a keyboard instrument, you might play the first three notes of "Doe, a Deer" from *The Sound of Music,* beginning on **C.** These are the first three notes of the major scale. Now *lower* the third tone by a half step—or begin playing on **A** and use all white keys—and you will hear how the melody would begin if it were based upon a minor scale.

Tonic

The first tone of a major or minor scale is called the **tonic.** It represents a kind of home base, from which a piece is likely to begin and on which it is even more likely to end. Each of the tones in a major or minor scale bears

(a) Smooth melody line   (b) Angular melody line

Figure P1.5

Melodic contours.

a specific relationship, relatively distant or close, to the tonic. For example, the fifth step of the scale, called the **dominant,** is the tone most closely related to tonic. It is heard frequently during a piece, and it seems to lead directly back to tonic, or home base.

Key

The tonic names the **key**—sometimes called the **tonality**—of a composition. For example, we say a piece is in the *key of A major,* meaning that the tonic note is A and the tones are primarily those of the major scale. Put another way, a piece based upon the D minor scale is said to be in the key of D minor.

Melodies of course have rhythm, because the tones of a melody occur in some order of long and/or short sounds. If a melody is particularly singable and memorable and seems complete in itself—as in a children's song or folk song—we call it a **tune.** A different kind of melody is a brief, fragmentary melodic idea, or **motive,** that recurs throughout a piece, particularly in instrumental music. Probably the most famous motive in Western music is the four-note "knocking" pattern that begins Beethoven's Symphony no. 5.

Melody is a linear concept in the sense that we could draw a line from one notated tone to another. Thus, a melody has a distinctive shape, or **contour,** which may be angular (with large leaps between the tones) or smooth (with tones that are closely connected) (fig. P1.5). Comparing the melody of "My country, 'tis of thee" (smooth) with that of "Oh, say, can you see" (angular) may clarify this distinction.

The melodies of European and American music are generally accompanied by vertical combinations of sounds that we call *harmony.*

Further Characteristics of Melody

Harmony is the simultaneous sounding of two or more different tones in a logical or meaningful (not necessarily beautiful) manner. The harmonic system that has governed most Western music for nearly four hundred years is based upon the tones of the major and minor scales, and is called the **tonal system** of harmony.

The purposeful combination of *three* or more different tones is called a **chord.**

HARMONY

The most basic chord in the tonal system consists of two superimposed thirds and is called a **triad** (fig. P1.6). Triads bear the same relationship to tonic and to each other as the tones upon which they are built. Thus, the strongest relationship is between the tonic triad (often represented by the Roman numeral **I**) and the triad built upon the fifth note of the scale, or the dominant (**V**).

Basic Chords of the Tonal System

Figure P1.6

Triads on each note of the C major scale.

I ii iii IV V vi vii I

Figure P1.7

Cadences: (a) Dominant (V) to tonic (I) in C major. (b) The cadence formula IV–I. (c) The cadence formula IV–V–I.

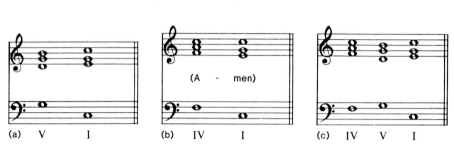

(a) V   I   (b) IV   I   (c) IV   V   I

In the context of a composition, the dominant triad seems to lead or pull toward the tonic. Therefore, many compositions end with the harmonic **cadence,** or ending pattern, **V–I.** (The root of a chord is typically in the bass, as in figure P1.7*a,* but the notes of the triad may be rearranged, or inverted, for melodic reasons.)

The next closest chord to tonic is the triad built upon the fourth, or **subdominant,** step of the scale, which provides a somewhat weaker drive toward tonic. The subdominant triad (**IV**) may resolve directly to tonic, as in the "Amen" at the end of a hymn (fig. P1.7*b*), or it may lead through V to I, as in figure P1.7*c*.

The I, IV, and V chords are particularly important not only at cadence points, but throughout traditional Western music. Many simple melodies are effectively accompanied by just these three closely related chords.

Texture

Harmony may be achieved by accompanying a melody with *chords,* or by combining a melody with one or more *melodic lines,* thus producing more than one tone at the same time. The manner in which a melody is, or is not, accompanied by harmony determines the **texture** of the music.

Monophony

An unaccompanied melody line is **monophonic** in texture, the prefix "mono" referring to one line of melody. If you sing a song in the shower or play a tune with one finger or in octaves on the piano, the resulting single line of melody is an example of monophony. Any number of voices and instruments may perform in monophonic texture, as long as they all perform the same melody, at the same time—that is, in **unison.**

Homophony

If, however, you accompany a song or piano tune with *chords,* the texture is **homophonic** (or "chordal"). This combination of melody plus harmony is the sound we experience when an organ accompanies congregational

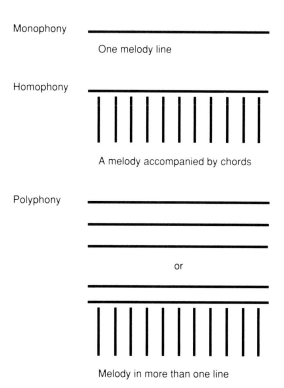

Figure P1.8

Texture in music.

hymns, a band plays "The Star Spangled Banner," or a singer strums chords on a guitar while singing a folk song.

Polyphony

Harmony in music is also achieved by combining two or more *melody* lines, in which case the texture is **polyphonic**. (The prefix "poly" indicates more than one of something occurring at the same time.) For example, we enjoy singing rounds (see page 69) because, simply by beginning a melody at different times, two or more voices produce harmony.

Both homophony and polyphony achieve harmony in music, but the textures differ in the manner in which the harmony is produced. Homophony is basically a chordal concept, whereas polyphony involves the combination of melodic lines. To put it differently, homophony may be considered a vertical, and polyphony a linear, technique (fig. P1.8).

The *quality* of a musical sound is called its **timbre**. Each musical instrument has a distinctive timbre, according to its size and the material of which it is made. For example, the timbre, or "color," of the sound produced by a violin is readily distinguished from that produced by a flute.

The manner in which an instrument is played often affects its timbre. Thus, the sound produced by plucking the string of a violin differs significantly from the sound made when the same string is bowed.

TIMBRE

TABLE P1.3 Dynamic Levels		
Levels of Volume		
Italian Term	**Abbreviation**	**English Meaning**
pianissimo	*pp*	very soft
piano	*p*	soft
mezzopiano	*mp*	moderately soft
mezzoforte	*mf*	moderately loud
forte	*f*	loud
fortissimo	*ff*	very loud

The timbre of a musical sound is also affected by its level of pitch. Notice how the high tones of the piano differ in timbre as well as pitch from its low tones. Similarly, men's and women's voices are distinguished in terms of timbre as well as in levels of pitch.

Dynamics

Another factor that affects the timbre of a voice or instrument is the loudness or softness of the sound, which is called its **dynamic level.** Of course, changes in dynamic level are often used by composers for purposes other than changes of tone quality. They can have powerful effects upon the emotions, for example. Dynamic changes might also be used in **program music**—instrumental music that "tells" a story or "describes" a scene—for extra-musical effects.

The Italian words **piano** and **forte** respectively indicate "soft" and "loud" in music. Other terms for dynamic levels, along with their abbreviations commonly found in written music, are included in table P1.3. These terms are frequently used, so you may refer to this list as you come across them either inside or outside the classroom.

ELEMENTS OF THE AMERICAN SOUND

The national origin of music is not always apparent, but sometimes we identify certain effects with a culture or nationality. During some periods of music history, composers generally emulated the style of whatever country currently dominated a particular kind of music. For example, "Italian" opera, "French" ballet, and "German" symphonic music were prodigiously produced by eighteenth- and nineteenth-century composers of various nationalities.

In the latter part of the nineteenth century, however, a wave of nationalism swept Europe. At that time, many composers wrote music based upon the folk and religious musics of their own culture in an effort to establish a characteristic national style. Some even wrote pieces in appreciative imitation of national styles *other* than their own. Today, increased opportunities for travel and communication greatly encourage the transfer of characteristics from one culture to the art of another, a process called **acculturation.**

However, Americans remained effectively isolated from the European experience until about the mid-nineteenth century, and so they could not be stimulated by significant developments in the arts abroad. The settlers, of course, were preoccupied with urgent matters of survival, which precluded much interest in music and art. Besides, in most cases, their religion was not supportive of the arts. And because the settlers came from various cultural backgrounds, a significant period of time had to elapse before a characteristic style could evolve in the New World.

During our century, certain musical effects are generally recognized as sounding American. They are certainly not reflected in all American music, but you may recognize some of these characteristics by considering them in terms of the elements of music.

Rhythm and Meter

American rhythms, metered or unmetered, are often more flexible than the rhythms of European music. Western composers have always varied rhythmic effects by placing accents between beats or on normally weak beats in the technique called **syncopation.** However, the bold and consistent syncopation of some American classical, as well as popular, music has a distinctive flavor. Much of the refreshing spontaneity we associate with some characteristically American pieces is in fact derived from their delightfully asymmetrical rhythms.

Melody

The long, irregular melodies of a number of American vocal and instrumental works are sometimes thought to reflect the wide-open spaces of our land. These flexible melodic phrases also seem to suggest the informality and the sense of personal freedom characteristic of American life.

Composers sometimes quote or imitate a familiar American melody for programmatic or nationalistic effect. For example, some Americans have used black spirituals, Indian melodies, cowboy songs, or early American hymn tunes as musical references to particular American experiences.

Harmony

No significant differences in the harmony of mainstream European and American composers are generally recognized. However, pioneer American composers were largely unaware of (and more significantly, not interested in) the conventional rules of Western (European) music. Therefore, the music of the first American composers (the First New England School, see pages 66–71) includes some refreshing harmonic surprises.

Timbre

Certain pieces of American concert music have borrowed the timbres of jazz, which evolved in this country from a combination of European, African, and American experiences. (The jazz influence is also reflected, of course, in many of the melodies and rhythms of American music.) Jazz musicians introduced a broad range of instrumental techniques, including the use of mutes and other devices, that significantly alter the timbre of musical instruments. Many of these effects are also heard in some twentieth-century American symphonic music.

Some Examples of Music with an American Sound

George Gershwin's *Rhapsody in Blue* (Optional Listening Example) effectively illustrates jazz effects in symphonic music. And *Adagio for Strings* by Samuel Barber (Optional Listening Example) includes the long, irregular melodic lines often considered characteristically American. We will study these pieces in some depth later in the course, but since you are already equipped to consider them in terms of their melodic style, rhythmic effects, tempo, changes in dynamic level, and timbres, you might enjoy hearing them now. What emotional reactions do they evoke—and how do they do so? Do you agree that they have an American flavor, and could you explain your opinion?

Of course, many subtle effects of the supposed "American sound" simply defy explanation. Syncopation and jazzy timbres are used by European composers without producing music we consider American in character. Perhaps you will sense in some American music a certain audacity, a saucy effect, an expansiveness, or a peculiar irregularity that simply "sounds American."

SUMMARY

Rhythm involves time relationships in music. Rhythmic notation indicates the proportional durations of tones in relation to others. The tempo of a piece may be indicated with descriptive terms or metronome markings.

Meter organizes rhythm into measures of a certain number of beats, the first of which is usually accented. The common meters are duple, triple, and quadruple.

A melody is a meaningful succession of tones, and represents the linear aspect of music. An unaccompanied melody line is monophonic in texture.

Harmony is a vertical concept, adding depth to musical sounds. Harmony is achieved by accompanying a melody with chords (homophonic texture) or by combining melodic lines (polyphony).

Timbre is the characteristic quality or color of a musical sound. Timbre is affected by many factors, including the pitch and dynamic level of the sound and the way an instrument is played.

The manner in which a composer combines the elements of music contributes to the style of a composition. A certain irreverence, an expansive melodic line, and a humorous glimmer are among the subtle, virtually indefinable, and apparently inimitable characteristics we recognize as distinctively American.

TERMS TO REVIEW

elements of music   The basic materials of which music is composed.

rhythm   The arrangement of time in music.

notes   The symbols with which music is written down.

rests   The symbols that indicate cessation of musical sound.

tempo   The rate of speed at which music is performed.

metronome   An instrument to measure tempo.

meter   The organization of rhythm into patterns of strong and weak beats.

measure   A unit containing a number of beats.

beat   Another word for pulse in music.

accent   A strong sound.

tone   A sound with a specific pitch.

frequency   The rate of a sound wave's vibration.

pitch   The highness or lowness of a sound.

melody   A meaningful succession of pitches.

interval   The distance between two tones.

octave   The interval of an eighth.

scale   A stepwise rising or ascending pattern of pitches within the range of an octave.

major, minor scales   The tonal scales, upon which most Western music has been based for nearly four centuries.

diatonic scales   The major and minor scales.

half step   The smallest interval on a keyboard, and the closest interval in traditional Western music.

whole step   An interval equal to two half steps.

tonic   The first and most important note of a tonal scale, often indicated by the Roman numeral I.

dominant   The fifth tone of the major or minor scale, the tone most closely related to tonic. Often represented by the Roman numeral V.

key or **tonality**   The name of the tonic upon which a tonal piece is based.

tune   A melody that is easily recognized, memorized, and sung.

motive   A short melodic phrase that may be developed.

contour   The shape or outline of a melody formed by its notes.

harmony   The simultaneous sounding of two or more different tones.

tonal system   The system of harmony that has governed Western music for nearly four centuries.

chord   A meaningful combination of three or more tones.

triad   The most basic chord in the tonal system. It consists of three alternate pitches, or two superimposed thirds.

cadence   A melodic or harmonic closing pattern.

subdominant   The fourth tone of the major or minor scale, represented as IV.

texture   The manner in which melodic lines are used in music.

monophony   One unaccompanied melodic line.

unison   The same pitch, performed at the same or at different octaves.

homophony   A melodic line accompanied by chordal harmony.

polyphony   The simultaneous combination of two or more melodic lines.

timbre   The characteristic quality of the sound of a voice or instrument.

dynamic level   The level of volume (loudness or softness) of a musical sound.

program music   Instrumental music that describes a story, scene, idea, or event.

piano   Soft.

forte   Loud.

acculturation   The process by which one culture absorbs characteristics of another.

syncopation   The occurrence of accents in unexpected places.

SUGGESTIONS FOR LISTENING

Duple meter:
John Philip Sousa, "The Stars and Stripes Forever," Listening Example 24, p. 147

Flexible, unmetered rhythms:
African drumming

Monophonic texture:
"Barbara Allen" (unaccompanied), Listening Example 6, p. 49
William Billings, "When Jesus Wept" (in unison), Listening Example 9, p. 70

Homophonic texture:
Martin Luther, "A Mighty Fortress Is Our God," Listening Example 4, p. 33

Polyphonic texture:
William Billings, "When Jesus Wept" (in canon), Listening Example 9, p. 70
John Knowles Paine, "Fuga Giocosa," Listening Example 20, p. 137

Contrasts in dynamic level:
Charles Griffes, *Pleasure Dome of Kubla Khan,* Optional Listening Example*

Motivic melody:
Johann Friedrich Peter, Quintet V, second movement, Optional Listening Example*

Program music:
Charles Griffes, *Pleasure Dome of Kubla Khan,* Optional Listening Example*

*Guides for Optional Listening Examples are in the Instructor's Manual and may be copied and distributed to students.

European music intended to sound American:
Maurice Ravel, *Violin Sonata*
Igor Stravinsky, "Ragtime"
Claude Debussy, "Golliwog's Cakewalk" from *Children's Corner*
Darius Milhaud, "La Création du Monde" ("The Creation of the World")

part 1

PREPARATION FOR
AN AMERICAN MUSIC

NORTH AMERICAN
INDIAN MUSIC

Chapter 1

The ancestors of today's North American Indians began arriving on this continent more than 12,000—some people believe as many as 40,000—years ago. By the time Christopher Columbus arrived in the New World, well over three hundred Indian cultures were living in what is today the United States. Thus, it is not surprising that there is no *one* Indian culture today. Native Americans, whom Columbus called Indians because he believed he had landed in the Indies, have many different kinds of music, ceremony, dance, art, and ways of maintaining and supporting life. Their languages were derived from more than a dozen different language families, and hundreds of local dialects have evolved.

Much of what Americans know about Native Americans has been learned from movies and television. Some recent movies, including the popular *Dances with Wolves* (1991), have presented a sympathetic view of the cultural norms, values, and ceremonies (the **lifeways**) by which Native Americans live. However, most members of mainstream American society have little understanding of Indian culture. One effective way for outsiders to appreciate the culture of the Native Americans is by understanding their arts.

VISUAL ARTS

Although early Indian cultures had little free time for recreational purposes, many Native Americans found time for artistic endeavors of a practical nature. For example, they made and often decorated utilitarian objects such as cooking baskets, pottery, and even music instruments. The materials they used, depending upon the location and the environment in which they lived, included wood, cane, earth, grass, gourd, hide, and metal.

Some early Indian paintings were made directly on the hides of shields, drums, or teepees. Others were done on hides that were carefully folded or rolled up and opened for viewing only when necessary. These paintings often depicted scenes of daily life, such as an encampment, a battle, or an important ceremony (fig. 1.1).

Written historical documents were not made by Indians prior to the late nineteenth century, but their early artistic endeavors show us much about lifeways prior to that time. For example, archeological excavations

Figure 1.1
American Indian hide painting of a person seated in front of a Peyote altar holding a rattle, feather, and staff. (© 1980 by J. Richard Haefer. Used by permission.)

have yielded decorated pottery such as that made by the Hohokam in Arizona over eight hundred years ago, illustrating dances similar to those practiced by their O'odham and Pima descendants today. Three-dimensional art is found in the Hopis' visual representations of cultural deities called *Kachinas* and in the decoration of utilitarian objects, as mentioned previously.

In the late nineteenth century, European drawing tools and techniques were introduced to many cultures, and by the mid-twentieth century, the well-known Institute for American Indian Arts was established in Santa Fe, New Mexico. Today the works of dozens of American Indian artists, such as **Fritz Scholder** and **Alan Hauser,** are in the collections of major art museums.

LITERATURE

Traditionally, Indian culture has been passed from one generation to the next by **oral tradition**—the spoken rather than the written word. In this way, Indians have maintained a large body of *oral literature,* including myths, legends, other kinds of stories, oration, and many kinds of poetry. Song texts are among the most prolific examples of Indian oral literature.

Tales

Traditional tales were recited at specific times of the year to remind the people of their history, moral values, and other cultural norms. Because some of these stories were extremely long—often lasting four to seven days or more—it is amazing to non-oral cultures that they were memorized and repeated, with little or no change, year after year, in large public ceremonies.

In addition to these large ceremonies, many short tales exist that are often humorous in nature. *Coyote* is a central figure in many cultures, and humorous stories about Coyote are often used to teach cultural values. One such tale, typical of many that describe the position and habits of natural creatures within Indian lifeways, concerns Coyote and another well-known character, *Trickster.*

> Coyote has tricked Trickster many times in the past, and now Trickster seeks revenge. He puts a horse soundly to sleep, and then sends Mouse to Coyote with a message: "Tell Coyote, 'My grandson, there is an animal dead over there, and I was unable to move him. Pull it to one side, and then we will be able to have it to ourselves.' " Mouse willingly delivers the message, and Coyote, delighted, runs to where the horse is asleep. As Trickster watches, Mouse ties the horse's tail to Coyote. Coyote begins to pull—and wakes up the horse, who is frightened at finding an animal tied to its tail. The horse jumps up and begins racing at full speed toward the village, dragging Coyote like a branch behind him. Trickster shouts, "Just look at him, our son-in-law Coyote! He is doing something disgraceful!" All the people run out and are very surprised to see Coyote tied to the horse's tail, bouncing up and down. The horse finally reaches his master, who unties Coyote; but Coyote is very much ashamed. He sits up, his mouth twitching, and without even returning to his lodge, leaves the village, never to live among people again. If a person sees him anywhere, he is ashamed, and when one gets very close to him, his mouth twitches in remembrance of his shame long ago.[1]

Written Literature

In recent years, a body of written Indian literature has developed as modern authors, often working within the university environment, have produced collections of poetry, short stories, novels, and nonfiction in the Western tradition. **M. Scott Momaday** and **Vine Deloria** have been most successful in the middle years of this century. Among the many younger Indian authors publishing today is the poet **Joy Harjo,** whose books have been well received.

MUSIC

In American Indian cultures, it is difficult to separate music from dance, ritual, and ceremony. In fact, most cultures do not have a word for music in their traditional language, speaking rather of *song,* or of *song and dance,* as part of *ceremony.* Therefore, if we are to understand the Indians' music, we must also understand their ceremonies, rites, and culture.

General Characteristics

Indian music is essentially song, and there are as many different sounds to Indian songs as there are Indian cultures. Of course, some cultures share similar music traits, and to Western listeners the music of all American Indians may sound alike at first.

Indian music is generally monophonic. That is, melodies may be doubled at the octave by male and female voices singing together, but there is no harmonic accompaniment. Rather, songs are usually accompanied by one or more rattles or drums, providing a percussive effect. Song texts may

---

1. From *The Trickster* by Paul Radin. Copyright © 1956, Schocken Books.

be in the native language (or, in the twentieth century, in English), or they may utilize a series of vocables based on consonant-vowel clusters such as *hey, yeh,* or *nay.*

Melodies generally begin at a high pitch and have a descending melodic phrase of varying shape. The *scales* on which melodies are based may have as few as four tones or as many as seven. Most melodic *intervals* are small, usually seconds and thirds.

Strophic Form

Normally, music is organized in some manner that provides a sense of structure or formal design. As in the other arts, *form* in music is based upon some combination of *unity,* or repetition, and *variety,* or contrast.

The form of many Indian songs is fairly simple. It is called **strophic,** indicating that there are two or more verses (strophes) of text, all set to the same melody. The balance between unity and variety in strophic form depends upon the text, which may be different for each verse or the same. Indian songs are often simply several repetitions of text to the same short tune.

There are several methods of classifying music instruments, but we normally recognize at least three families of instruments: *percussion, wind,* and *strings.* Percussion instruments are struck or rubbed in some manner—for example, drums by a drumstick, a cymbal by another cymbal, rattles by seeds inside the instruments. Sound is produced in wind instruments by activating the column(s) of air, usually by blowing into or across an opening in the instrument. String instruments may be bowed, strummed, or plucked.

North American Indians use **sound instruments,** as they call them, to support or "hold up" songs, but there is little purely instrumental music. Only flute songs exist as melody alone, with no text, and the flute is said to sing the melody. Sound instruments fall into all three instrument families, but the basic types are rattles, rasps, drums, whistles, and flutes.

Sound Instruments

Percussion Instruments

Rattles, the most common and widespread music instrument of the American Indians, may be either *container* or *suspension* in nature. **Container rattles** are made of gourd, hide, bark, pottery, or other material into which is placed some type of "rattle element," like small pebbles or sacred corn or beans. They are played either by shaking them in time to the song or by swinging them in a circular motion to produce a continuous sound, and sometimes both means of sound production are used in the same song.

The carving and decorating of music instruments has more than aesthetic significance to Indian cultures. The decorations on the container rattle in figure 1.2, for example, depict the closeness of the Northwest Coast Indians to nature, particularly to the sea.

For **suspension rattles,** objects such as deer hooves or shells are suspended from a stick. These instruments are frequently associated with ceremonial activities, such as healing rites or the girl's puberty ceremony.

Figure 1.2

Two Northwest Coast carved wooden rattles from the Tlingit Culture, carved with double birds' heads. These date from the late nineteenth century and come from the area around Sitka, Alaska. (© 1980 by J. Richard Haefer. Used by permission.)

Rasps are normally made from a long stick of wood into which notches have been carved. The stick is then rubbed with another stick or a piece of bone (such as the shoulder blade of a sheep) to make a rasping sound. To amplify the sound, the rasp may be placed on an inverted basket or on a piece of hide over an open hole in the ground.

Indian drums are of two types: the *frame drum* and the *log drum.* **Frame drums,** which are larger in diameter than in thickness (fig. 1.3), are made from a strip of wood or an old cheese crate and are often painted and decorated. They may have one or two heads made from deer or other animal hide, and they are held in one hand and played with the other. **Log drums** are made from a hollowed-out log, and may be either tall and thin or large in diameter and short in height. The latter (similar to a bass drum) is most often found in the Plains area and is the **powwow** drum of today, while the former is found in the Southwest, especially among the Pueblos. Other types of drums, such as *water drums* and *inverted basket drums,* are found in various parts of the country.

Wind Instruments

Wind instruments include the *whistle* (which produces only a single tone) and the *flute* (which produces several tones). Other wind instruments, like *panpipes* (several tuned pipes glued or tied together) and *trumpets,* may be found in isolated areas throughout the country.

Whistles are made of wood, cane, or bone, and may be used in ceremonies such as the Sun Dance. The **flute** is the primary melodic instrument of the American Indians. Flutes are made of various types of wood, and they are often elaborately carved and decorated, especially to symbolize various birds. The flute in figure 1.4 is decorated with feathers, human hair, and paint, all of which are sacred to the Plains Indians.

Figure 1.3

Frame drum of the Northern Plains Indians. This Cheyenne Indian frame, or tambourine, drum and drumstick feature a painting of a red-winged blackbird. (© 1980 by J. Richard Haefer. Used by permission.)

Figure 1.4

Decorated flute of the Northern Plains Indians. This Kiowa Indian flute with a carved wind cap is decorated with painting, feathers, and braided hair. (© 1980 by J. Richard Haefer. Used by permission.)

The flute is used especially in the Plains area as a "love instrument," the sound of the flute communicating the love of the male flute player to his chosen young woman. In one charming custom, the flute player stands behind the young woman, according to the direction in which the wind is blowing, so that the wind may carry his love directly to her heart.

STYLES OF NORTH AMERICAN INDIAN MUSIC

Although the characteristics discussed here apply generally to the music of North American Indians, there are significant differences in the manner in which the music of various Indian cultures is performed and in the sounds that are produced. In order to understand the differences in music styles among Indian cultures, it may be best to speak of music *style areas*—geographical or culture areas that share similar music sounds. Accordingly, North American Indian music can be divided into eight different style or sound groups, each group including one or more cultures whose music shares similar sound traits. Table 1.1 is a partial list of the different cultures found in each style area.

The Plains

The best-known style of Indian music is that of the Plains area. Here the singing voice is very tense and utilizes the high **falsetto** range (above the normal singing range) of the male singer. The sound is also quite nasal, and pulsations may be used to stress the rhythm of the melody.

Plains Indians' melodies descend in a **terraced** fashion, moving downward in a stairstep-like pattern. Since the first part of a song does not recur consistently in successive renditions, the form is called **incomplete repetition.** Accompaniment is provided by the singers, who play small hand drums, a large log drum, or rattles in a style that is unique, the instruments sounding slightly off the beat of the sung melody.

The significance of a Plains Indian song often exceeds its musical or aesthetic value. For example, songs are an important part of ceremonies like the Sun Dance and must be properly performed to make the ceremony authentic. A young man sent out on a vision quest during puberty rites may seek a song to be his own; and songs that belong to an individual bring him great power and are never sung by others.

Southern Plains style is similar to that of the North, although the pitch range is usually lower. Listening Example 1 is a modern Northern Plains song, similar to the traditional song style of the Plains. The "Flag Song" is like a national anthem, used to begin each powwow.

The East

The music of the East (generally that area east of the Mississippi River, excluding the Great Lakes) is similar to that of the Plains, but with considerably less tension and a lower pitch. Formal structures in the East are more symmetrical, with short phrases of equal length. Eastern songs also tend to have more text material, although vocables or consonant-vowel clusters may be found in some songs, especially the stomp dance songs of the Southeast. **Responsorial singing style,** or **call-and-response,** in which a solo voice alternates with a chorus of singers, is also found in the East.

TABLE 1.1
Representative Cultures Sharing Music Style Traits

The Plains		The East	
Northern	**Southern**	**Northeastern**	**Southeastern**
Arapaho	Comanche	Iroquois	Cherokee
Blackfoot	Kiowa	Nations	Creek
Cheyenne	Western	Wabanaki	Seminole
Crow	Cherokee		Shawnee
Dakota (Sioux)			

The Great Lakes	The Southwest/ Southern California	The Athapaskan
Menomini	Hopi/Zuni/Other "mesa" pueblos	Apache
Ojibwa (Chippewa)	Maricopa	Navajo
Winnebago	O'odham (Papago)	
	Pima	
	Rio Grande Pueblos (from three	
	language families)	
	Yavapai	
	Yuma	

The Great Basin/ Northern California	The Northwest Coast	Eskimo/Inuit and Athapaskans
Paiute	Bella Coola	Eskimos of Alaska, Canada,
Pomo	Kwakiutl	and Greenland
Shoshoni	Nootka	Northern Athapaskans
Ute	Salish	(Slave, Kutchin, Dogrib)
	Tlingit	

In the Northeast, songs are usually sung in the *long house,* or traditional long brush house of the area, while in the Southeast, songs are often sung outside, accompanying games or around the campfire. Songs of southeasterners may be a little more complex than those of their northern neighbors.

The Great Lakes

The music of the Great Lakes Indians, who are situated between the Plains and the Northeast, shares traits of both adjacent song areas. Here songs occur within the legends of the origins of "the people," as members of these cultures refer to themselves, and they are also used in various societies, including those that specialize in healing the sick. Generally, the pitch level for songs is lower than that of the Plains, and the tension is less.

LISTENING EXAMPLE 1*
Modern Northern Plains Song

Title "Flag Song"

Performers Parker Singers

Culture Chippewa-Cree from Box Elder, Montana

Style Northern Plains powwow

Medium Male and female singers (the former predominate). The males strike a single large drum while singing. Notice the high, pinched, nasal sound of the Northern Plains singing voice.

Rhythm There is a steady pulse, but no metrical accent. Near the end of the song are *hot beats*, or accented beats, and an increase in tempo.

Melody/Form The shape of the melody is a short descending pattern, which is repeated throughout the song. Each repetition begins with a call and response.

Text The text consists of a series of vocables or consonant-vowel clusters.

*Listening Example selections are on the ninety-minute cassette that accompanies this text.

The Southwest

The Southwest, although smaller geographically than the Plains, is a much more complex area, with many different cultures living in the states of Arizona and New Mexico. Here highly complex societies were developed by peoples who continued to live in the same area for many centuries. Because they were agricultural societies that did not need to follow the migration trails of various animals as did the Plains Indians, cultures like the Hopi, Zuni, Taos, and other Rio Grande city people developed large city complexes called **pueblos** that were often well hidden from dangers high on flat-topped hills, or *mesas*.

Together with more complex rituals and ceremonies, the pueblo Indians also developed more complex songs, which often include complicated rhythmic relations and changing tempos. Their scales tend to be **pentatonic,** using five tones to the octave. Forms may be incomplete repetition, or long **through composed** style, meaning that as the text evolves, the music, too, changes continuously. The singing style is sometimes tense with pulsations, as on the Plains, but the pitch level is usually very low, almost like a growling voice. Pueblo songs are normally accompanied by the log drum played by one or two singers.

Listening Example 2 is a dance song of the Hopi, who live on top of three mesas in northern Arizona.

Less well-known groups in the Southwest include the Pima and O'odham of southern Arizona and the Yuman cultures of the Colorado River area, all of whom use highly developed song texts and often organize their songs into *cycles*. The songs are usually in incomplete repetition form for

---

LISTENING EXAMPLE 2
Hopi Dance Song

Title   "Hopi Butterfly Song"

Description   The Butterfly is a communal social dance. Dancers in two lines (one male, the other female) are dressed in elaborate costumes with bright colors and paintings symbolizing various natural elements crucial to Hopi lifeways (fig. 1.5). Although this is a social dance, the Hopi are still communicating with the deities that surround their life in the mesas. Clouds and lightning are symbolized, because they represent the life-giving rain essential for growing crops in the desert Southwest, and various animals are also represented in the dance costumes.

The complexities of Hopi life stand out in their music. Thus, when listening to this example, you can clearly hear the differences between this song and the more common powwow song of Listening Example 1.

Figure 1.5

Hopi-style butterfly dancers dancing in pairs. The ladies wear elaborate headgear. The men hold gourd rattles and have bells attached to their legs. (© 1980 by J. Richard Haefer. Used by permission.)

the O'odham (**AABCD AABCD BCD BCD**), and in repeated form with pitch variations for the Yumans (**AAAAA'AAA'A.**) In the latter example, **A'** uses the same melody as **A,** sung a fifth higher—the so-called *rise* in Yuman music.

Recent studies indicate that in O'odham culture, the rhythms and even the melodies of these songs may be highly dependent upon the texts, while the Yumans use a more complex rhythm, especially for dance songs. Songs in these cultures are usually accompanied by a gourd rattle or a basket drum.

The Athapaskan

The Southern Athapaskans include members of the Navajo and Apache cultures, who migrated into the Southwest at a relatively late date from the Northern Plains area of Canada. Although their languages are from the same family, Apache and Navajo music and culture have many differences. Two distinct singing styles may be found among the Navajo—the high-pitched, tense, nasal style of the Yei-bei-chai, and the lower, less tense style of most other Navajo songs. Apache songs can be distinguished by the alternation of a refrain using vocables, with verses having Apache language texts. Both cultures celebrate elaborate rituals for the coming of age of female members of the society, and Navajo culture also has many ceremonies or "ways" to help maintain the balance between humanity and nature.

The Great Basin

In the Great Basin of Nevada, Utah, and northern California are found the simplest of American Indian songs. Here song ranges tend to be narrow, and form to consist of repetitions of paired phrases (**AABBAABB**). Cultures of this area traditionally lived in small bands and survived by hunting and gathering, and their social structures and ceremonies were usually simple.

Songs of the Great Basin Indians accompany games, such as the gambling game called *handgame,* or they may be used for healing ceremonies. The Great Basin style influenced late-nineteenth-century **pan-Indian** songs, such as those from various cultures used in the Ghost Dance and Peyote ceremonies.

The Northwest Coast

Like the Southwest, the Northwest Coast area is one of the most complex in North America, and here ceremonial activity, songs, dances, and art were highly developed aspects of society. Several music style traits are unique to this area, especially the use of small intervals (whole and half steps), complex song forms based on short phrases, intricate rhythmic accompaniments, and some polyphonic singing.

The Northern Athapaskans and Eskimo/Inuit

In the most northern reaches of the United States and Canada live the northern Athapaskan cultures (related to those of the South) and the Eskimo/Inuit peoples.The music of the former is similar to their southern relatives, while that of the Eskimos reflects both the simple nature of their environment and sometimes, especially rhythmically, a more complex style. Of special interest is the *someak,* or hand drum, of the Eskimo, a large drum with a narrow frame covered with the bladder of the walrus.

A Culture Rich in Diversity

For years, Western listeners have thought of Indian music simply as something different from the European tradition. But even this brief description of traditional singing styles shows that the music of the North American Indian is quite varied and cannot be heard as one sound. Today **ethnomusicologists,** or scholars who study the music of other cultures, realize that each Indian culture not only has its own collection of songs and sound instruments, but that each is based upon a system of norms and culture values

Figure 1.6

Modern powwow dancers. Entrance dance/parade for a contemporary Indian powwow at a modern university campus. Lead dancers carry the United States and individual state flags, and are followed by the contest dancers. Each dancer has a number identifying him to the judges when dancing. (© 1980 by J. Richard Haefer. Used by permission.)

leading to a unique theory and experience of music. Only by studying and learning these new music theories can we ultimately come to understand the traditional musics of the Indian people.

CONTEMPORARY INDIAN SONG

The late nineteenth and twentieth centuries have seen many changes in North American Indian music. Among the earliest of these changes was the development of pan-Indian song styles, such as those of the Ghost Dance and Peyote ceremonies. These evolved as the introduction of the horse, and later the automobile, increased intertribal contact, and Indian peoples began to share their dances, songs, and even ceremonies. The new acculturation led to practices such as those of the Native American Church, or Peyote cult, which uses Plains-style singing with stylized consonant-vowel clusters (almost like text) in a ceremony that combines elements of traditional religious practices with elements drawn from Christian rites.

The modern powwow is common not only on the reservations, where Indians used to be required to live, but also in cities ranging from New York to California and from Montana to southern Florida. Many Indians follow the powwow circuit from one place to the next, often traveling 15,000 miles or more to sing, dance, and rodeo. Powwow songs are of the Plains style (as in Listening Example 1), and the costumes (fig. 1.6) are elaborate, befitting a public display of Indian culture and values.

NEW VERNACULAR MUSICS

Some Indian cultures or groups have adopted elements of contemporary popular or vernacular musics, modifying them to suit their needs and desires. Indian rock bands like **Xit,** country-western groups (the **Navajo Sundowners**), and gospel quartets flourish on many reservations today.

Other groups modify European styles to develop a music of their own. For example, the **waila** (Listening Example 3), or "chicken scratch" music of the Pima and O'odham of southern Arizona, was originally borrowed,

---

LISTENING EXAMPLE 3
Waila

Title "Hohokam Polka"

Performers Joaquin Brothers

Culture O'odham (Papago) of Sells, Arizona

Style Contemporary

Genre Polka

Medium Waila or "chicken scratch" band: saxophone, accordion, electric guitar and bass, and drum set. Each instrument has a distinctive timbre, and all are uniquely blended into the scratch band sound. The melody is performed by the saxophone.

Texture Polyphonic

Rhythm Steady pulse with regular duple meter accent. The accordion and rhythm guitar play on the off-beats, with the bass on the beat.

Melody/Form Short, regular phrases repeated in pairs with some variation (**AABBAA . . .**).

---

in the nineteenth century, from the Norteño music of northern Mexico. Today it is the social dance music of these two Indian cultures and has mostly replaced traditional round dancing for all social dance affairs—wedding celebrations, Saint's dance, graduations, anniversaries, and so on. The replacement has been, however, within the cultural norms or values of the society, and most of the attributes of traditional round dancing have been transferred to waila. Accordingly, the dance is performed counterclockwise; dances begin at sundown and end at sunrise; certain songs "belong" to certain parts of the night; and waila is danced to bring happiness and joy to the people—all according to round dance tradition.

It may be seen that, although there are many differences in the music of various Indian peoples, and although changing times affect the music played and consumed by Native Americans, many of the *values* of song remain constant: Song unites the people as Indian, authenticates various ceremonies necessary for life as an Indian, and helps keep humanity and nature in balance. For these cultures, therefore, song is a necessity for life.

RELATIONSHIPS BETWEEN INDIAN AND WESTERN ART MUSIC

In the late nineteenth and early twentieth centuries, several mainstream American composers used Indian themes as the source or inspiration for art or concert music. However, it is probably more significant that several American Indians have developed their own style of Indian music, writing within the mainstream of the Western European art music tradition.

Accomplished Indian composers include **Edward Wapp** and, most notably, **Louis Ballard.** Ballard, of Quapaw/Choctaw descent, has taught for many years at the Institute of American Indian Arts in Santa Fe. He has composed for chorus, band, and orchestra, often using Indian instruments to mix traditional Indian sound with the sound of the modern symphony orchestra. His composition *Why the Duck Has a Short Tail* uses an Indian legend in a musical setting for band and narrator.

Today, of course, Indian students are studying music at universities and conservatories throughout the country and applying their native gifts and experience to composing and performing music within the Western music tradition. To name just two, **Carlos Nakai** is a Navajo-style flute player who is becoming very successful performing music in a jazz-Indian-fusion style; and **John Kim Bell,** a Caughnawaga Indian, is associate conductor of the New York Philharmonic Orchestra.

At the same time, it appears that American listeners are becoming more aware of and sensitive to the values of a music born and nurtured in the land they share with the Native Americans, yet more foreign to their experience than the music of many distant cultures. North American Indian pride is effectively celebrated in both traditional and contemporary music, dance, and literature. Descendants of those who immigrated to the New World after the American Indians, as well as recent arrivals to this continent, may well be grateful that the American Indians share freely the arts by which humankind receives the most gracious blessings.

SUMMARY

There is no one North American Indian music, but rather a whole series of musics, including song, dance, and ceremony, that differ widely throughout the continent. The song styles are as many and varied as the sound instruments that hold up the songs.

Contemporary Indian music reflects not only the ancient, traditional songs and dances, but also various new styles. Today's songs include those that are traditional in nature and those that have been borrowed from European neighbors. Even when it is new, song remains a potent source of power in Indian culture, confirming Indian-ness, validating ceremonies, and helping keep people "right" and in balance with nature and with the deity who controls all.

TERMS TO REVIEW

lifeways   The cultural norms, values, and ceremonies by which people live.

oral tradition   The passing on of traditions (songs, dances, rituals, ceremonies) by word of mouth rather than by written documents.

strophic form   A song form with two or more verses of text set to the same melody.

sound instruments   Music instruments that hold up or support the songs in Indian cultures.

container rattles   Sound instruments consisting of a container made of gourd, hide, or other material, with a rattle element inside. They are shaken or swung to make a sound.

suspension rattles   Sound instruments consisting of a group of objects (shells, hooves) suspended from a stick that is shaken to produce the rattle sound.

rasp   A sound instrument consisting of a stick with notches cut into one side. It is scraped by another stick or object.

frame drum   A narrow frame covered by a membrane and struck with a drumstick or beater. The drum may or may not have a handle.

log drum   A drum made from a hollowed-out log. It may have one or two heads, and may be either tall with a small diameter or short with a large diameter. The tall drum is played by one or two people. The short drum, called a **powwow drum,** is played by several people.

powwow   A contemporary pan-Indian gathering for singing, dancing, rodeo, carnival, and other celebrations.

whistle   A wind instrument that produces only a single pitch. It is often made from an eagle bone.

flute   A wind sound instrument capable of producing a series of pitches. The flute is the only true melody instrument found in American Indian cultures today.

falsetto   The singing voice above the normal (full or chest voice) range.

terraced descending melody   A melodic pattern that moves down in a stairstep-like pattern.

incomplete repetition   A formal structure or pattern in which the first part is not repeated in successive renditions of the song. It may be illustrated graphically as **AABCD BCD.**

responsorial singing style or **call-and-response**   A solo voice alternates with a chorus of singers.

pueblos   Towns or cities built by Indians living in the American Southwest. The term also refers to the people living in these towns.

pentatonic   A five-note scale within the range of an octave. There are many conceivable patterns.

through composed   A song form that has new music for each verse or throughout the song.

ethnomusicologist   A scholar who studies the music of other cultures.

pan-Indian styles   Ideas, song, and ceremonies used by Indian people of different cultures. For example, a pan-Indian powwow may include people from many different tribes.

waila   The contemporary dance genre of the Pimas and O'odham of southern Arizona, adopted from the Norteño style of Mexican music in the later nineteenth century.

KEY FIGURES

Native American Artists
Fritz Scholder
Alan Hauser

Native American Writers
M. Scott Momaday
Vine Deloria
Joy Harjo

Native American Performers
Xit (rock band)
Navajo Sundowners (country-western)
Carlos Nakai (flutist)

Native American Composers
Edward Wapp
Louis Ballard

Native American Conductor
John Kim Bell

SUGGESTIONS FOR FURTHER LISTENING

Records produced by:
Canyon Records, 4143 North Sixteenth Street, Phoenix, AZ 85016

Indian House, P.O. Box 472, Taos, NM

Smithsonian Folkways, Smithsonian Institution, L'Enfant Plaza, Washington, DC

EUROPEAN PRECURSORS OF AMERICAN MUSIC

Chapter 2

The music of that part of the Americas that was to become the United States has roots in the artistic styles and experiences of many cultures. Because the predominant influence upon American concert music was European, it is important for the student of American music to know something about the music brought to America by the European settlers.

HISTORICAL PERSPECTIVE

Life in Medieval and Renaissance Europe (approximately the sixth through the sixteenth centuries) was dominated by the Roman Catholic church, whose music consisted largely of stylized settings of the Latin *liturgy,* or service text, called **plainsong, plainchant,** or simply **chant.** In the sixth century, a pope who took the name Gregory organized the existing chants according to the church season they represented (Christmas, Easter, etc.), and ever since, that grand collection of music has been called **Gregorian chant.** One of the most significant bodies of music in Western history, Gregorian chant has provided melodic material for religious and secular music through the centuries.

Modes

Gregorian chants, like most music of the Medieval and Renaissance periods, were based upon pre-tonal scales called **modes,** each of which is a seven-note scale within the range of an octave. If you start on any white note on a keyboard and play up or down an octave, using white keys only, you will have played one of the modes.

As we have seen, the mode on **A** later became the minor scale and the mode on **C** became the major scale when those modes were used according to the rules of the tonal system. The other modes also included five whole and two half steps, but the different order in which they occur gives music based upon each mode a distinctive sound, one mode sounding as different from another as the major scale sounds from the minor scale.

THE PROTESTANT REFORMATION

In 1517, a devout German cleric named **Martin Luther** (1483–1546) (fig. 2.1) publicly protested against and proposed reforms of certain practices of the Roman Catholic church, including some having to do with music. In this way, he initiated the **Protestant Reformation**. Luther loved the beautiful chants, as well as the elaborate choir pieces that are also an invaluable

Figure 2.1

Martin Luther and his family. Luther is shown playing a lute. (EKM-Nepenthe.)

part of the church's heritage. However, these were always performed in Latin, and Luther insisted that some church music should be sung in the **vernacular,** or common language of the people. After all, few members of the German congregation understood Latin, and few could sing the flexible rhythms and sophisticated melody lines of Gregorian chant, which were intended for performance by trained choirs.

Luther proposed that each worship service include some songs with sturdy tunes, simple structures, and vernacular texts, as well as some Latin chant and choir pieces. The new religious songs he introduced, called **chorales,** were enthusiastically sung by the new "Lutheran" congregations, and chorales remain an important part of Protestant church music today.

Chorales

A chorale is a kind of **hymn**—that is, a religious poem set to music suitable for congregational singing, in strophic form. Luther and his colleagues set German translations of Catholic hymns as well as their own original verses to old hymn tunes, folk and popular tunes of the day, or newly composed melodies.

LISTENING EXAMPLE 4
Chorale

Composer   Martin Luther

Title   "A Mighty Fortress Is Our God"

> Although Luther encouraged the joyful singing of simple tunes and light-hearted texts in church, the chorale for which he is best known is a serious expression of confidence and trust in a strong and steadfast God. The words, as well as the tune, express fervent religious faith.

Form   Strophic

Texture   Homophonic

Rhythm   The rhythm of Luther's chorale was syncopated and complex. In time, however, congregations smoothed out the irregularities, and the rhythm of the chorale as it is usually sung today is simple and symmetrical (fig. 2.2).

Text of First Verse

(German)	(Free translation)
Ein' feste Burg ist unser Gott,	*A mighty fortress is our God,*
Ein' gute Wehr und Waffen;	*A Bulwark never failing;*
Er hilft uns frei aus aller Not,	*Our Helper He amid the flood*
Die uns itzt hat betroffen.	*Of mortal ills prevailing.*
Der alte böse Feind,	*For still our ancient Foe*
Mit Ernst er's jetzt meint,	*Doth seek to work us woe,*
Groß Macht und viel List	*His craft and power are great*
Sein grausam Rüstung ist,	*And, armed with cruel hate,*
Auf Erd ist nicht seinsgleichen.	*On earth is not his equal.*

Manner of Performance

At first chorales were sung in church only in unison, because it was thought that the pleasant sounds of harmony would distract the congregation from concentrating on the words. Chorales were also performed without instrumental accompaniment, or **a cappella,** for the same reason.

However, polyphonic versions of the chorales were enjoyed informally in people's homes. And before the end of the sixteenth century, homophonic settings were accepted for congregational singing or performance by a church choir in some Lutheran churches.

Luther wrote many chorale texts himself, and he is thought to have composed the tune for one of the most familiar of all chorales, "A Mighty Fortress Is Our God" (Listening Example 4). Like many other chorale tunes, Luther's famous melody has been used frequently in large choral, orchestral, and organ pieces to the present day.

Figure 2.2

The original and modern rhythms of Luther's "A Mighty Fortress Is Our God."

The original, syncopated rhythm

Regular rhythm, as "A Mighty Fortress Is Our God" is performed today

PSALM TUNES

Soon Protestants in other northern European countries adopted the practice of singing church music in their own vernacular languages. In Switzerland, the followers of **John Calvin** (1509–1564) developed a new kind of congregational song called the **psalm tune.**

Calvin believed that the only purpose for music in a church service was to enhance the expression and understanding of a religious text, so he insisted—unlike Luther—that *all* church music should be sung in the congregation's common language. He was also concerned that church music not stir emotions or draw attention to itself, since it was intended to move God, not people. Accordingly, musical instruments had no place in Calvin's worship service, because they are incapable of expressing words and simply enhance music's sensuous appeal.

Further, Calvin believed that the only texts suitable for singing in church were the **psalms.** These 150 inspirational verses found in the Old Testament of the Bible are poetic in style and expression, but neither metered nor rhymed. To render them suitable for singing, Calvin and his colleagues retranslated the words of each psalm into verses having a regular number of lines with particular patterns of weak and accented beats.

Psalters

The metered and rhymed psalm verses were printed in books called **psalters** for use in congregational singing. Some psalters contained notated melodies, while others had only the words, which could be sung to familiar tunes. The first collection of psalm tunes was printed in Switzerland in 1539, and the first edition of the famous *Geneva Psalter* appeared in that city in 1551. The texts were in French, which was the vernacular language of the Geneva congregation.

Some of the tunes in the *Geneva Psalter,* like the tunes of many chorales, were borrowed from other religious sources. Other tunes resembled, and may have been derived from, secular songs. It was not considered necessary to provide a separate tune for each of the 150 psalms, since all verses with the same metrical pattern could be sung to the same melody. The *Geneva Psalter* contained 125 tunes, and all of the psalms could be sung to at least one of them.

LISTENING EXAMPLE 5
Psalm Tune

Composer   Louis Bourgeois (c. 1510–c. 1561)

Title   "Old Hundred." The title refers to the tune's association with Psalm 100, various translations of which continue to be sung to the tune today. In many hymnals a verse known as the Doxology ("Praise God from whom all blessings flow") is also set to this tune.

Form   Strophic

Meter   Each verse consists of four lines, with eight syllables in each line. This is called **long meter.** (Any psalm in long meter could be sung to any long meter tune.)

Texture   In most hymnals and psalters today, the tune appears in a homophonic, or chordal, setting. However, polyphonic versions were enjoyed even in early Calvinist homes, where the tune might also have been played upon or accompanied by instruments.

Rhythm   While the melody has remained unchanged for centuries, the arrangement of long and short notes has been altered. Early congregations enjoyed irregular rhythmic patterns that were considerably more interesting than the regular, symmetrical patterns prevalent in psalms and hymns today. Modern Protestants generally sing "Old Hundred" to one of two well-known rhythmic patterns, neither of which has the variety or vigor of the earliest settings.

Among the tunes in the *Geneva Psalter* was a setting of Psalm 100 (Listening Example 5). This tune, known today as "Old Hundred," has become the most famous psalm tune of all. (Another famous psalm tune, "Windsor," is an Optional Listening Example.)

In England, King Edward VI (reigned 1547–1553) permitted Protestants to practice their Calvinist form of worship, including the singing of psalm tunes. However, when Queen Mary Tudor replaced him on the throne, only Catholic services were allowed, and English Protestants were severely persecuted. Some fled to Switzerland, where they became familiar with the tunes in the *Geneva Psalter.*

In 1558, Elizabeth I came to the English throne, and many Protestants returned to England under her more liberal rule. A new English psalter, known as ***Sternhold and Hopkins*** (from the man who had printed the first metrical psalter in English and the man who contributed the most translations to the new version), was printed for their use in 1562. This compilation became the most important religious text next to the Bible for more than a century. It included some tunes from the *Geneva Psalter,* as well as several folklike melodies that might have been derived from popular songs

THE ENGLISH EXPERIENCE

of the day. There were seventeen metrical patterns to which the verses could be set. The psalters used by the Separatists, who found even Elizabeth's rule repressive and fled to Holland, had even greater metric variety.

Sternhold and Hopkins and the psalter printed in Amsterdam known as **Ainsworth** (fig. 2.3), contained tunes of a merry mood and lively tempo. Some had the syncopated rhythms of popular Renaissance dances, causing skeptics to refer to them as "Geneva jigs" and Shakespeare to write in *The Winter's Tale* of a Puritan who "sings psalms to hornpipes." The attractive tunes sung at worship on Sunday also provided entertainment at home, where they were often accompanied by a variety of musical instruments or sung in polyphonic settings.

EUROPEAN MUSIC COMES TO AMERICA

During the second half of the sixteenth century, French and English explorers arrived on both coasts of the New World and settled parts of Florida and the Southwest. Artists who accompanied them made maps and painted pictures of Indians and exotic nature scenes that helped persuade other Europeans to travel to the new country. The French Huguenots in the East and Sir Francis Drake's men in California encouraged the American Indians to join them in singing their joyful psalm tunes and hymns.

About the same time, Spanish missionaries also arrived in California, where they tried to convert the Native Americans to Christianity. Within a hundred years of their first arrival, Catholic missions were established throughout much of California and in what is today New Mexico.

Music was an important part of the religious training of the Indians, who sang in choirs, played in church orchestras, and even learned to make instruments. They were taught traditional Spanish music, hymns, and Gregorian chant, and at Christmastime, they participated in musical nativity plays. A large number of instruments have been found at some of the mission sites, as have manuscripts of Mass settings and other church music of varying levels of complexity.

Native Americans drove the Spaniards out of New Mexico in 1680, but the missions remained active in California until the Mexican government ordered them closed in 1833. Throughout that time, music of the Catholic church was performed by the missionaries and their Native American students in the Mass and other religious services. The Indians seem to have learned quickly and enjoyed their performances, and the reports of most visitors who heard them were enthusiastic.

However, it was the music of the Pilgrims and the Puritans that profoundly affected the early American music experience and provided inspiration for countless American compositions to the present day. The Pilgrims sailed from Holland and the Puritans from England in the early seventeenth century, bringing to the New World their well-worn psalters, and their psalm tunes supported the predominant music experience in America for well over a hundred years.

Music at the Spanish Missions

SUMMARY

Martin Luther initiated the Protestant Reformation in 1517 by proposing reforms of certain practices in the Roman Catholic church. For example, he believed that church music should include chorales, which have easy tunes and are sung in the people's own language.

Calvinists only included the unaccompanied, unison singing of psalm tunes in their services. These, like chorales, are strophic in form and sung in the vernacular language. Metered and rhymed translations of all the psalms were printed in psalters, which often included tunes as well.

Spanish and French missionaries taught Native Americans to sing some of the music of the Catholic church, but it was the psalm tunes of the Pilgrims and Puritans that dominated the early American music experience in New England and had the most far-reaching effect on American music.

TERMS TO REVIEW

plainsong, plainchant, or **chant**   Music to which portions of the Roman Catholic service are sung. Chant is sung in unison and in flexible, unmetered rhythm.

Gregorian chant   The collection of chants organized by Pope Gregory in the sixth century.

mode   One of the seven-note scales that may be played on a keyboard beginning on any white key and playing up or down the octave using white keys only.

Protestant Reformation   A sixteenth-century movement of protest against certain procedures of the Catholic church.

vernacular   The common language.

chorale   A hymn, characteristic of the German Protestant church.

hymn   A religious verse set to music suitable for congregational singing. A hymn is strophic in form, and is sung in the vernacular language.

a cappella Unaccompanied choral music.

psalm tunes Tuneful settings of the psalms in versions suitable for congregational singing.

psalms One hundred fifty inspirational verses found in the Old Testament.

psalter A collection of the psalms in metered and rhymed verse, suitable for setting to simple tunes.

Geneva Psalter The first complete psalter. It was published in French by Calvinists in Geneva, Switzerland, in 1551.

long meter Four-line verse with eight syllables per line.

Sternhold and Hopkins The Puritans' psalter, published in England in 1562.

Ainsworth The Pilgrims' psalter, published in Holland in 1612.

KEY FIGURES

Martin Luther

John Calvin

Louis Bourgeois

OPTIONAL LISTENING EXAMPLE*

Psalm tune:
"Windsor" (Psalm 15)

SUGGESTIONS FOR FURTHER LISTENING

Chorales:
Hassler/Bach, "O Sacred Head, Now Wounded"
Cruger/Bach, "Jesu, meine Freude"

Compositions based upon chorale tunes:
Felix Mendelssohn, Symphony no. 5 ("Reformation"), fourth movement
J. S. Bach, Chorale Prelude, "Ein' feste Burg"

Psalm tunes:
Old 124th (Psalm 8)
Old 112th (Psalm 34)

*Guides for Optional Listening Examples are in the Instructor's Manual and may be copied and distributed to students.

AT THE TIME
OF THE SETTLERS

Chapter 3

W hen the Pilgrims and Puritans arrived in the area now known as New
England, they had left behind a rich and varied cultural experience that
was generously supported by royalty and the Catholic church. The artistic
style that was prevalent in Europe at that time, and that remained so
throughout the seventeenth century, is known as the **Baroque.**

[handwritten annotations above "Pilgrims" and "Puritans": Holland, England]

THE STYLE OF
THE BAROQUE

The art of the Baroque is filled with tension, drive, activity—in a word,
drama. Baroque painters often directed the viewer's eye right off the canvas,
as if resisting the boundaries of measured space. Sculpted figures of the
period seethe with tension and strain, caught in the midst of dramatic action.
Baroque buildings jut and protrude, projecting a sense of instability. And
much of the decorative ornamentation of the period is so elaborate and
complex that it is almost dizzying in effect.

Baroque Music

Contrast is a primary characteristic of the music, as well as the art, of the
Baroque period. Secular music was as important as sacred music; there
were as many fine instrumental as vocal compositions; and homophony was
of equal importance with polyphony. Contrasts of timbre, alternation of
free and metered rhythms, and abrupt changes of dynamic levels were also
characteristic of this dramatic style. It is hardly surprising that the extravagant form of music drama called opera was introduced during the
Baroque.

In the New World

The settlers in the new land generally shared simple tastes more typical of
the preceding period, the Renaissance. They had left Europe, after all, just
as the Baroque was emerging as the newly preferred style. They knew little
of the tonal system of harmony, because Gregorian chant, Renaissance
church music, and many folk tunes were based upon modal scales. Some
Lutheran chorales and psalm tunes were modal as well.

Nevertheless, although the settlers generally avoided the extravagant
characteristics of the Baroque, some among them loved art and music and
made them a significant part of their new life.

John Quidor, *The Return
of Rip Van Winkle.*
Although painted in the
nineteenth century, the
teeming motion and
elaborate detail of this
delightful American
painting are reminiscent
of art in the Baroque
style. (Andrew W. Mellon
Collection, © 1992
National Gallery of Art,
Washington, c. 1849.
Canvas, 1.010 × 1.265
[39¾ × 49¾].)

The triumphant conclusion of Monteverdi's *The Coronation of Poppea.* The extravagant staging, classical garments, and stylized gestures are characteristic of opera as it was conceived in the Baroque. (Photograph by Hans W. Fahrmeyer.)

The more we learn about Puritan society, the more we realize how inappropriate is the stereotype of them as plain and wholly serious people. Recent research indicates that their society included sophisticated men and women of keen wit and high intellect. The well-to-do, educated Puritans who arrived in the New World about 1630 brought their personal libraries with them, and as colonists they soon began to produce literature of their own. This largely consisted of didactic religious tracts, but also included memoires, essays, and poetry.

The New World's first poet was a woman named **Anne Bradstreet** (1612?–1672) (fig. 3.1). The wife of a colonial governor and the mother of eight, she yet found time to compose a significant body of fine poetry, despite serious illness and the rigors of colonial life. There is no indication that her peers found this an unwomanly pursuit; on the contrary, she was admired then as now for her learned and well-crafted poems.

The Pilgrims and Puritans were practical people with little use for articles that were purely decorative. Art for art's sake held no interest for them, and art was specifically excluded from their churches as a potential distraction from God.

Yet the early American experience was rich in artistic expression. While churches and meetinghouses were plain, their adjacent graveyards often contained elaborately carved and decorated headstones. In their homes, the Pilgrims and Puritans made functional articles objects of beauty. Fine needlework covered tables and beds and provided protection from cold New England drafts. Furniture was often beautifully carved, dishes were hand painted, and even toys were elaborately constructed for the delight of children. Landscape painting had little meaning for the settlers, who were more anxious to tame and control nature than to depict its charms. Portraits,

LITERATURE IN THE COLONIAL PERIOD

COLONIAL ART

which served the practical purpose of preserving a likeness, were valued. However, even the market for portraits was limited, and few early artists were able to earn a living as portrait painters. Farmers, shopkeepers, carpenters, silversmiths, or house- and sign-painters sometimes painted portraits on the side, their materials crude and their training rudimentary. They considered themselves craftsmen rather than artists, but many of their works are highly valued today.

There is often a linear quality and a rather attractive "flat" appearance to these early portraits, lending them a distinctive—an American—flavor, unlike the sophisticated products of their European contemporaries. It is interesting to note, however, that the subjects of these early American portraits are often dressed in elaborate finery, suggesting an attraction to worldly goods surprising in the staid Puritan society (fig. 3.2).

Gravestone in a colonial churchyard. (The Bettmann Archive, Inc.)

Figure 3.2

Elizabeth Davis, *Mrs. Hezekia Beardsley.* (Yale University Art Gallery, Gift of Mrs. E. A. Giddings.)

Figure 3.3

Robert Feke, *The Isaac Royall Family*, 1741. (Harvard Law Art Collection.)

Robert Feke is widely considered America's first important painter. His birth and death dates are unknown, but it is presumed he was born in the New World early in the eighteenth century. Apparently self-taught, Feke revealed a strong sense of form and technique. His works lack the depth and polish of contemporary European paintings, but they are charming in their simplicity and clarity of line (fig. 3.3).

RELIGIOUS MUSIC

Many of the settlers had enjoyed playing and listening to musical instruments in their European homes. However, the small ships that brought them to New England had no room for large luxuries, and few musical instruments were carried to the New World. Thus, the colonists were largely unable to experience instrumental performances in their new environment. Besides, because travel was costly, time-consuming, and dangerous, it was seldom undertaken for less than pressing concerns, and the settlers soon lost touch with significant musical events abroad.

As we have seen, however, psalm tunes provided music for both worship and entertainment. The psalters of the Puritans and Pilgrims included a variety of attractive tunes to which the rhymed and metered psalms could be sung.

The *Bay Psalm Book*

In a surprisingly short time, the settlers developed an American taste and tongue. The language of the old psalters began to seem stilted and old-fashioned, and the Puritans especially felt the need for a new—an American—translation. The first book printed in the New World was a psalter

Figure 3.4

Pages from the *Bay Psalm Book,* the first book printed in the American colonies. (© Historical Pictures/Stock Montage.)

popularly called the ***Bay Psalm Book*** (fig. 3.4), which appeared in Cambridge, Massachusetts, only twenty years after the settlers landed at Plymouth Rock.

In true Puritan fashion, the authors of the *Bay Psalm Book* produced verses that were literal in translation and serviceable for worship. Intended for everyday use by plain people, the new psalter made no pretense at literary elegance. Whereas *Sternhold and Hopkins* had included seventeen different meters, the *Bay Psalm Book* had only six. No tunes were printed, though the names of tunes to which each text could be set were given in the comfortable assumption that everyone knew the familiar melodies.

Lining Out

In time, of course, the old psalm tunes were remembered differently in various towns and villages, and people—few of whom could read music—began to disagree as to how they should be sung. In order to learn the tunes as they thought they should be rendered, some congregations adopted the practice of **lining out.** A leader sang one line of a psalm tune, which was then repeated in unison by the congregation, and each succeeding line of the psalm was performed in this manner.

The song leaders, who did not necessarily have pleasing voices or particular musical ability, were sometimes moved to embellish tunes in a tasteless or inappropriate manner. Some apparently chose starting pitches that were too high or too low, causing people to "squeak above" or "grumble below" their comfortable singing ranges. Members of the congregations, probably bored by slow tempos and by the repetition of each line of a psalm, also embellished the melodies freely, greatly distorting the effect of the original tune.

In hopes of remedying this regrettable situation, thirteen tunes were printed in the ninth edition of the *Bay Psalm Book* (1698). This was far fewer than had been included in the popular early psalters, and the melodies in the *Bay Psalm Book* were rhythmically simpler and less interesting than earlier versions. Nevertheless, each of the psalms could be set to one or more of these tunes, depending upon the meter of their verses. Because one tune could be used for several different texts, tunes were often named for English cathedral or university towns (such as "Oxford," "York," or "Windsor"), rather than according to the words of a particular psalm.

Each edition of the *Bay Psalm Book* after 1698 included music, but still few people knew how to read music notation. Besides, many had become accustomed to altered versions of the old tunes and were loath to forsake what had become their usual way of singing them. For a time there was strong resistance to all efforts to impose the "regular" style of performance—that is, singing the tunes as they were written.

SECULAR MUSIC

The terms "sacred" and "secular" were more closely related in the early American experience than they are today. The church or meetinghouse provided a place for social diversion as well as worship, and the chief forms of entertainment—music and dance—took place there.

Neither did the settlers distinguish as clearly as we do between religious and vernacular music, singing psalm tunes at home as well as in church. At home the tunes were often performed in harmony and accompanied by musical instruments, such as guitars, trumpets, and drums, which were becoming increasingly available in America by the late seventeenth century. A precursor of the modern violin called the **viol** and small keyboard instruments called **virginals** (fig. 3.5) were also found in some New England homes.

The Pilgrims were generally less affluent and less educated than the Puritan settlers, and their tastes were not as sophisticated. They particularly enjoyed music of a secular—today we would say popular—nature, especially folk songs and dances. (Puritans, too, apparently participated in some of this worldly entertainment, since their ministers sometimes complained of the pleasure their parishioners derived from singing ballads and work songs.)

Figure 3.5

Double spinet, or virginal, made by Ludovicus Grovvelus (Lodewijck Grauwels). Early virginals were oblong boxes small enough to be placed on a table, but late in the eighteenth century, the term was applied to various keyboard instruments. (The Metropolitan Museum of Art; The Crosby Brown Collection of Musical Instruments, 1889.)

Among the settlers were farmers, laborers, servants, and others who came to the New World not so much for religious freedom as to escape poverty, famine, political persecution, or even criminal prosecution. These people often avoided the urban experience, settling instead in rural areas where they soon became isolated from the mainstream of American development. They sang the songs and danced the dances they remembered from their homelands—the music of the "folk."

Folk music is variously defined as music that appears to have been spontaneously created, or whose origin has been lost or forgotten. More recently, songs and other pieces composed in the style of folk music have entered the folk repertoire.

The style of folk music may be generally described as simple and unpretentious, easily remembered, and easily performed. Folk music appeals to inexperienced listeners and sophisticated musicians alike. In fact, its strong melodies and attractive irregularities of rhythm and meter offer a wealth of material to the composer of concert or religious music.

Folk music in America has many ethnic sources, including British (English, Scottish, Irish, Welsh), German and other European, and African-American music. Many traditional songs were preserved, but they often acquired new words and a new "flavor," reflecting American dialects and

FOLK MUSIC

The Sources of American Folk Music

the American experience. The traditions thus begun survive today in certain rural and mountain areas, where the style of singing and playing instruments is remarkably close to that of seventeenth-century Britain.

Thus, some of the songs, dances, and instrumental pieces of the folk came to this country from abroad, and some developed here. Some are very old, and others are much more recent. By definition, the origin of folk music is obscure.

Instrumental Folk Music

The folk music of the American colonists included fiddle tunes and other happy instrumental pieces. Gigs and reels were among the many country dances performed to fiddle (or less often, flute) accompaniment.

Psalm Tunes

The psalm singing of the New Englanders was, in effect, a kind of folk tradition, for psalm tunes were of a folklike nature and were generally learned from oral experience. As we have seen, the psalm tunes were in strophic form, with four-line stanzas, as is common to much folk song. Besides, psalm tunes were freely ornamented and varied in performance, as typically occurs with songs in the folk tradition.

Mennonite Hymns

German Protestants called **Mennonites** brought their hymnals to America when they settled in the seventeenth century, and their hymns, too, have many characteristics of folk music. Their sturdy tunes were always sung in unison, unaccompanied by musical instruments. The rhythms were quite flexible, and the tempo very slow. Some hymn texts were actually set to German folk songs, while others were sung to Latin hymns or newly composed tunes.

The slow tempo at which the Mennonite hymns were sung encouraged the embellishment and alterations also typical of folk music. In fact, some of these lovely old hymns are considered part of the folk repertoire in Mennonite and Amish settlements today.

Folk Songs

Songs more commonly included in the realm of folk music include *lullabies,* lovely and lilting in their haunting simplicity. An example you may recognize is "The Mockingbird" ("Hush little baby, don't say a word; Papa's gonna buy you a mockingbird"). There are also *nonsense songs,* delightfully silly and entertaining. Sea *chanteys* describe the harrowing voyage from Europe to the new land, or the dangerous labors of the sailor or fisherman. (A well-known example is "Blow the Man Down.")

Many American folk songs relate *historical* or *topical events,* with titles such as "Billy the Kid," "The Erie Canal," "The John B. Sails," or "The Wreck of Old Number Nine." *Singing games* (for example, "Did You Ever See a Lassie" and "Go in and out the Window") are also a kind of folk song.

LISTENING EXAMPLE 6
Ballad

Title   "Barbara Allen" (sometimes "Barbery Ellen" or another similar name)

Composer   Anonymous

Form   Strophic. As in most ballads, there are several four-line stanzas.

Text   The story is of the young "Sweet William" who is dying for love of "hard-hearted Barbara Allen." She loves him too, of course, and soon joins him in death. A red rose and a green briar miraculously grow and join above the ill-fated lovers' adjacent graves. The words are not always the same, since the song has been handed down through centuries by oral tradition.

Melody   The melody, like the words, exists in several versions. It is based upon a pentatonic scale that uses only the tones of the five black notes of a keyboard. Many children's songs and folk melodies are based upon this simple scale.

Texture   This song is often performed with no accompaniment. Sometimes simple chords are strummed on a guitar, banjo, or other instrument. A piano may provide accompaniment if a chordal texture is desired.

Rhythm   There is a steady underlying pulse and a general sense of quadruple meter. The rhythm is refreshingly irregular, and the phrases are sometimes asymmetrical, adapted to suit the informal text.

Ballads

A **ballad** is a story told in song. The narrative is characteristically very simple and direct, offering little background or detail. The listener is simply plunged into the midst of a situation that allows free reign to a fertile imagination.

Ballads are sung from memory, with or without instrumental accompaniment. Because a ballad is in strophic form, the accomplished ballad singer often adds verses at will to prolong the entertainment and perhaps to add local or timely interest to the tale. The tune as well as the words may be altered as the song is passed from town to town and from one generation to the next.

An astonishing number of folk ballads have survived, apparently virtually intact, since the Medieval period that spawned them. Curiously, some have been better preserved in America than in the land where they originated. An example of such a ballad, brought to America from England and long since adopted into the American vernacular experience, is "Barbara Allen" (Listening Example 6).

THE BLACK EXPERIENCE

Figure 3.6

A banjar. (Courtesy of Kephart's Music Center, Dubuque, Iowa. Photography by Bob Coyle.)

Blacks were first brought to America early in the seventeenth century, at the same time the Pilgrims and Puritans were settling in New England. The first blacks landed in Virginia, where they were put to work as indentured servants, their services purchased for a period of time after which they would be released and become independent. However, by 1700, slavery had become common throughout the thirteen colonies.

In New England, slaves were treated with some leniency, at least in comparison with those in the South. For example, they were allowed free time to entertain themselves and their masters with their own style of singing, dancing, and playing musical instruments. Many had brought small, simple drums and string instruments with them on the slave ships, where they had sometimes been compelled to perform music to keep themselves occupied and—vain effort—to keep their spirits up.

One of these instruments was the banjar, a primitive but versatile precursor of the **banjo** (fig. 3.6). Even in their adversity, black slaves found the time and the inclination to scoop the seeds out of a gourd or calabash, stretch across it a skin (coonskin or whatever was available), attach a long handle or neck, and lay four strings across the bridge to the neck. Eventually they developed this adaptation of the earlier African instrument into the banjo, which was to provide untold entertainment for black and white Americans for generations to come.

Although harsher conditions were suffered by the plantation slaves in the South, even there, Sunday was largely observed as a day of relaxation and music making. Throughout the Colonial period, many blacks attended white churches, sitting in segregated sections and lustily singing the Protestant hymns that were also enjoyed by their white masters.

The music of the blacks excited widespread admiration—not always, however, to the advantage of the blacks. Lists in Colonial newspapers of slaves for sale and of runaways often referred to their musical abilities, adding to their desirability as commodities to be owned and abused.

Work Songs and Field Hollers

During the week, blacks—free or slave—sang work songs to relieve tension and depression, to focus attention on music they enjoyed (and away from work they did not enjoy), and to set the pace and coordinate movements for collective efforts. Whether working in cotton fields, on river levees, or in other arduous situations, they often produced a long, loud shout that came to be called a **field holler.**

Field hollers were dramatic cries charged with emotional content. They were **improvised,** or conceived and performed simultaneously, so they varied considerably, but they typically ended with a rising inflection. Some field hollers had words, but most used neutral syllables that carried effectively over distances, establishing wordless but heartwarming contact with fellow workers.

Thus, the music of the first African-Americans, like the music of the white settlers, was generally of a functional nature—associated with religion, or with work, or performed to accompany dance. Most of the music of the blacks was vocal, though it was often accompanied by drum or banjo. Sometimes rattles or bits of shell or bone were added to simple instruments to enhance their rhythmic effect. Melodies were simple and often pentatonic, and some pitches were the "bent" or flexible tones later called blue notes (see pages 229–30). Rhythms were often complex, with a driving, exciting quality that almost compelled bodily movement. Many songs were performed in a call-and-response manner, with a leader singing a line that was echoed or responded to by the participating group.

SUMMARY

The earliest colonists appreciated art and literature, and produced works of aesthetic as well as practical value. The singing of psalms was the predominant music experience in early America, and the first book printed in America was a psalter, commonly called the *Bay Psalm Book*. Lining out proved an effective means of teaching the tunes to those who couldn't read music. However, the practice interfered with the musical effect, and people often preferred their own versions of the psalm tunes.

Blacks first arrived in America about the same time as the New England settlers, bringing with them their own music customs and instruments. Other newcomers also brought the folk music of their native lands, which was preserved and adapted to the American experience.

TERMS TO REVIEW

Baroque   The dramatic, emotional artistic style prevalent from about 1600 to 1750.

Bay Psalm Book   The first book printed in America, a psalter that first appeared in 1640.

lining out   Each line of text is sung by a leader and echoed by the congregation.

viol   A bowed string instrument, precursor of the modern violin.

virginal   A small keyboard instrument, similar to a harpsichord.

folk music   Usually music of unknown origin, transmitted orally and enjoyed by the general population.

Mennonites   A German Protestant sect.

ballad   A folk song, strophic in form, that tells a story.

banjo   A string instrument related to the banjar that was brought by blacks from Africa.

field holler   An emotional vocal phrase, sung as a long, loud shout, which was developed by blacks as a kind of communication with fellow workers.

improvisation   The simultaneous invention and performance of music.

KEY FIGURES

Colonial Poet
Anne Bradstreet

Colonial Portraitist
Robert Feke

SUGGESTIONS FOR FURTHER LISTENING

Ballads:
English, "Scarborough Fair"
Anglo-American, "The Foggy Dew"
American, "Wayfaring Stranger," "Lonesome Road"

Chantey:
"Blow the Man Down"

Play song:
"Skip to My Lou"

Lullaby:
"The Mockingbird"

Modern compositions based upon ballads:
Roy Harris, American Ballads (for solo piano); "Folksong" Symphony

part 2

THE EIGHTEENTH CENTURY

THE AGE OF CLASSICISM

Chapter 4

Throughout Western history, two basic styles have alternately dominated artistic expression. One, highly subjective and emotional, is called "romantic." The other, more restrained and objective, is called "classical." Both styles are emotionally expressive and intellectually significant, differing primarily in their relative degree of subjectivity or objectivity.

CLASSICAL AND ROMANTIC STYLES

Ancient Greece is often called "the cradle of Western civilization," and indeed much of the European experience is rooted in the cultural and intellectual achievement of that early civilization. Among the qualities of ancient Greek art that Westerners have particularly admired are its perfection of form, its balanced designs, the artists' control of their medium and subject, and their restraint in expressing overt emotion. These came to be known as "classical" qualities, and the art of later periods dominated by these characteristics is called **classical** in style.

While the West has periodically turned for inspiration and instruction to the ancient Greeks (and the Romans, who adopted the classical approach to art), at other times classical balance and objectivity have been less valued than a highly individual, or subjective, style of art. These are the periods we call **romantic.**

HISTORICAL PERSPECTIVE

The first several centuries of the Medieval period are sometimes referred to as the Dark Ages, for the rigors of survival during those difficult years precluded significant interest or accomplishment in the arts (table 4.1). The thirteenth century, however, was acutely concerned with aesthetic achievement, and many great works were produced. The fourteenth century was an even more exciting period of fervent creativity, as exhibited by vivid artworks that were dramatic in expression and lively in execution.

This relatively romantic approach was replaced in the succeeding period, the Renaissance, by a cool, restrained, classical style. Then the stylistic pendulum swung again, rendering the Baroque a romantic period of highly dramatic and deeply personal artistic expression. Throughout this fervent Age of Faith, as the Baroque period is also called, devout Catholics and Protestants alike were guided by intense emotional and intuitive experience.

TABLE 4.1
Major Stylistic Periods

Stylistic Period	Approximate Dates
Medieval (or Middle Ages)	500–1450 A.D.
Renaissance	1450–1600
Baroque	1600–1750
Classical	1750–1820
Romantic	1820–1900
Twentieth century	1900–Present

Before 1750, however, romanticism began to decline, and the Baroque was succeeded by an objective, orderly, and largely secular period known as the Age of Reason or the **Classical period.** No longer trusting God to solve their problems and right their wrongs, the political, social, and intellectual leaders of the new age assumed responsibility for improving the conditions of life. Artists, too, approached their works with emotional restraint.

Certain religious sects also became intensely involved in practical humanitarian activities. In both Europe and America, for example, the Methodists and other Protestants sought to relieve the harsh conditions of the poor and sick, and the Quakers actively worked for the emancipation of slaves in the New World.

AMERICA IN THE EIGHTEENTH CENTURY

Paradoxically, the eighteenth-century period of emotional restraint was also a time of violent revolution, with Americans joining several European nations in rejecting rule by authority and establishing a republican form of government. We note, however, that the leaders of the American Revolution were enlightened intellectuals who avoided inflammatory rhetoric and unnecessary violence for its own sake. The classical influence in eighteenth-century America is evident in the cool and reasoned language of the Declaration of Independence, which begins, "When in the course of human events it becomes necessary for one people to dissolve the political bonds which have connected them with another. . . ."

From about 1750 until 1825, artists on both sides of the Atlantic adopted this orderly, balanced, and emotionally restrained approach. Thus, the Age of Reason in social and political affairs became the Age of Classicism in the arts.

Literature

During the eighteenth century, New Englanders produced literature more secular, reasonable, and bland than the impassioned verses and tracts of the early settlers. The new intellectuals gave serious consideration to subjects

Classical influence is reflected in the orderly layout of streets and the prevalence of Greco-Roman architectural style in Washington, D.C. (National Park Service/ Department of Interior.)

previously thought trivial or even frivolous. Certainly they produced sermons, tracts, essays, and poems that were logically organized and reasonably expressed, but witty discourses on the joys of dubious entertainment increasingly appealed to the secular tastes of the eighteenth-century realist.

Architecture

America's founders, led by Thomas Jefferson and influenced by outstanding French **neoclassical** architects, designed Washington, D.C., to be an orderly city of wide and regular streets with grassy parks and shady trees. Neoclassical is the term used for new art based upon the styles of classical Greece and Rome, such as Washington's state buildings, designed with simple lines and graced with classical columns. Although not constructed until the early years of the nineteenth century, America's capital city is clearly representative of the ideals of the Classical period during which it was planned.

Painting

Eighteenth-century America produced artists of more training and sophistication than the folk artists of the earlier colonial period. Their finest works, however, retained an innocence, honesty, and decorative sense that distinguished them from the more elegant European works of the same period, and we view them now as distinctively American in style.

John Singleton Copley (1738–1815), America's greatest colonial artist, was largely self-taught. He developed a highly personal style rooted in the American tradition and governed by classical order and reserve. As he

John Singleton Copley, *Mrs. Thomas Boylston,* 1766. (Courtesy of the Harvard University Portrait Collection, Harvard University, Cambridge, Massachusetts. Bequest of Ward Nicholas Boylston in 1828.)

became increasingly, though reluctantly, involved in events relating to the impending American Revolution, Copley sailed for Europe in 1774. He intended to return to America when peace was attained, but in fact, spent the rest of his life abroad.

In Europe, Copley studied with the famous American expatriate **Benjamin West** (1738–1820), who encouraged him to produce paintings of historical and heroic subjects. These were indeed more elegant and polished than Copley's early American portraits, but they were far less distinctive and interesting.

However, one of Copley's later paintings, *Watson and the Shark* (1778), is of particular interest, for in it Copley produced a warm and sympathetic portrayal of a black man attempting to assist a white man desperately floundering in the water (see plate 2). The black man has thrown

a rope, which Watson has missed catching, as the shark looms menacingly nearby. (Notice how the black man's outstretched arm mirroring that of Watson contributes to the symmetry and the drama of the painting.) Such a subtle and sympathetic rendering of relations between blacks and whites was unusual in that time, and Copley's painting is in every way a masterpiece.

Charles Willson Peale (1741–1827) also studied for a time in Europe with Benjamin West. He then returned to America and became the leading artist in Philadelphia for many years. He fought in the American Revolution and painted fine portraits of the leaders of the young nation. Peale's painting *The Staircase Group* (fig. 4.1) is so realistic a portrayal of his sons on a staircase that George Washington is said to have bowed to the boys as he passed the painting one day.

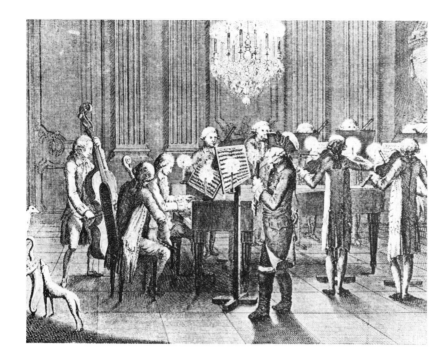

An eighteenth-century chamber music concert. (The Bettmann Archive, Inc.)

Peale revealed the classical thirst for knowledge in his boundless curiosity about a broad range of subjects. Further, he had the classical inclination to implement his ideas; for example, he established the first American museum of natural history, in Philadelphia in 1802.

MUSIC IN THE CLASSICAL STYLE

Eighteenth-century music compositions are usually modest in length and organized according to a clearly delineated form. Their melodies generally have symmetrical phrases—that is, a phrase four measures in length is usually answered by another four-measure phrase. Harmonies, too, are clearly defined and logically organized. Although warmly expressive, the great music of this period is never overly emotional; restraint and control are consistent characteristics of the Classical period.

Although eighteenth-century composers produced attractive vocal and choral works and various kinds of music theater pieces, their instrumental music was of even more significance. European composers of the latter part of the eighteenth century composed a wealth of music for orchestra, for small or chamber ensembles, and for solo instruments. Orchestras were small, and **chamber music**—that is, music for a small number of instruments with one instrument per line of music—was particularly appreciated.

Chamber Music

The title of a chamber music composition often reflects the number and kind of instruments involved, as in "string quartet" or "woodwind quintet." Performers in a chamber ensemble must be particularly proficient, since each is independently responsible for one line of music.

Chamber music is demanding upon listeners as well. A chamber ensemble replaces the full and sensuous effect of a symphony orchestra with a softer, more delicate sound, and it is necessary to follow each line of music in order to fully appreciate the performance. A special rapport between players and audience enhances the intimate, personal experience of listening to chamber music. (Listening Example 13 in chapter 6 is from a chamber music composition.)

MUSIC IN EIGHTEENTH-CENTURY AMERICA

In New Orleans, New Mexico, and California, where French or Spanish influence was dominant, Catholic church music was important, but elsewhere in America, Protestant psalms and hymns remained the predominant music throughout much of the eighteenth century. Public concerts were performed in some of the larger American cities beginning in the late 1720s, about the same time they began to be held in Europe. Music theater became popular in some areas during the 1730s. Growing numbers of professional musicians from Europe provided performance and educational opportunities previously denied colonial Americans.

For most of the eighteenth century, however, there was hardly any interest in formal concert music in America, and Americans were scarcely aware of the outstanding composers of their time, the Austrians **Wolfgang Amadeus Mozart** (1756–1790) and **Franz Joseph Haydn** (1732–1809).

Informal Music

As secular tastes encouraged the development of music for aesthetic and entertainment purposes, Americans enjoyed an increasing variety of musical experiences. Music in eighteenth-century New Orleans must have been particularly rich and varied, for African, Indian, Caribbean, French, and Spanish cultures were all part of life in that colorful city. In rural areas, combined work-social affairs such as barn raisings, maple sugaring, and cornhusking were often accompanied by singing, fiddling, or other musical activities and followed by dancing.

Work songs, play songs, religious songs, and patriotic songs dominated American music throughout the eighteenth century, though instrumental music was also of significance during this time. More and more Americans had musical instruments in their homes, including viols and violins, guitars, oboes, and flutes. Aside from the small virginals, popular keyboard instruments included harpsichords and early pianos called **fortepianos,** some of which were built in America. The fortepiano was smaller and more delicate than the modern instrument, but as its name implies, it was able to produce varied dynamic levels according to the touch of the performer.

Children and young ladies learned to sing and play simple pieces by taking lessons from immigrant professional musicians. Servants, both black and white, were sometimes chosen for their musical abilities and were expected to contribute to music making in the home. Music publishing had become an important business by the latter part of the century, producing

Figure 4.2

A band of drummers.
(© Fridmar Damm/Leo
de Wys, Inc.)

quantities of sheet music appropriate for the amateur performer. This consisted mostly of simple vocal and piano pieces sometimes referred to as "household music."

Music for social dancing was sometimes supplied by talented blacks, who also played at dancing schools, in taverns, and for formal balls. The favored instrument to accompany dancing was the **fiddle.** Smaller and lighter than the modern violin, the eighteenth-century instrument produced a louder and more vibrant sound than was considered appropriate for genteel listening and thus was heard more often in the barnyard or ballroom than in the parlour.

Military Bands

The first American military bands, established during the Revolutionary War, consisted only of drums and small flutes called **fifes.** Aside from performing their military duties, these early bands (fig. 4.2) played to boost the morale of the troops and probably to entertain the public at parades and informal concerts as well. Among the most popular of the tunes they played was "Yankee Doodle" (Listening Example 7).

Blacks and Indians had participated in America's earliest battles, and Indians were among the troops on both sides in the American Revolution. Nevertheless, George Washington initially prohibited blacks from joining colonial troops, presumably for fear of uprisings. However, when the English avidly solicited the service of blacks, promising freedom to those who joined the Royalist army, the colonists felt constrained to offer the same inducement, and blacks then joined the colonial army in significant numbers. Black

LISTENING EXAMPLE 7
Fife and Drum

Title   "Yankee Doodle"

Tune   The origin of the tune and the meaning of its title are unknown. It was composed some time before the Revolution, either in Britain or America, and first appeared in print in 1782. (The words are also anonymous and were often changed for partisan purposes. In fact, the British first sang the song to make fun of the Yankees, who later adopted it as their own!)

Meter   Duple

Form   Strophic. The first section of the tune is played and repeated; then the second section, in a version popular during the Revolution, is played and repeated. As the example tapers off, the corps begins to repeat the first section of the song.

Timbre   The high-pitched fifes carry the stirring tune, while the drums mark the rhythm with distinctive beats and rolls.

recruits were often assigned to play in the fife and drum corps, whose duties extended far beyond lifting spirits, raising morale, and quickening the steps of the amateur soldiers. They announced the beginning and end of the day, meals, and other activities; and on the battlefield, they transmitted commands that could not otherwise be heard over the noise of musket fire.

In 1792 the first laws were passed standardizing the formation of military bands. European bands, including those giving concerts in America, had long had a variety of woodwinds and brasses as well as percussion instruments; now the typical American military band also included brass instruments. However, members of the brass family only assumed significant melodic responsibilities after they were fitted with valves, about 1830, since it was difficult to play melodies on the earlier, valveless instruments.

Music Published for Bands

Early American bands provided an important stimulus for music publishing in America, although much of the music printed for American bands was written by European composers. Besides marches and dance tunes, programmatic pieces were particularly popular at band concerts, with "battle" pieces featuring the sounds of gunshots, cries of the wounded, trumpet calls, and other warlike effects being especially admired.

SUMMARY

Artistic style has alternately experienced classical and romantic periods. During the eighteenth century, intellect replaced emotion as a reliable guide to truth, and the arts reflected this return to classicism. European and American literature became increasingly practical and secular, while architects emulated classical Greek and Roman styles, and painters produced balanced, objective, and realistic works.

Music in the Classical period also exhibited logic and emotional restraint. Chamber music was important, though of limited interest in America, where the outstanding European composers of the time were scarcely known. Religious, household, and band music were more significant than concert music in eighteenth-century America.

TERMS TO REVIEW

classical style A restrained, objective style of art.

romantic style An emotional, subjective style of art.

Classical period The period from about 1750 to 1820, also known as the Age of Reason.

neoclassical style The eighteenth-century style of painting and architecture inspired by the arts of ancient Greece and Rome.

chamber music Music for a small number of instruments, with one instrument per line of music.

fortepiano The early piano, smaller and less sonorous than the modern instrument.

fiddle A precursor of the violin, smaller and lighter than the modern instrument. (The term is also used today as a colloquialism for the violin.)

fife A small flute.

KEY FIGURES

American Painters
John Singleton Copley
Benjamin West
Charles Willson Peale

European Composers
Wolfgang Amadeus Mozart
Franz Joseph Haydn

OPTIONAL LISTENING EXAMPLE*

Johann Friedrich Peter: *Quintet V,* second movement (chamber music by eighteenth-century Moravian composer)

---

*Guides for Optional Listening Examples are in the Instructor's Manual and may be copied and distributed to students.

PIONEER AMERICAN COMPOSERS

Chapter 5

The singing of psalm tunes remained the prevalent music practice in Protestant churches throughout the first hundred years of the American experience. Naturally, the melodies were altered over the years, as individual congregations developed their favorite versions of old tunes. Comfortable with their own familiar ways, congregations firmly resisted their leaders' encouragement to sing the tunes in the "regular" way (as they had been written), much preferring the "usual" (in a sense, the American) versions to which they had become accustomed. The tunes as *they* knew them were dear to their hearts, and arguments flared between advocates of the regular and the usual styles of singing.

EARLY EFFORTS AT REFORM

The first attempts to teach New Englanders to read the tunes printed in their psalters were made by some of their better-educated ministers. These minister/teachers printed collections of tunes, prefaced by detailed instructions on how to read music notation.

Traditional Music Notation

For centuries, European music has been written on a **staff** of five lines and four spaces, each line and space representing a particular tone. We read up or down the staff the same way we would climb up or down a ladder, and in fact, the word "scale" comes from the Italian word for ladder. A sign called a **clef** is written at the beginning of the staff to establish the specific pitches indicated by each line and space. The two most commonly used clefs are the **treble** (𝄞) for higher tones and the **bass** (𝄢) for lower tones. The range of pitches indicated by each clef is shown by the relative position of the tones on the incomplete keyboard in figure 5.1.

New Systems Introduced by Americans

Although the traditional system of music notation is quite easy to learn, some eighteenth-century amateur teachers attempted to devise even simpler methods. One, based upon the four syllables then commonly used to sing pitches (*fa, sol, la,* and *mi*), placed on the staff the first *letter* of each syllable (*f, s, l,* or *m*) instead of the traditional note heads.

The slightly later **shape-note notation,** introduced just after the turn of the nineteenth century, evolved from the letter method of notation. The shape-note system assigned a different shape (square, circle, diamond, or

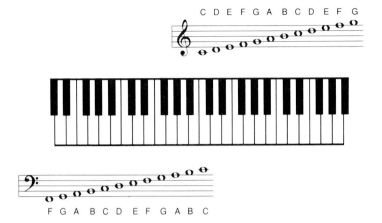

Figure 5.1

Pitches notated in the treble and bass clefs. Certain tones, including "middle C," may be notated in either the bass or treble clef.

△ = fa (used for the 1st and 4th degree of scale)
𝑜 = sol (used for the 2nd and 5th degree of scale)
□ = la (used for the 3rd and 6th degree of scale)
◊ = mi (used for the 7th degree of scale)

Figure 5.2

An arrangement of "Old Hundred" in shape-note notation. The words are placed under the melody line. (From B. F. White and E. J. King, *The Sacred Harp,* 1844. Copyright © Sacred Harp Publishing Company, Atlanta, GA. Reprinted by permission.)

triangle) to each of the four syllables, placing *them* on the staff in lieu of initial letters (fig. 5.2). Although never adopted as the usual way of notating music, the shape-note method proved an effective teaching tool. It continues in use today with informal singing groups in certain rural, urban, and suburban areas across the country.

The efforts of the teaching ministers were soon supplemented, and eventually assumed, by talented amateur musicians known as **singing school masters.**

America's earliest music teachers had no formal music instruction themselves but were self-taught music amateurs who earned most of their living as shopkeepers, merchants, farmers, or in other trades. Some of them became itinerant teachers, traveling from town to town and holding informal singing schools in the local meetinghouse, church, or school.

THE SINGING
SCHOOL
MOVEMENT

People were glad to welcome a singing school master to their town, for singing schools became popular social as well as educational events. Interested men, women, and young people attended the singing lessons several times a week for two or three months. At the end of this period, the class gave a performance, demonstrating their accomplishments to the town's proud public. Then the singing school master traveled on to another place.

The singing school movement, which began in Boston about 1720, experienced its greatest activity throughout New England from 1760 to 1800, finally spreading north into Canada and south through New York, New Jersey, Pennsylvania, Maryland, and into the Carolinas. In fact, the singing school masters offered widespread instruction and inspiration—especially in rural and remote areas—well into the nineteenth century.

The singing school masters were necessarily hardy and independent individuals. They devised their own teaching materials, compiling collections of familiar psalm tunes and other religious songs, and composing tunes of their own. Some wrote extensive introductions to their music primers, including information about the syllables to be sung and the elements of music. They were the first Americans to write music in a distinctively American style, and they are collectively referred to as members of the **First New England School** of composers.

Music of the First New England School

A "school" of artists generally includes people who live at about the same time, in the same country or area, and who share certain artistic goals and similarities of style. The First New England School composers lived in the late eighteenth century in New England, and their goal was to provide musical textbooks for use in their singing school classes. Most of their simple, folklike songs had religious texts and so were suitable for congregational singing as well as for simple entertainment at home.

The best songs of these "Yankee pioneers" were as rugged, naive, and honest as the sturdy tunesmiths who wrote them. Untouched by the influence of their sophisticated European contemporaries, they relied upon old, familiar techniques and their own honest taste. Colonial Americans, after all, had been out of touch with European music since the early seventeenth century, the very time that tonality was becoming the harmonic system of the Western world. Although aware of the major and minor scales, the singing school masters did not know all the rules of the tonal system. Nor did they feel obliged to conform to those they understood, frequently basing their melodies upon modal or pentatonic scales. The European rules of harmony that governed relationships between "tense" and "relaxed" (or *dissonant* and *consonant*) sounds were also quite unfamiliar to the American pioneers, whose harmonies were often conceived according to personal taste rather than formal precedent. Thus, their music is filled with refreshing surprises for twentieth-century ears accustomed to consistently tonal effects.

Certain combinations of musical sounds have the effect of being passive, or at rest. These are the sounds we call **consonant.** Other harmonies sound relatively tense, or active, and are sometimes used to provide a sense of drive or direction in music. These sounds we call **dissonant.**

It is important to understand that dissonance and consonance have nothing to do with "good" or "bad" sounds, but refer only to the relative degree of activity or tension the composer intends or the listener perceives. These concepts are entirely subjective, differing widely from one time, culture, or individual to another. Dissonance and consonance work together to provide variety and stability in musical compositions. For example, dissonant sounds sometimes create tension that then resolves to a consonant harmony, much as a dancer expressively tenses and then relaxes certain muscles.

Because the First New England School composers wrote to please their own ears, it is not surprising that some of their musical decisions were refreshingly unorthodox. The singing school masters were aware that conventional relationships between consonant and dissonant sounds had been established by European music theorists, but they chose to be independent of such rules. To make this point, William Billings wrote a song titled "Jargon," in which he obviously delighted in using outrageous harmonies sure to offend the sensibilities of those with delicate taste.

The best known of the early New England composers was **William Billings,** a tanner of hides who became a famous singing school master and composer in his day. He was the first American to produce a tunebook consisting entirely of his own compositions. This was *The New England Psalm Singer,* printed (by Paul Revere) in 1770 (the year of the great German composer Ludwig van Beethoven's birth).

Billings had attended singing school himself, and he continued to study music and to improve the quality of his compositions throughout his career. However, he considered "nature" the best teacher, and he confidently judged the quality of a piece according to how much he liked it. His contemporaries considered Billings eccentric but talented above the ordinary. He had many admirers, but he failed to realize much profit on his tunebooks, for there was no effective copyright protection in his day. Forced to work as a street cleaner late in life, Billings died a poor man.

William Billings was a nationalistic composer, in the sense that he wrote to suit his own American tastes and made no attempt to imitate European styles. He often wrote on American subjects and produced a number of stirring patriotic songs, some of which describe specific events of the American Revolution. Such a song was "Chester" (Listening Example 8), a favorite of the Revolutionary period and sometimes referred to as the first American popular song. It first appeared in the collection printed in 1770, but Billings added topical verses after the war broke out. Many people became familiar with "Chester" through stirring band performances, and the song was one of the most popular pieces in the early band repertoire.

LISTENING EXAMPLE 8
Revolutionary War Song

Composer   William Billings

Title   "Chester"

Form   Strophic. There are several four-line stanzas.

Meter   Quadruple. "Chester" was the principal marching song of the New England troops during the Revolutionary War.

Melody   The strong tune lies within the range of an octave. It begins with the last four notes of the ascending major scale—the third phrase also uses these four notes only. The second phrase uses the lower notes of the octave, and the fourth phrase uses the complete descending major scale.

Texture   Homophonic. The melody lies in the **tenor,** or next-to-the-lowest voice, as was the custom in homophonic vocal music of the eighteenth century. We are accustomed to hearing the melody of a song in the **soprano** (highest) voice, with the **alto** or **contralto** (lower female voice), tenor, and **bass** (lower male voice) providing harmony. Here we must listen carefully to distinguish the melody line from the other voices, which simply provide harmony and have no melodic interest of their own.

Timbre   "Chester" may be sung a cappella, but it was probably accompanied by instruments in its usual eighteenth-century performance.

Text   Three verses of the words, which were written by Billings, will indicate the stirring spirit and martial mood of his text.

> *a*   Let tyrants shake their iron rod,
> And Slav'ry clank her galling chains.
> *b*   We fear them not, we trust in God.
> New England's God forever reigns.
>
> The Foe comes on with haughty stride,
> Our troops advance with martial noise.
> Their vet'runs flee before our youth,
> and Generals yield to beardless boys.
>
> What grateful off'ring shall we bring,
> What shall we render to the Lord?
> Loud Hallelujahs let us Sing
> And praise his name on ev'ry Chord.

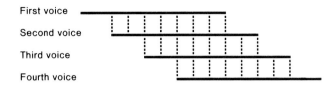

First voice

Second voice

Third voice

Fourth voice

POLYPHONIC MUSIC

By the time of the First New England School, congregational singing in church was often accompanied by an organ or other music instrument(s). Since harmony was no longer excluded from music performed in church, homophonic versions of psalm tunes and hymns were generally accepted in the worship service. People had long enjoyed singing polyphonic settings of religious tunes in their homes, and gradually these, too, came to be sung in church.

Canons

A **canon** is a melody that forms a polyphonic composition when performed with "staggered entrances"—that is, when successive voices begin the melody at later times (fig. 5.3). As the second (and sometimes the third and fourth) voices enter, they form meaningful harmonies with the first voice and with each other, each voice continuing to the end of the melody and then dropping out. (Here "voice" refers to a line of music, whether sung or played by musical instruments.) A canon that continues to make harmonic sense when repeated indefinitely is called a **round.** "When Jesus Wept," one of Billings's best-known songs, is a circular canon or round (Listening Example 9).

Fuging Tunes

Late in the eighteenth century, a new kind of song called a **fuging tune** became very popular, and by 1810, about one thousand fuging tunes had been written.

A fuging tune consists of two sections, which we will call **A** and **B** (fig. 5.4). The first section (**A**) is chordal, or homophonic, in texture—that is, the melody lies in one voice (usually the tenor), and the other three voices (soprano, alto, and bass) provide chordal harmony.

The second section of a fuging tune (**B**) begins with staggered entrances. Because each line in this section has melodic interest, the texture is polyphonic. But unlike a canon, in which each voice performs the *same* melody, entering and dropping out in turn, a fuging tune has four *independent* lines of music, and the voices end together on a chord. The second section is repeated, rendering the form of a fuging tune **ABB.**

"Sherburne" by **Daniel Read** (1757–1836) was an immensely popular fuging tune in the late eighteenth century (Listening Example 10). Read, a comb maker who also owned a general store, became well known as a composer and singing school master, and was probably the most popular composer of fuging tunes. "Sherburne" remained widely known until the Civil War period, and it is still sung today, particularly in some rural parishes.

LISTENING EXAMPLE 9
Canon

Composer William Billings

Title "When Jesus Wept"

Form A four-part circular canon or round. There are four phrases, any two or more of which form harmony when performed together.

Texture Monophonic when the melody is performed in unison; polyphonic when performed in canon.

Meter Triple

Timbre The canon may be performed by four women's voices, four men's voices, or by a mixed chorus of soprano, alto, tenor, and bass.

Text Billings wrote the words, as well as the music, of this famous canon. The ending is particularly effective; the last voices sing the moving words in unison, the other voices having dropped out in turn.

> *When Jesus wept, the falling tear*
> *In mercy flow'd beyond all bound;*
> *When Jesus groan'd, a trembling fear*
> *Seiz'd all the guilty world around.*

Figure 5.4

A fuging tune. Section A is homophonic in texture, as represented by the dotted vertical lines. Section B begins with staggered entrances (polyphonic texture) but ends with chords. Section B is repeated.

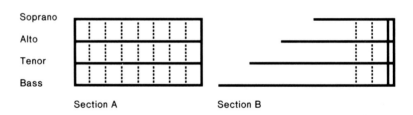

Soprano
Alto
Tenor
Bass

Section A   Section B

Besides Billings and Read, there were many singing school masters and composers in the First New England School. Although these practical men conceived of their music as teaching material rather than art, we value it today as strong, beautiful, and genuinely American in character.

LISTENING EXAMPLE 10
Fuging Tune

Composer   Daniel Read

Title   "Sherburne"

Texture   The first section, consisting of the first two lines of text, is homophonic in texture. (The fact that the words are sung in the four voices simultaneously implies chordal texture or vertical combinations of sound.) The second section (third and fourth lines) begins with staggered entrances, each melodic line imitative of, but not identical to, the others. (Different words in different voices enhance our ability to hear the music in a linear fashion.) The last few syllables are sounded simultaneously in all the voices, and the section ends on a chord. The second section is repeated.

Text   The words are those of a famous hymn written in 1700 by Nahum Tate.

> *While shepherds watched their flocks by night,*
> *All seated on the ground,*
> *The angel of the Lord came down,*
> *And glory shone around.*

SUMMARY

Early efforts to improve the quality of singing in New England's churches included the introduction of new methods of music notation. Shape-notes remain in use in certain rural areas today and are being introduced in some urban and suburban regions as well.

Many of the singing school masters were also members of the First New England School of composers, whose music was different in style and purpose from that of their European contemporaries. Often based upon modal or pentatonic scales, their folklike melodies were appealing and easy to sing. William Billings and Daniel Read were among the many Yankee pioneers who produced quantities of psalm tunes, hymns, fuging tunes, and patriotic songs that were enjoyed at singing school, at church, and in the home.

TERMS TO REVIEW

staff   Five lines and four spaces upon which music is notated.

clef   A sign placed on the staff that fixes the pitch of each line and space.

treble clef (𝄞)   Usually used to notate higher pitches.

bass clef (𝄢)   Usually used to notate lower pitches.

shape-note notation   A method that assigns a shape to the notated pitches of fa, sol, la, and mi, placing them on the staff in normal fashion.

singing school movement   An effort by music amateurs to teach New Englanders to read music and to sing. The movement began in the early eighteenth century.

First New England School   America's first composers. Also known as Yankee pioneers and singing school masters, they lived in New England in the late eighteenth century and wrote music for practical purposes.

consonance   Musical sounds that seem to be passive or at rest.

dissonance   Musical sounds that imply tension, drive, or activity.

soprano   The high female voice.

alto or **contralto**   The low female voice.

tenor   The high male voice.

bass   The low male voice.

canon   A polyphonic composition in which all of the voices perform the same melody, beginning at different times.

round   A circular canon, or one that may be repeated indefinitely.

fuging tune   A song in two sections, the first homophonic and the second polyphonic in texture.

KEY FIGURES

William Billings
Daniel Read

SUGGESTIONS FOR FURTHER LISTENING

Fuging tunes and other songs by other Second New England School composers, such as:

Timothy Swan
Andrew Law
Jeremiah Ingalls
Jacob Kimball
Supply Belcher

Modern compositions based upon the music of the First New England School, including:

William Schuman, "New England Triptych" "Chester Overture," Listening Example 37, p. 224

Henry Cowell, eighteen pieces, each titled "Hymn and Fuging Tune"

Otto Luening, "Fuging Tune for Wind Instruments"

Ross Lee Finney, "Hymn, Fuging and Holiday"

THE BROADENING MUSIC EXPERIENCE

Chapter 6

By the latter part of the eighteenth century, American amateurs were actively involved in many phases of musical activity, but professional performances continued to be dominated by foreign musicians. Musical societies were founded in a number of larger cities for the purpose of presenting instrumental or choral music—mostly by European composers. For their concerts, which were usually private affairs attended by invitation only, the amateur members were often joined by professional foreign musicians.

The efforts of the musical societies were supported by well-to-do patrons and musical amateurs, such as the famous statesman **Thomas Jefferson** (1743–1826). Jefferson was a fine musician who participated enthusiastically in music activities but insisted in the classical way that the arts must be relevant to life. An accomplished architect who designed buildings to be beautiful as well as efficient, Jefferson apparently considered the musical arts an essential part of the human experience as well. Jefferson played the violin, as did Patrick Henry. They sometimes performed duets to entertain themselves, their friends, and (before the Revolution) illustrious representatives of His Majesty's government in Williamsburg, Virginia.

Most early Americans agreed with Jefferson that art—especially American art—must be practical to be worthwhile. John Adams, in fact, referred to art as a luxury inappropriate for the people of a young democracy, although he admired a well-written sermon, political document, or tract. **Benjamin Franklin** (1706–1790) warned that Americans should not cultivate a taste for the arts before they were able to produce them; he clearly considered Europeans to be superior in this regard.

Even Franklin, however, contended that poetry, painting, and music might be useful under certain circumstances. He wrote verses to set to tunes that he enjoyed, learned to play the guitar and the harp very well, and even invented a musical instrument called the **armonica** or the **glass harmonica** (fig. 6.1). This consisted of a row of bottles of graded sizes, filled with liquid and placed on a spindle that the performer kept turning through a trough of water by working a pedal. A delicate sound was produced by rubbing the tuning bottles or glasses with the fingers. The glass harmonica, which

PRESTIGIOUS
MUSICAL
AMATEURS

Figure 6.1

Benjamin Franklin playing his glass harmonica. (Art & History Archives, Berlin.)

was later adjusted to be played with a keyboard, was extremely popular in Franklin's day and through the early years of the next century. Mozart is said to have enjoyed playing upon it—he even composed several pieces of music for the novel instrument. (See Listening Example 11.)

Franklin also wrote about music, as he wrote about everything of interest to him. He complained that America had no musicians of the caliber of outstanding European performers, and that even concerts performed by Europeans in America were inferior to the performances Franklin heard in England and on the Continent.

AMATEUR
COMPOSERS

The first secular songs published in America were by Europeans, many from England, and they were usually associated with the theater. But about the same time that the singing school masters were writing religious songs to use as teaching tools, other amateur American composers began to write music that had neither religious nor practical purpose.

LISTENING EXAMPLE 11
Glass Harmonica

Composer   Wolfgang Amadeus Mozart

Title   Adagio in C, K. 617a (old K. 326). As you already know, *adagio* means slow. Here, the very slow tempo of the piece allows time for the distinctive drawn-out "ring" of the rubbed glasses to carry effectively.

The "C" in the title refers to the tonic note and the key of the piece, which is C major. (A lowercase letter is normally used to indicate a minor key.)

The "**K.**" refers to the catalogue in which all of Mozart's known works are organized in chronological order, as nearly as L. von Koechel could determine their dates of composition or publication. The **Koechel catalogue** was published in 1862 and has been revised since then to reflect more recent scholarship. Thus, the original **K. numbers** have in some cases been changed.

Francis Hopkinson was an extraordinary eighteenth-century American. He was our first Secretary of the Navy, and he was one of the signers of the Declaration of Independence. He was also concerned with the artistic dimension of American life, and he wrote several **art songs**—that is, songs intended for concert or recital performance (amateur or professional) as opposed to folk or popular pieces. The text of an art song is a poem, presumably of literary merit, by a known poet. Because the music is intended to enhance the meaning of the poem, it may be expressive or dramatic rather than necessarily "beautiful." Since the essence of an art song lies in the text, and since translations inevitably lose nuances of meaning and sound, art songs are nearly always performed in the language in which they were written.

Francis Hopkinson was a zealous patriot in the political sense, but his songs were conceived in conscientious imitation of the English songs of his day. Unlike the sturdily independent singing school masters, Hopkinson held the "cultivated" eighteenth-century American view that the colonists were inferior in the arts and should emulate European styles. His song titled "My Days Have Been So Wondrous Free" (Optional Listening Example) is of historical but little musical interest today.

Although Hopkinson appears to have been the first American to attempt songs of this nature, soon others also composed songs that were European in style. The texts, however, were often based upon American subjects—several in honor of George Washington, for example. Most early American art songs were suitable for performance by amateurs.

When the famous Methodist missionaries and hymn writers **John** and **Charles Wesley** arrived in America in 1735, they were accompanied by a number of **Moravians** who wished to settle here. Having been severely

Francis Hopkinson (1737–1791)

The Moravians

persecuted for their religious beliefs and practices in Moravia and Bohemia, the Moravians came to America to serve as Christian missionaries to the blacks and Indians. They settled first in Georgia, and then moved north to found Bethlehem, Pennsylvania. Other Moravian communities were soon established nearby.

Music had always been an important part of the Moravians' experience, and they continued to compose and perform beautiful music in their new land. Hymn singing and other religious music were integrated into their daily lives. They also wrote songs and instrumental music and gave the first performances in America of important European symphonic and choral works. Their strong German and Czech heritage was reflected in the music they composed, which was sophisticated and complex beyond that of other early Americans. Moravian musicians were amateurs only in the sense that they wrote music for the love of it (as the root of the word amateur implies), rather than for money. Their compositions and performances were of the very highest quality.

The first important American-born Moravian composer was **John Antes** (1740–1811). He composed a number of beautiful religious pieces called *anthems,* some of which are sung and well recognized yet today (see Listening Example 12).

Anthems

An **anthem** is a religious song, longer and more complex than a fuging tune and intended to be sung by a trained soloist or choir rather than a church congregation. The text of an anthem is often biblical. The form is usually through composed (see chapter 1). That is, as the text unfolds, there is new music throughout the piece, with little or no repetition of melodic phrases.

Antes was also the first American-born composer of chamber music, of which the Trio in E-Flat Major (Listening Example 13) is a fine example. Unlike the First New England school composers, the Moravians were well-versed in the European rules of theory, and they thought in terms of the tonal system of harmony. Thus, in the title and in the *key signature* at the beginning of the score, Antes identified the key in which his Trio no. 1 was written.

Key Signatures

In order to achieve the major or minor scale pattern on tonics other than C or A respectively, certain steps of a scale must be raised or lowered. A **sharp** (♯) indicates that a note should be *raised* one-half step; a **flat** (♭) means that it should be *lowered* one-half step. For example, to play a major scale beginning on G, we must raise the seventh step to F *sharp,* in order to preserve the pattern of half and whole steps of the major scale.

LISTENING EXAMPLE 12

Anthem

Composer   John Antes

Title   "Surely He Has Borne Our Griefs"

Form   Through composed

Meter   Quadruple. Although there is a steady sense of pulse throughout this moving anthem, the tempo is often greatly relaxed at the ends of phrases to heighten the emotional expressiveness of the piece. The term for this expressive "robbing from" and "returning to" the tempo is **rubato.**

Harmony   The anthem is in the key of C minor, meaning that the tonic note is C and most of the melodic and harmonic material is based upon the C minor scale. However, notice how Antes varies the effect by occasionally using a major chord, as at the end of the first phrase on the word "griefs."

Also notice how pungent dissonances, as on "wounded" in the third phrase, enhance the meaning of the text by evoking an emotional response. The sopranos' high pitch on "wounded" and in the last phrase on "stripes" also has an emotional impact upon the listener.

Accompaniment   Whereas most early American composers expected accompanying instruments simply to double the voice lines, Antes wrote full instrumental accompanying parts for his anthems. Here there is a four-part accompaniment for string ensemble, although it may be played on an organ or piano instead. There is no instrumental introduction, but the instruments play an interlude between the two large sections (beginning after "iniquities"). Their ending material, with its descending melodic line, slowing of tempo, and lessening of dynamic level, brings the anthem to a moving close.

Text   Surely He has borne our griefs and carried our sorrows. He was wounded for our transgressions. He was bruised for our iniquities. The chastisement of our peace lay upon Him: And with His stripes we are healed.

The sharps or flats required to produce the major or minor scale beginning on a particular tonic are called the **key signature** for that key. (Thus, the key signature of G major is F♯ [fig. 6.2].) The composer indicates the key of a piece by placing the required sharps or flats, if any, on the staff just after the clef.

LISTENING EXAMPLE 13
Chamber Music

Composer   John Antes

Title   Trio no. 1 in E-Flat Major for Two Violins and Cello, op. 3. (Excerpt from 3rd movement.)

Although this is Antes's Trio No. 1, the op. 3 in the title indicates that it is his third **opus**, or published composition.

The third (last) movement of this trio is in the mood, tempo, and meter (duple) of a robust country dance. The violins carry the sprightly melody and provide simple harmony and embellishment, while the deeper-pitched cello supports them with strong, detached strokes and occasional sustained tones. Notice the balanced phrase structure (a series of phrases of equal length, sometimes giving a question-and-answer effect), typical of the Classical style of music.

About twenty-five seconds into the movement, you may hear an expressive, sustained tone in the cello, followed almost immediately by the repetition in the violins of a brief melodic phrase at successively lower pitch levels. This repetition of melody at different levels of pitch is called **sequence**, and it is one of the most common and most easily identified melodic techniques of melody in all genres of music.

Shortly after this, you will hear an echo effect, achieved by sudden changes in dynamic level in all three instruments.

A good way to develop listening techniques would be to listen to this brief excerpt repeatedly, concentrating on a different aspect each time. Follow the violins once, then listen primarily to the cello; count the beat; listen for changes in dynamic level; try to recognize melodic sequence. It soon becomes easier to notice and appreciate many significant effects at once.

Figure 6.2

The sharp placed on the F line of the staff in the key signature indicates that all Fs will be sharp unless otherwise marked.

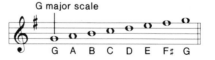

News of the Moravians' outstanding performances of choral and instrumental music spread quickly, and people came from other settlements to hear their concerts. George Washington and Benjamin Franklin were among the Moravians' most fervent admirers. John Wesley and Charles Wesley reflected the influence of the Moravians in the variety and quality of the hymns they wrote for their hymnal published in 1737. Many of these beautiful hymns are included in the hymnals of Protestant denominations today and remain widely known and loved.

Public concerts in eighteenth-century America were indeed concerted efforts by amateur and professional performers who produced a variety of vocal and instrumental entertainment. These concerts, which lasted three or more hours, were attended by an elite audience, able to pay the price of admission and to appreciate the long and varied performances.

However, even the best-educated American audience had very limited experience with music. Therefore, early concerts consisted of simple and popular pieces. Short, accessible works from the Baroque period were performed, as well as newer pieces from the **Mannheim School,** a group of European composers whose works were conceived for performance by the finest orchestra in Europe at the time, located in Mannheim, Germany. Marches, dance tunes, and stirring programmatic pieces were interspersed with folk songs and popular songs from the contemporary theater. Battle pieces written for the keyboard (harpsichord, organ, or piano), as well as for bands, were among the most popular concert attractions.

Professional Composers

Many talented and accomplished European musicians immigrated to the United States seeking professional opportunity, and they greatly enriched the American concert experience before and after the turn of the nineteenth century. **Benjamin Carr** (1768–1831), a composer, singer, conductor, organist, pianist, and music publisher, arrived soon after the Revolution. Aside from his many other activities, Carr also ran a music store in Philadelphia that became the leading center of music activity after the war.

James Hewitt, whose birth and death dates are the same as those of Beethoven (1770–1827), became a theater director and music publisher. He catered to the prevailing American taste by composing a number of programmatic battle pieces, including an orchestral work titled "Overture in Nine Movements, Expressive of a Battle" and an organ piece called "Battle of Trenton."

Alexander Reinagle (1756–1809) taught music for a while in New York City before settling in Philadelphia as director of a theater company. He also composed attractive instrumental pieces and directed a series of City Concerts that presented the music of outstanding European composers, as well as that of the prestigious emigrants.

The last movement of Reinagle's Sonata in E for the Piano Forte is in the form of a *rondo* (Listening Example 14).

Rondo

Although a **rondo** may include any number of sections, the letters **ABACA** illustrate the general concept of the form. That is, the opening melodic material returns (comes round) a number of times, alternating with other, contrasting sections. Because the mood of a rondo is often bright and the tempo fast, the form is often chosen as an effective close to a multimovement work.

LISTENING EXAMPLE 14
Rondo

Composer Alexander Reinagle

Title Sonata in E for the Piano Forte, third movement. (A **sonata** is a multimovement composition for one or more solo instruments. **Pianoforte** was an early name for the modern piano.)

Form Rondo (or, since the contrasting sections are extended and rather complex, modified rondo).

Tempo Allegro

Meter Duple

(**A**) The gay opening theme includes two balanced phrases. It is repeated, with only slight variation, to provide classical balance and to enable the listener to memorize it and recognize its return. The left hand plays a simple accompaniment, including some measures of the **broken-chord** pattern called **Alberti bass.**

The extended (**B**) section includes graceful running passages. Notice the strong accents in one passage. (**A**) returns; there is another contrasting section (**C**), including contrasts between forte and piano passages. A slow and quiet **cadenza,** or solo passage for the right hand alone, anticipates the return of (**A**).

EARLY AMERICAN THEATER

Many of America's earliest professional musicians were associated with both the theater and the concert hall. While the songs and instrumental interludes they composed for theatrical works were performed in concerts as well as for theater performances, it was theatrical performances that made their works popular and afforded them a living.

Charleston and Williamsburg were early centers of music activity, both southern cities having active theaters well before the middle of the eighteenth century. The prevailing religious influence in the South was Anglican, and the English church—unlike the Calvinists—had largely abandoned Oliver Cromwell's seventeenth-century scruples regarding theatrical performances.

A general ban on theater performances prevailed throughout the colonies at the time of the Revolution, but after that period, music theater developed a growing popularity. Interest in music and the theater moved north to New York and then to Philadelphia, which soon dominated the musical scene. The Quakers' disapproval of theatrical performances was overruled by the enthusiasm of such influential patrons as George Washington, who justified his fondness for theater by declaring that it had the practical effect of elevating one's manners.

This was hardly apparent at performances, however, where informality to the extent of rowdiness prevailed. Those sitting in the cheaper seats, called the gallery, yelled freely at the actors and musicians, demanding to hear their favorite songs and criticizing the performance in the frankest terms. Bottles and fruit were tossed into the orchestra pit or onto the stage, and although soldiers were hired to keep order, pandemonium frequently reigned.

The eighteenth-century American stage offered a potpourri of entertainment, with performances lasting four or five hours and usually including a main drama and a shorter, lighter, and often comic piece as well. Music was added even to nonmusical plays, and musical entertainment was provided between the dramatic pieces and after the comedy. Sometimes a march was played at the end, leading the audience out of the hall to attend a dance.

Most of the plays performed in eighteenth-century America were English pieces adapted to suit American taste. Shorter and lighter than contemporary European works, they also included more comedy. The most popular type of performance, called a **ballad opera,** was a simple, unsophisticated musical play in which spoken dialogue was used instead of the *recitative* (a sort of "sung speech") of serious opera, and popular songs of the day were interspersed throughout the show. John Gay's *Beggar's Opera,* the first musical play of this kind, became as popular in America as it had been in England since it opened in 1728.

Francis Hopkinson wrote a short theater piece in 1781, which may have been America's earliest original music theater work. (It is likely, however, that Hopkinson simply set new words to music that already existed.) In any case, the American popular music stage was dominated for a considerable period by foreign professionals such as Alexander Reinagle, who had significant effect upon the development of music in America.

SUMMARY

Americans' musical tastes became more secular and more varied during the eighteenth century, as music supplied entertainment in the home, at concerts, and in the theater. Many people learned to play instruments and sing simple songs, and musical societies were formed for the purpose of performing instrumental and choral music.

Talented amateurs participated in informal recitals and composed songs and keyboard pieces. The Moravians' music was of a complexity and quality unprecedented by other early American compositions. Public concerts were long and varied affairs, and music theater had also become a popular form of entertainment by the middle of the century. The important musicians associated with the early American theater were Europeans who adapted popular European plays and ballad operas to suit the less sophisticated American taste.

TERMS TO REVIEW

armonica or **glass harmonica**   A musical instrument invented by Benjamin Franklin, consisting of tuned, wet glasses that were rubbed to produce sound.

K. numbers   These refer to the **Koechel catalogue,** in which Mozart's works are organized in approximately chronological order.

art song   A secular song intended for concert or recital performance.

Moravians   Europeans who settled in Pennsylvania and whose music compositions and performances were of highly professional quality.

anthem A through-composed religious song, usually with a biblical text, for performance by a choir rather than a congregation.

rubato Expressively taking from and then adding to the tempo. (The word "rubato" means "robbing.")

sharp (♯) Raises a tone one-half step.

flat (♭) Lowers a tone one-half step.

key signature The number of sharps and flats in a key.

opus The opus number indicates the chronological order in which a piece was written or, more often, published.

sequence The repetition of a melodic pattern at one or more different levels of pitch.

Mannheim School A particularly accomplished group of composers of orchestral music in early eighteenth-century Mannheim, Germany.

rondo An instrumental form consisting of three or more sections in which the first melodic material (**A**) alternates with other melodic sections (**B,** etc.), as for example, **ABACA.** The tempo is usually fast and the mood happy.

sonata A multimovement composition for one or more solo instruments.

pianoforte An early name for the modern piano; larger and stronger than the earlier fortepiano.

broken chord The notes of a chord played in succession, one at a time.

Alberti bass A broken-chord accompaniment pattern.

cadenza A solo passage. In a keyboard piece, a cadenza is a passage for one note at a time.

ballad opera An English form of music theater in which comedy and satire were set to popular tunes.

KEY FIGURES

Musical Amateurs
Thomas Jefferson
Benjamin Franklin
Francis Hopkinson

Moravian Composer
John Antes

Hymn Writers
John Wesley
Charles Wesley

Immigrant Professional Musicians
Benjamin Carr
James Hewitt
Alexander Reinagle

SUGGESTIONS FOR FURTHER LISTENING

Music for glass harmonica:
Mozart, *Adagio and Rondo,* K. 617, for glass harmonica, flute, oboe, viola, and cello

American instrumental music in classical style:
Benjamin Carr, *Sonata I,* for piano or harpsichord
Federal Overture

Battle piece:
James Hewitt, "Battle of Trenton," for organ

Music by Moravian composers:
Johann Friedrich Peter
Johannes Herbst
John Antes
Jeremiah Denckem
Edward W. Leinbach

part 3

THE YOUNG REPUBLIC

ROMANTICISM IN AMERICA

Chapter 7

Even before the turn of the nineteenth century, there were signs of change from the reasoned and orderly approach of the Classicists toward the emotional, intuitive style we call **romanticism.** The Romantic period of music (the capital letter distinguishes the nineteenth-century period from the romantic style in general) is usually considered to have extended from about 1825 to 1900. However, fierce *independence,* a worshipful love of *nature,* and fascination with the *unknown*—all romantic characteristics—were significant facets of American expression well before that time and after.

ROMANTICISM IN AMERICAN LIFE

Having won their independence from England, Americans asserted their intention to retain that condition by resisting the French and British in assorted skirmishes during the early years of the nineteenth century. They also vigorously fought the notorious Barbary pirates, and in the Monroe Doctrine of 1823, vowed to resist foreign interference anywhere in the western hemisphere.

Nature, formerly viewed as a menacing force to be conquered and tamed, now became a source of reverent admiration. The natural beauty of the American continent in particular was exalted and idealized in the American literature, painting, and music of the Romantic period.

Unlike the classicist, who finds satisfaction in the methodical achievement of reasonable, limited goals, the romantic is endlessly intrigued with the unknown. Thus, romantic curiosity was among the influences that encouraged pioneer men and women to extend the frontier ever farther west. In spite of great perils and difficulties, they pushed on in the high spirit of optimism characteristic of the romantic personality. Perhaps the early settlers' sense of adventure was bred into later generations of Americans, or perhaps the vast and wild land encouraged freedom and independence. For whatever reasons, romanticism seemed then—as it does now—to be characteristic of the American personality.

The Rise of the Common Folk

The brave men and women who extended the American frontier encountered harsh and dangerous conditions that afforded little cultural or educational opportunity. However, they developed a fierce respect for the integrity and rights of the individual. Puritans, Quakers, and other Protestants living in the cities of the Northeast shared the frontier folks' work

George Caleb Bingham, *Fur Traders Descending the Missouri.* Oil on canvas. H. 29, W. 36½ in. (The Metropolitan Museum of Art, Morris K. Jessup Fund, 1933. [33.61].)

ethic and concern for the common people. This belief in individual rights and responsibilities, essential to the American creed, is among the basic tenets of romanticism.

Movement toward Reform

During the nineteenth century, a strong reform movement rose, vigorously addressing human and civil rights issues. Women became active in a number of social causes, including the abolition of slavery, the founding of the American Temperance Society (1826), improvements in conditions in prisons and asylums, and increased aid to the disabled.

In 1829, people in the cities and on the frontier definitively rejected aristocratic leadership by electing a popular hero, Andrew Jackson, president of the United States. Under President Jackson, a new American nationalism evolved, as artists and writers, encouraged by their patrons' new interest in American art for art's sake, began to produce works on a wide variety of American subjects.

THE ARTS IN NINETEENTH-CENTURY AMERICA

Comparisons may be readily drawn between the various arts of any stylistic period, but the relationships between Romantic literature, painting, and music are particularly strong and significant. Artists of this period drew inspiration from close association with each other and showed unprecedented interest in each other's work.

In fact, artists were in some sense more dependent upon each other at this time than ever before, for the artist's position in society had undergone significant change. Formerly viewed as servants of the church or aristocracy, both of which supported artists by requisitioning works to be executed according to the desires (demands) of the patron, artists began to consider themselves not only independent of, but somehow superior to, such patronage. In a sense, artists viewed themselves as a special class. Yet, in truth, they were newly dependent upon the approval of a public audience, which lacked both the training and the experience of the earlier limited, even private, audiences of the church, court, or salon. Thus, it is understandable that during the Romantic period, artists relied upon each other not only for moral support, but sometimes also for support of a more practical kind.

Although musicians remained tied to European—specifically, German—traditions, literary and visual artists began to evolve characteristically American styles.

Literature

Steamship transportation to Europe was available from about the 1830s, but it was not very safe or reliable. Most Americans, therefore, remained effectively isolated from European culture. Little diplomatic exchange took place, and few foreigners emigrated during the mid-century period. Refreshingly free from European dominance, American literary figures began to develop their own distinctive ways to express the American experience, and a genuinely American literature evolved.

The prolific literary activity of this period reflected the new American nationalism, as poets and novelists wrote on American subjects placed in American settings. **James Fenimore Cooper's** *The Last of the Mohicans* was one of many works about the American Indian. **Edgar Allan Poe** and **Nathaniel Hawthorne** reflected another passion of the Romantics in their fascination with abnormal psychology. The poets **William Cullen Bryant** and **Henry Wadsworth Longfellow** and the essayists **Ralph Waldo Emerson** and **Henry David Thoreau** portrayed nature as good and beautiful, expressing in characteristically American ways ideals similar to those of the British Romantics Robert Burns, William Wordsworth, Percy Bysshe Shelley, John Keats, Samuel Taylor Coleridge, and Lord Byron.

New York City became the major center of intellectual and artistic activity. There, and in other large cities, the theater thrived. Journalism, too, became an important means of communication and a stimulus for humanitarian reform.

Meanwhile, Boston housed an important group of writers and philosophers known as **Transcendentalists** who, in the romantic way, trusted intuition over reason as the guide to truth. The Transcendentalists also shared the Protestants' and frontier folks' belief in the integrity and ability of the individual. Love of nature and pride in America's natural beauty were fervently expressed in their literary and philosophical works.

The Visual Arts

During the early years of the nineteenth century, surveyors and engineers explored and carefully mapped the wilderness areas of upstate New York, New England, and the West. The Erie Canal (fig. 7.1) was opened in 1825,

Figure 7.1

The Erie Canal. (The Bettmann Archive, Inc.)

and steam railroads soon offered further means of travel. Painters sometimes accompanied explorers and adventurers, and their depictions of the wild beauty of these untamed areas stirred the romantic imagination of city dwellers.

The new appreciation of art for its own sake encouraged American painting and sculpture of an unprecedented variety. Artists and patrons alike began to consider a broader range of subjects than before. American painting in this post-Revolutionary, **federal period** reflected the new American nationalism and the romantic love of nature, as artists captured the clear light, blazing sky, and vast open spaces of the American landscape.

The same democratic spirit that elected Andrew Jackson president stimulated appreciation for scenes of everyday life, especially as experienced in the country. Cornhusking, dancing, and all manner of working and playing were charmingly depicted by folk and formal artists. **George Catlin** (1796–1872) was an artist-explorer who vividly portrayed the vast American wilderness, complete with Indians and wild animals. **John James Audubon** (1785–1851) shared Charles Willson Peale's scientific interests, producing realistic watercolors of American birds in their natural poses and settings. There were few professional women artists, but **Margaretta Angelica Peale** (1795–1882), a cousin of Charles Willson Peale, was admired as a painter of lovely still lifes (fig. 7.2).

Samuel Morse (1791–1872), like Audubon and C. W. Peale, was interested and talented in both science and art. A promising painter who studied in Europe and produced several fine paintings upon his return to America, Morse was discouraged at the Americans' preference for landscapes of local scenery over the large European-style "history paintings" he favored. He finally turned his attention to another form of communication and invented the telegraph. Morse was also influential in making the pre-photographic process known as daguerreotype popular with Americans, who often appreciated the new and the mechanical more than the purely artistic.

Figure 7.2

Margaretta Angelica Peale, *Still Life with Watermelon and Peaches,* 1828. Oil on canvas, 13 × 19⅛ in. (33 × 48.5 cm.). (Smith College Museum of Art, Northampton, MA. Purchased with funds given anonymously by a member of the class of 1952.)

The first important group of American artists, known as the **Hudson River School,** was led for a time by **Thomas Cole** (1801–1848), whose devout religious feeling and pride in the beauty of America are reflected in his large landscape paintings. In particular, the spaciousness and grandeur of the Catskill and Adirondack Mountains are beautifully captured in his works. Like so many of the great Romantics, Cole associated closely with other artists, producing works such as his *Scenes from The Last of the Mohicans* (fig. 7.3), based upon the novel by his friend James Fenimore Cooper.

Kindred Spirits by **Asher B. Durand** (1796–1886), who succeeded Cole as leader of the Hudson River School, also represents a romantic mating of the arts. This painting portrays the artist Cole (for whom the painting was a memorial) and the poet William Cullen Bryant standing together and admiring the natural beauty of the Catskill Mountains (see plate 1).

Sculpture, too, became popular as Americans sought to idealize the great figures of this important period, but American sculptors produced little that was original or characteristically American in style. Architecture reflected the strong romantic interest in the past, as state and other public buildings were designed in ancient Greek and Roman style. However, the important architects of the federal period were Europeans.

MUSIC

Many Romantics were prodigiously talented in several of the arts, and some who became famous as composers also produced paintings or literary works of varying levels of quality. A mating of the arts also occurred when composers or painters based their works upon a literary idea. An art song, for example, was the setting of a poem to music. Program music, which often

Figure 7.3

Thomas Cole, *Scenes from Last of the Mohicans.* (Courtesy of the New York Historical Society, N.Y.C.)

depicted scenes from literature, was prevalent among instrumental compositions of the nineteenth century. Certain kinds of music theater—especially operas and operettas—constituted an even more complex mating of visual, literary, and musical arts.

In order to express their artistic ideals, Romantic composers handled the elements of music differently from the manner in which the Classicists had used them.

Melody

Melodies in Romantic music are often long and lyrical, and melodic phrases are asymmetrical rather than balanced in the Classical way. Nineteenth-century composers were more likely to repeat their long, songlike melodies with variation or embellishment than to develop intellectual or motivic ideas.

Harmony

Chordal harmony became fuller and more dissonant in the nineteenth century. Just as our palates enjoy spicier seasonings as we become accustomed to highly flavored foods, our ears become adapted to richer sounds and pungent dissonances. Romantic composers added new tones to the chords of tonal harmony, thus achieving varied and colorful effects.

Rhythm

Romantics treated rhythm more freely than the Classicists had done, preferring to avoid the "tyranny of the barline," or the regularly recurring pattern of a certain number of beats per measure with an accent on the first. The love of freedom and stress on individuality also encouraged Romantic composers to use **irregular meters** (five or seven to the bar, for example), **changing meters** (a different number of beats in succeeding measures), or **polymeters**—two or more meters at the same time.

Timbre

About the same time that painters began to use color for expressive rather than realistic purposes, composers began to explore the timbres, or "colors," of sounds. Thus, the music of the nineteenth century includes increasingly rich and imaginative instrumental effects.

As technological changes increased the capabilities of woodwind and brass instruments, more of them were included in the symphony orchestra. The percussion section of the orchestra was also greatly expanded, and it then became necessary to add more strings in order to balance the sound. Accordingly, the Romantic orchestra was not only larger than that of the Baroque and Classical periods, but it also included a richer variety of timbres. When you attend orchestral performances today, you will probably notice that pieces written in the eighteenth century are played by a small or **chamber orchestra,** whereas Romantic pieces require a much larger ensemble.

The Foreign Influence

As we have seen, nineteenth-century American writers and artists developed certain indigenous styles of expression, but American composers continued to turn to Europe for inspiration and instruction in their art. The zeal for reform that gave rise to labor movements and the Temperance Society also led musicians to scrupulously avoid the irregularities characteristic of the music of the self-taught singing school masters. Yet too insecure to indulge in a nationalistic style, American musicians of the Romantic period sought to emulate the German masters who also dominated European music of the nineteenth century.

SUMMARY

By the turn of the nineteenth century, Americans had become more romantic than classical in their style of expression. Among the influences that led to expansion of the American frontier were the romantic characteristics of strong independence, love of nature, and fascination with the unknown. The zeal to improve the conditions of life was also a romantic trait, which gave rise to humanitarian reform and labor movements as well as efforts to abolish slavery throughout the Romantic period.

Under the presidency of the popular Andrew Jackson, a strong sense of nationalism evolved, significantly affecting American literature and art of the period. New York City became the center of intellectual and artistic activity, while the Boston Transcendentalists produced moving literary and philosophical works.

Unlike art and literature, however, American music of the Romantic period was dominated by European, particularly German, ideals. American composers sought to correct the irregularities of music produced by the First New England School and to reform the naive taste of the American public.

Plate 1

Asher B. Durand, *Kindred Spirits*. In a scene exemplifying the Romantic image, the painter Thomas Cole and the poet William Cullen Bryant share their admiration for the beauty of the Catskills. Love of nature, nationalism, and the close mating of the arts are among the Romantic characteristics beautifully expressed in this moving painting. (Collection of The New York Public Library. Astor, Lenox and Tilden Foundations.)

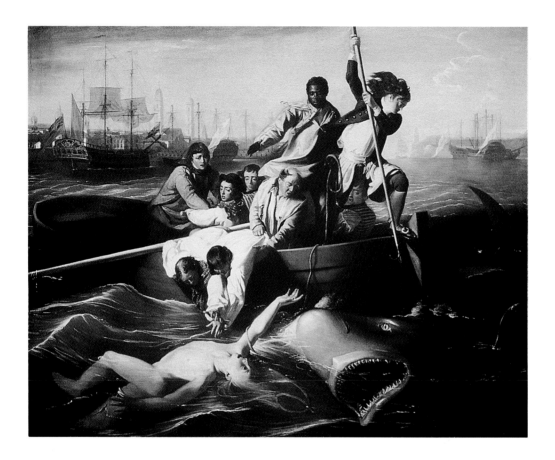

Plate 2

John Singleton Copley, *Watson and the Shark,* 1778. Oil on canvas, 72½″ × 90¼″ (184 × 229.5 cm). Although largely self-taught, Copley effectively captured the seething action and dramatic interplay of emotions between the desperate characters in his masterful painting. (Gift of Mrs. George von Lengerke Meyer. Courtesy, Museum of Fine Arts, Boston.)

Plate 3

The Sargent Family,
American School, 1800,
canvas, 0.974 cm ×
1.280 cm. Folk artists, like
the singing school
masters, accomplished
highly attractive art in
their efforts to provide a
practical service—here, to
preserve the likenesses of
this young American
family. (Gift of Edgar
William and Bernice
Chrysler Garbisch,
© 1992 National Gallery
of Art, Washington.)

Plate 4

Thomas Eakins, *Max Schmitt in a Single Scull,* oil on canvas. In this nineteenth-century painting, Eakins captured the spaciousness, clear air, and brilliant light characteristic of the American atmosphere. (The Metropolitan Museum of Art, Purchase, Alfred N. Punnett Endowment Fund and George D. Pratt Gift, 1934.)

TERMS TO REVIEW

romanticism   Emotional, subjective style of art. The period from about 1820 to 1900 is referred to as the Romantic period of music.

Transcendentalists   Philosophers and literary figures who relied upon intuition as the guide to truth.

federal period   The period in American history that succeeded the American Revolution.

Hudson River School   The first important school of American artists.

irregular meters   Meters other than duple, triple, or quadruple.

changing meters   A different number of beats to the measure within a piece or section.

polymeters   Two or more meters performed simultaneously.

chamber orchestra   A small orchestra with a few instruments per line of music.

KEY FIGURES

Authors
James Fenimore Cooper
Edgar Allan Poe
Nathaniel Hawthorne

Poets
William Cullen Bryant
Henry Wadsworth Longfellow

Philosophers and Essayists
Ralph Waldo Emerson
Henry David Thoreau

Artists
George Catlin
John James Audubon
Margaretta Angelica Peale
Samuel Morse
Thomas Cole
Asher B. Durand

THE MOVE TO REFORM MUSIC

Chapter 8

The educated American's sense of cultural inferiority had developed into a full-fledged complex by the turn of the nineteenth century, by which time the unself-conscious works of the singing school masters were largely disparaged. Fuging tunes were considered old-fashioned, and their polyphonic sections were thought to obscure understanding of the text.

Professional American musicians of this period conscientiously imitated European forms and styles of music in an effort to improve the condition of music in their young country. In music collections published in America during the first half of the nineteenth century, European works and their American imitations largely replaced indigenous American pieces. Simplified notation systems, including shape-notes, were generally abandoned in favor of the traditional European system of writing music.

CLASSICAL VERSUS POPULAR MUSIC

Before the nineteenth century, Americans had drawn little if any distinction between music intended for popular entertainment and music considered serious, cultivated, or "art." Fuging tunes, for example, provided both entertainment at home and instructive material at singing school, and hymns and psalm tunes were sung at social as well as religious occasions.

In the nineteenth century, however, differences between serious and popular music and between religious and secular music became significant. Patriotic Civil War songs and minstrel songs and dance tunes were the natural expressions of unself-conscious folk, but American concert music was conceived in imitation of European styles, especially German Romanticism.

THE GENTEEL TRADITION

For culturally insecure Americans, it became important to establish their gentility, though of course the zeal to be proper negated the possibility of producing genuinely expressive and significant art. Superficiality, artificiality, and extreme sentimentality are among the characteristics ascribed to the music and art of the "genteel tradition."

Most concerts in America were performed by European musicians who had the twofold mission of improving American taste and raising money for themselves. Concerts usually took place in the larger, well-established cities, where genteel folk asserted their respectable, refined, and fashionable tastes by conspicuous attendance at music performances.

Throughout the early nineteenth century, people increasingly acquired musical instruments in their homes, and musical instruction became more widely available. Collections of rather simple pieces by European and American composers, suitable for playing by amateurs at home or in a village band, were published in growing numbers.

However, instrumental concert music was not yet well accepted in America. Recognizing that concertgoers of the period sought entertainment rather than edification, clever entrepreneurs such as P. T. Barnum (1810–1891) recruited performers who would thrill the naive American audience. Vocal music was particularly well appreciated, and people flocked to performances by well-known European singers.

The typical concert of the early to mid-nineteenth century was very long—lasting several hours, in fact—and included a wide variety of pieces, mostly vocal. Favorite art songs and opera excerpts were interspersed with sentimental ballads of a more popular nature, with the new brass bands, in which valved brass instruments played melodies as well as chords, providing further variety and light relief. But the joys of orchestral music eluded the American audience until later in the century.

Instrumental versus Vocal Music

Music for choirs and vocal soloists was enthusiastically received, and choral societies proliferated throughout the nineteenth century. The Boston Handel and Haydn Society, one of the earliest and most long-lived of these organizations, presented outstanding concerts of choral music by European masters. Many other musical societies in Charleston, Boston, New York, Philadelphia, and even Newport, Rhode Island, also promoted choral music. They published collections of choral music, offered singing lessons, and presented concerts of great European choral works, often accompanied by a symphony orchestra.

Among the kinds of dramatic choral music heard by these early American audiences were relatively short works called *cantatas* and longer compositions called *oratorios*.

Choral Music

Cantata

A **cantata** is a multimovement piece for chorus, one or more soloists, and organ or orchestra. It tells a story or describes an event, which may be on a religious or secular subject. A well-known American cantata from the late nineteenth-century period is "Hora Novissima" by Horatio Parker.

Oratorio

An **oratorio** is also a multimovement dramatic work for chorus, soloists, and orchestra. It is usually longer than a cantata and is based upon a religious subject. The best-known oratorio is *Messiah* by George Frideric

Handel, portions of which are performed around the world at Christmas and Easter time.

Oratorios were particularly admired by the nineteenth-century American concert audience. The Handel and Haydn Society presented Handel's *Messiah* and Joseph Haydn's *The Creation* as early as 1817, and these works were widely praised by the public, though critics found the performances inferior to those heard in Europe.

Late in the century, cantatas and oratorios by American composers were occasionally performed, but the preference for European works remained strong. The famous *Boston Handel and Haydn Society Collection of Church Music* was compiled by Lowell Mason, the leader of the movement to reform music in America.

LOWELL MASON (1792–1872)

Lowell Mason was the son of a singing school master and schoolteacher, from whom he inherited a talent for music and for teaching. Having attended singing school as a child, Mason continued the study of music as a young man by taking private lessons with a German musician while working at a bank. He learned to play several instruments, became a church organist and choirmaster, and began to compose rather conventional but quite attractive anthems and hymns.

Although music had not previously offered Americans significant business opportunities, it became apparent soon after 1800 that money could be made in that field. For example, Mason's collection, which included some of his own religious songs and several that he had arranged from melodies by famous European composers, sold extremely well. Amazed at the amount of money the book earned, Mason soon left his bank job and turned his professional attention to music.

It was Mason's intention to improve and modernize musical taste and experience in America by providing hymns and other religious music of a better (that is, more European) quality than the works of the pioneer composers. He was sensitive, however, to the needs of an unsophisticated public, and he conformed in some ways to their expectations.

Old-Fashioned Techniques

Mason seemed surprisingly comfortable with certain old-fashioned practices. For example, he sometimes used a system of musical shorthand called **figured bass** (fig. 8.1) that had served throughout the Baroque and early Classical periods but proved inadequate to notate the complicated harmonies of Romantic music and was seldom used after 1800. And although he clearly preferred people to learn the traditional, European system of music notation, Mason yet used—or allowed his publisher to use—shapenote notation in some of his popular collections. He also wrote some of his hymns in three-part harmony, which was familiar to ordinary people, rather than in the modern standard four-part arrangement of soprano, alto, tenor, and bass. He even sometimes placed the melody in the middle voice, as the singing school masters had done, instead of in the top voice, as modern listeners were coming to expect (and as we are accustomed to hearing today).

(a)

(b)

Figure 8.1

(a) A figured bass.
(b) A "realization" of the
figured bass.

Recognizing the public's fondness for fuging tunes and other early American songs of which he disapproved, Mason wisely included some of them in each volume he published. Thus, of course, all of his books sold well, and he became a wealthy man.

Less daring and original than the efforts of the Yankee pioneers, Mason's attractive, rather sentimental hymns appealed to the taste of his day. A number of them, in fact, remain among the most familiar hymns today. "Nearer, My God, to Thee," "My Faith Looks up to Thee," "Work, for the Night Is Coming," and "When I Survey the Wondrous Cross" are still widely known and included in the hymnals of many denominations.

Mason's "Missionary Hymn" (Listening Example 15) illustrates in text as well as music the Romantic zeal to instruct and improve.

Lowell Mason's Hymns

Music Education in the Schools

Lowell Mason believed that children should not depend upon the New England singing school system for their music education, as he had. He thought, in fact, that instruction in reading and singing music should be provided to all American children by the public schools. It was largely due to his efforts that music was first included in the Boston public school curriculum in 1838, and other school districts soon followed Boston's example.

Mason was also a pioneer in providing training for music teachers. He made voice lessons readily available to adults and children in the Boston area, conducted performances of choral music, continued to publish collections of choral music and hymns, composed religious vocal music, and generally promoted the improvement of musical taste and performance in America.

Thomas Hastings (1784–1872) is said to have written close to one thousand hymns, the most famous of which is "Rock of Ages, Cleft for Me." He also wrote hymn texts and set them to the music of European composers. Like Mason and others of that time, he frequently selected secular tunes for this

IMPORTANT PEERS OF LOWELL MASON

LISTENING EXAMPLE 15
Hymn

Composer Lowell Mason

Title "Missionary Hymn"

Form Strophic. There are four verses, each with four melodic phrases.

Meter Quadruple

Melody The tune begins with the first, third, and fifth note of the major scale played in order (one-three-five). Performed simultaneously, three alternate tones, or the interval of a third superimposed upon another third, form a chord called a triad, the most basic chord in the tonal system. Many melodies begin with a **broken triad** such as this.

Harmony The harmony consists of simple, mostly major chords. Mason avoided the irregular harmonies and surprising dissonances of the singing school masters. Thus, although his harmony is technically more correct, it is also less interesting than that of the Yankee pioneers.

Accompaniment Mason wrote a keyboard accompaniment, including an introduction and closing section, with broken chords similar to an Alberti bass pattern. However, the hymn was often performed in three- or four-part harmony with a simple chordal accompaniment, as we generally hear it today.

Text (first verse)

From Greenland's icy mountains,
From India's coral strand;
Where Afric's sunny fountains
Roll down their golden sand;
From many an ancient river,
From many a palmy plain,
They call us to deliver
Their land from error's chain.

---

purpose. However, since he believed that music best served to enhance the sentiment of a religious text without calling undue attention to itself, his own tunes and harmonies are simple and unaffected.

Another successful music educator, composer, and compiler of religious tunebooks was **William B. Bradbury** (1816–1868). His tune titled "Woodworth" is often sung today with a text beginning "Just As I Am, without One Plea." "Sweet Hour of Prayer" is another of Bradbury's familiar hymns.

SUMMARY

Musicians in early nineteenth-century America considered European music superior to American music and therefore attempted to imitate the German Romantic style. Lowell Mason, who led the movement to reform musical taste in America, wrote attractive though quite conventional hymns, brought music education into the public school system, and systematically attempted to raise the level of musical awareness and appreciation.

Even Mason, however, sometimes used the convenient but old-fashioned technique of musical shorthand called figured bass. As an astute businessman, he included popular fuging tunes in his collections of music and sometimes allowed his publishers to use shape-note notation in order to make his books accessible and attractive to a wide audience.

Music societies presented performances of the great European oratorios. The so-called genteel society attended the societies' private performances, as well as concerts of a varied nature. Instrumental music was less well received, although novelty pieces played by the new brass bands were considered entertaining.

TERMS TO REVIEW

cantata A relatively short choral work on a religious or secular subject, accompanied by organ or orchestra.

oratorio A dramatic work based on a religious subject and performed by vocal soloists and chorus with orchestral accompaniment.

figured bass A system of musical shorthand by which composers indicated intervals above the bass line with numbers instead of notated pitches.

broken triad The notes of a triad played in succession.

KEY FIGURES

Lowell Mason
Thomas Hastings
William B. Bradbury

SUGGESTIONS FOR FURTHER LISTENING

Hymns by Lowell Mason:
"Nearer, My God, to Thee" ("Bethany")
"My Faith Looks up to Thee" ("Olivet")
"Work, for the Night Is Coming" ("Diligence")
"When I Survey the Wondrous Cross" ("Hamburg")
"Watchman, Tell Us of the Night" ("Watchman")

Melodies beginning with a broken triad:
"The Star Spangled Banner"
Louis Moreau Gottschalk, "Le Bananier," Listening Example 19, p. 122
Daniel Decatur Emmett, "I Wish I Was in Dixie's Land," Optional Listening Example*

*Guides for Optional Listening Examples are in the Instructor's Manual and may be copied and distributed to students.

OF, BY, AND FOR
THE PEOPLE

Chapter 9

People in the rural areas of America remained largely unaffected by the music reform movement, simply continuing to enjoy their accustomed ways of reading and singing psalm tunes and hymns. Country folk firmly resisted Lowell Mason's attempt to replace shape-notes, which used only four syllables, with the European seven-syllable system using **do, re, mi, fa, sol, la,** and **ti.** The singing schools, which remained popular through much of the nineteenth century, used tunebooks printed in shape-note notation, which as we have already noted, continues to be the preferred system in some areas today.

Because frontier America was virtually isolated from European experience throughout the post-Revolutionary period, it is not surprising that a distinctive, rather primitive music evolved that suited the purpose and pleased the ears of rural folk. While city people sang the stately, dignified, European-style hymns of Lowell Mason and his colleagues, country dwellers greatly preferred folk hymns and spiritual songs.

REVIVAL MOVEMENTS

A religious revival movement known as the **Great Awakening** had begun in the South during the previous century. It had spread widely through the North and West, promising ample rewards and ultimate salvation to faithful and virtuous Christians.

In the nineteenth century, a similar movement, known as the **Great Revival** or the **Second Awakening,** developed rapidly. Rural Presbyterians, Baptists, Methodists, and others were attracted by the thousands to huge, emotional camp meetings that lasted for several days (fig. 9.1). Itinerant preachers called *circuit riders* led the praying, shouting, singing, and often a kind of frenzied dancing at these social, recreational, and religious events. Camp meetings were refreshingly democratic affairs in which men and women, blacks and whites, adults and children participated with enthusiasm. Life in the South, in the country, and on the frontier was exceedingly difficult, and the popular camp meeting songs were a treasured source of comfort and inspiration.

Figure 9.1

George Bellows, *Billy Sunday.* This lithograph depicts the famous revivalist preaching to a fervent camp meeting crowd. (Courtesy National Portrait Gallery, Smithsonian Institution, Washington, D.C./Art Resource, N.Y.)

Spiritual Songs

The songs sung at camp meetings included hymns by the English composers **Isaac Watts** and Charles Wesley, as well as popular American folk hymns. For those who could read music, songbooks printed in the popular shape-note notation were available, with the melody printed in the middle voice according to old-fashioned custom.

One of the most popular songbooks, still in use in many rural and some urban and suburban areas today, was *The Sacred Harp,* first published in 1844. Many of the tunes included there were those of popular British ballads, to which Americans had set their favorite religious verses— hence, the folksy, tuneful nature of these lovely melodies.

"Amazing Grace" (Listening Example 16) is often called a folk hymn. Its composer is unknown, but the song appeared in print at least as early as 1831. It remains widely known and loved today.

Negro Spirituals

Blacks, free or slave, who had been converted to Christianity participated enthusiastically in the exciting camp meetings, singing the whites' psalm tunes and hymns with sincerity and fervor. They also developed a kind of religious folk song of their own called a **spiritual** (Listening Example 17).

The melodies of the black spirituals were simple and folklike. The texts of some spirituals were joyful, while others expressed loneliness and pain. Many offered hope for eventual release—from slavery, oppression, the harsh realities of the black experience in America, even from life itself. The "promised land" waiting somewhere "over Jordan" was a recurring theme.

Many spirituals were originally improvised and performed in the African style of call-and-response. That is, a leader sang one line, which was then repeated by the group, or the leader sang the verses, and the group responded to each verse with a simple refrain. Thus, the spirituals were easily learned, and many of them became familiar to and well loved by blacks and whites alike.

LISTENING EXAMPLE 16
Folk Hymn

Title   "Amazing Grace"

Composer   Anonymous

Form   Strophic

Melody   The haunting melody, using only the notes of the pentatonic scale, is often embellished, much as jazz singers embellish the melodies they play or sing. Slides, scoops, and other effects similar to, and sometimes borrowed from, black music are freely improvised.

Meter   Triple

Tempo   Slow

Text   The words were written by John Newton, an English evangelist overwhelmed with remorse for his earlier life as a slave trader. They promise God's forgiveness, even for such a "wretch" as he.

> *Amazing grace, how sweet the sound*
> *That saved a wretch like me.*
> *I once was lost, but now I'm found,*
> *Was blind, but now I see.*

White Spirituals

Folklike white spirituals were similar in form and style to the spirituals sung by blacks. These, too, involved much repetition, allowing even those who could not read words or music to learn them quickly and sing along. Some spirituals (white or black) had many verses, in each of which only one or a few words changed—for example, the word "father" becoming "mother," "sisters," "brothers," or "friends" in succeeding verses.

SECULAR SONGS

Each geographical area of America produced and enjoyed songs that expressed the typical experience of the people. As New Englanders became heavily involved in sea trade and traffic, sailors' work songs, or chanteys, appeared. On the frontier, people sang songs about freedom, equality, danger, and the beauty of nature in the wild. There were miners' songs, railwaymen's songs, and songs about the Gold Rush of '48. Slaves in the South produced their own characteristic music, expressive of their particular loneliness and suffering.

Lullabies served every segment of the population. Play and party songs, too, were enjoyed by rural adults as well as children.

In the cities, concerts and Italian opera continued to attract genteel or cultivated audiences. The theater, however, appealed to a far wider population.

LISTENING EXAMPLE 17

Negro Spiritual

Title   "Nobody Knows de Trouble I've Seen"

This folk hymn of tribulation retains its improvisatory flavor, and indeed the words of succeeding verses may vary considerably in performance, as led by a soloist in call-and-response fashion.

There is a simple chorus:

Nobody knows de trouble I've seen,
Nobody knows but Jesus.
Nobody knows de trouble I've seen,
Glory Hallelujah.

This alternates with short verses, the first of which is:

"Sometimes I'm up, sometimes I'm down,
Oh, yes, Lord.
Sometimes I'm almost to de ground,
Oh, yes, Lord."

All participants sing the familiar chorus, and all participate in the refrain, "Oh, yes, Lord," of the verses.

The hauntingly beautiful tune is based upon the pentatonic pattern that can be played on the black notes of a keyboard and that seems particularly comfortable to sing.

Several kinds of songs by European and American composers were included in nineteenth-century theatrical performances. Selections from popular English ballad operas and from the Italian opera repertory were much enjoyed, as were occasional art songs, highly sentimental ballads, and patriotic tunes. Although composers began to distinguish between music intended for professional performance and music to be sung and played at home, for the general public the differences between popular and classical or formal and informal music remained much less distinct than they are today.

THE POPULAR THEATER

Even before Ireland's potato famine of the 1840s drove thousands of people to emigrate, the Irish had flocked to America's shores in huge numbers, seeking economic opportunities unavailable in their homeland. The ruggedly beautiful melodies and nostalgic texts of their folk ballads appealed strongly to Americans. Songs such as "Believe Me If All Those Endearing Young Charms" and " 'Tis the Last Rose of Summer" offered a refreshing change from the formal art songs of European and American composers.

The Scottish culture, too, offered a treasure trove of song. The poet Robert Burns (1759–1796) had set his own verses to some lovely folk tunes that became popular in America before the Civil War. Although their melodies are more difficult to sing than the lilting Irish ballads, Burns's "Comin'

Ballads from Great Britain

Scene from *The Black Crook,* a wildly popular musical show of 1866, as depicted on the sheet music cover to the "Black Crook Waltzes." (Billy Rose Theatre Collection, The New York Public Library at Lincoln Center. Aster, Lenox and Tilden Foundations.)

thro the Rye" and "Auld Lang Syne" soon became and yet remain among the best-known songs in America.

England contributed generously to the American repertoire. The most popular song in both England and America during much of the nineteenth century was "Home, Sweet Home," written by an English composer, Sir Henry Bishop.

Patriotic Songs

Some of America's most enduring patriotic songs were composed during the period between the Revolution and the Civil War and are associated with events from that time. These songs were frequently included in theatrical entertainments, and they became, and in some cases remained, extremely popular.

"The Star Spangled Banner"

The words to "The Star Spangled Banner" were written by a young lawyer, **Francis Scott Key** (1780–1843), under the most dramatic circumstances. During the War of 1812, Key boarded a British vessel moored in Chesapeake Bay in order to plea for the release of an important American prisoner. The British agreed to release the prisoner before sailing for England, but they held both him and Key on board through the night while they attacked the city of Baltimore. In two stirring verses, the emotional young lawyer described the agony of suspense he experienced while witnessing the attack, and his overwhelming pride and relief at the sight of the American flag waving high the next morning.

Of course, Key little imagined that many years later (during the Spanish-American War, 1898), his song would be designated the official national anthem of the American armed forces—especially since he had

LISTENING EXAMPLE 18
Patriotic Song

Title   "Hail, Columbia"

Composer   Philip Phile, whose tune was originally known as the "President's March." The tune was very famous in its own right, and was often included in theatrical performances. Several instrumental pieces included excerpts from this famous march.

Form   Strophic

Meter   Duple

Text   Joseph Hopkinson set his stirring verses to Phile's tune in honor of George Washington's election in 1789:

> *Hail, Columbia, happy land!*
> *Hail! ye heroes, heav'n born band,*
> *Who fought and bled in freedom's cause,*
> *Who fought and bled in freedom's cause,*
> *And when the storm of war is gone,*
> *Enjoyed the peace your valor won;*
> *Let independence be your boast,*
> *Ever mindful what it costs;*
> *Ever grateful for the prize,*
> *Let its altar reach the skies.*
>
> Chorus: *Firm, united let us be,*
> *Rallying round our liberty,*
> *As a band of brothers joined*
> *Peace and safety we shall find.*
>
> (There are two more verses.)

set his romantic text to the melody of a popular Irish drinking song! Still less did he imagine that, in 1931, President Hoover would sign a bill making Key's song the American national anthem. Some have suggested that the melody's wide range and large intervals render it more difficult to sing than is appropriate for a national anthem. But defenders respond that the dramatic nature of the melody (however lowly its origin) and the effort required to sing it properly make it truly distinctive and ideally suited for the purpose.

"Hail, Columbia"

In some cases, patriotic songs served political as well as artistic aims. For example, when France and England went to war with each other in 1798, American allegiance was divided. Some rallied to the side of the newly democratic French republic; others felt tied to England by affection and tradition. But the words to "Hail, Columbia" (Listening Example 18), written by Francis Hopkinson's son Joseph, so exalted the wonders and accomplishments of America that emotional audiences were effectively united by stirrings of national pride.

SUMMARY

Lowell Mason's efforts notwithstanding, country folk continued to practice and enjoy their accustomed ways of reading and singing music. The singing schools remained popular in rural areas, using shape-note songbooks such as *The Sacred Harp* as teaching materials.

During the Great Revival, people of all ages, both black and white, attended religious camp meetings, where hymns and spirituals were enthusiastically sung. Secular songs became popular, too, often reflecting the experience of everyday life.

In the cities, theaters offered popular entertainment that was primarily musical. A typical performance included the singing of sentimental ballads, particularly those of British origin, as well as stirring patriotic songs of the day.

TERMS TO REVIEW

do, re, mi, fa, sol, la, ti   The syllables of the major or minor scale.

Great Awakening   An eighteenth-century revival movement that sought to Christianize whites and blacks alike.

Great Revival or **Second Awakening**   A continuation and intensification of the evangelistic movement begun in the eighteenth century.

The Sacred Harp   A popular collection of hymns and spiritual songs.

spiritual   A folklike religious song with a simple tune. The text often includes repeated phrases.

KEY FIGURES

Isaac Watts
Francis Scott Key

SUGGESTIONS FOR FURTHER LISTENING

Hymn texts by Isaac Watts:
"From All That Dwell Below the Skies"
"O God, Our Help in Ages Past"
"Joy to the World!"
"When I Survey the Wondrous Cross"

Hymn texts by Charles Wesley:
"Come, Thou Long-expected Jesus"
"Hark, the Herald Angels Sing"
"Jesus Christ Is Risen Today"
"Love Divine, All Loves Excelling"

part 4

THE CIVIL WAR ERA

SONGS OF THE NORTH AND SOUTH

Chapter 10

The reform movements begun in the early part of the nineteenth century were stronger than ever by the 1860s. Workers, increasingly well organized, forced enactment of tough new labor laws. Feminists, too, marched and demonstrated, demanding improved education opportunities for women, liberalized property rights, equitable divorce laws, and the right for women to vote. While urban Northerners were increasingly repelled by slavery, Southerners considered the system essential to the plantation economy upon which they depended, and there seemed no grounds for compromise on this volatile subject.

As Americans were finally forced to confront the problems that led inexorably to the Civil War, the literary, visual, and musical arts reflected every facet of these and other social issues.

THE VISUAL ARTS

From about 1850 to 1875, while European artists explored the myriad effects of light, American painters, too, learned to use light as a means of expression, their best work capturing the clear atmosphere and wide spaciousness characteristic of the American scene. They idealized nature in the romantic way, considering it morally uplifting and taking pride in the grandeur of the American landscape. Andrew Jackson's optimism and the idealism of the American pioneer were reflected in moving scenes of mountain splendor and rural calm.

Frederic Edwin Church (1826–1900), Thomas Cole's only pupil, painted New England with a scientific accuracy akin to Peale's and Audubon's fascination with natural history. Church and some of his contemporaries pursued their search for a new frontier all the way to South America, which they rightly considered part of the New World.

The best-known American artist of his day was **James McNeill Whistler** (1834–1903) who, discouraged by the lack of a market for serious art in his own country, spent most of his life in Europe. Although highly eccentric in dress and manner, Whistler was widely admired for his great talent, and he became a leading figure in both European and American art.

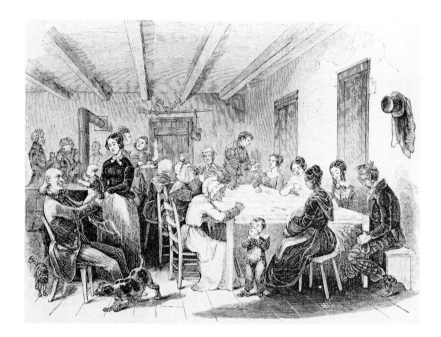

Figure 10.1

Nineteenth-century folk art. (North Wind Picture Archives.)

Figure 10.2

Edmonia Lewis, *Bust of Abraham Lincoln.* (Courtesy City of San José Public Library, CA.)

American still-life painting also matured and flourished, largely independent of European influence. Folk art became more individual and expressive than ever (fig. 10.1). American practicality produced fine craftsmanship, and articles such as weathervanes, shop signs, and pieces of furniture were made as beautiful as they were useful.

Americans also produced distinctive pieces of sculpture during this time. *The Greek Slave* by **Hiram Powers** (1805–1873) was seen as an American expression of sympathy for the Greek War of Independence as well as for slaves in the American South. Social consciousness was also apparent in *The Indian (The Chief Contemplating the Progress of Civilization)*, by **Thomas Crawford** (1813–1857). Although there were few professional women artists at the time, **Edmonia Lewis** (1845–1909), whose mother was Indian and whose father was black, produced a number of sculpted pieces of social and political relevance, including a stunning bust of Abraham Lincoln in 1867 (fig. 10.2).

LITERATURE

The year 1852 produced one of the most famous and influential novels of any period, *Uncle Tom's Cabin,* by **Harriet Beecher Stowe.** This book, which gave rise to the expression "Uncle Tom" to denote a black who accepts a servile position under whites, stirred heated reaction from people on both sides of the abolition question. The poets **John Greenleaf Whittier** and **James Russell Lowell** joined Emerson and Thoreau in a literary crusade against slavery. Meanwhile, **Sidney Lanier** (1842–1881) wrote moving verses from a Southerner's point of view. From the time Abraham Lincoln was elected

Figure 10.3

A melodeon. (The
Bettmann Archive, Inc.)

president in 1860 until he was assassinated in 1865, sermons, speeches, poems, articles, and proclamations addressed all sides of the slavery issue.

The famous humorist and author **Mark Twain** (1835–1910) was also an amateur musician who sang and played the piano, an instrument he claimed to particularly dislike. Apparently he associated the piano with the upper classes, with whom he did not identify. It is also possible that his sensitive, if untrained, ear was offended by the sound of poorly tuned pianos, because few instruments were afforded the regular attention of a professional tuner.

In any case, Twain's stories frequently refer to the singing of simple songs and the playing of homely keyboard instruments, such as the one variously called a **reed organ, parlor organ, cabinet organ, cottage organ,** or **melodeon** (fig. 10.3). The player of this instrument pumped one or two treadles, producing the wind that made the sound possible. The timbre could be varied through the use of levers or buttons called **stops.** The reed organ, which was cheaper and required less maintenance than a piano, was very popular in Twain's day.

MUSIC

By the middle of the nineteenth century, Americans were enjoying many kinds of music. They sang hymns and other religious and secular songs, attended military band concerts and balls, danced to the fiddle, played keyboard instruments, attended singing schools in the country, or joined urban musical clubs or societies. Even in the recently settled Great Plains area, music was occasionally played by explorers, trappers, traders, and missionaries. Music stores opened in frontier towns as well as in established cities, and instruments and sheet music sold well.

The most widely shared music experience was singing. There were aboli-
tionist (antislavery) songs, sentimental songs, patriotic songs, and religious
songs. Small collections called "pocket songsters" were printed and widely
distributed. Soldiers sang to relieve their loneliness and boredom, children
sang play tunes, and nearly everyone sang songs of faith.

Before and after the Civil War, several singing families toured through the
United States, performing songs of many kinds. Like the twentieth-century
European Trapp family portrayed in the Broadway musical *The Sound of
Music,* these traveling groups performed in churches, meetinghouses, and
concert halls.

 The most popular singing family was the **Hutchinson Family,** who first
came to public attention when the thirteen Hutchinson children presented
a highly successful performance of religious and secular music at a New
England meetinghouse in the early 1840s. Three Hutchinson sons later
formed a trio, and still later, their sister Abby joined their ensemble. This
popular quartet toured through New England for several years. The texts
of their songs, some of which they wrote or adapted themselves, addressed
some of the most radical social causes of the day—temperance, women's
suffrage, and the abolition of slavery—though their music was refined, genteel, and sentimental. When Abby married and retired from the group, other
members of the family formed various ensembles, and the Singing Hutchinsons remained famous in America and Europe for decades.

 Among the songs the Hutchinsons performed were secular, humorous
songs in strophic form called **glees.** The melody of a glee was usually in the
top voice, and the other two or three voices provided chordal harmony. Glees
were introduced in Europe during the eighteenth century, and were originally sung by men only. By the mid-nineteenth century, many glee clubs
had been formed in American cities, often including women as well as men,
and they sometimes sang more serious choral literature as well as glees and
other lighthearted fare.

The most popular of all songs representative of this turbulent period were
those included in the **minstrel shows.** In fact, the first big popular hit in
America was a minstrel song called "Jim Crow," written by **Thomas Dartmouth "Daddy" Rice,** the father of American minstrelsy. (It was only later
that the name of his song became a hostile term synonymous with discrimination against black people.)

 White men playing comic characters in blackface—their skin darkened by cork or coal—had been popular in England in the late eighteenth
century. Minstrel acts, as they were called, were soon commonly included
in American circus and showboat performances as well. Americans also
enjoyed brief minstrel performances between the acts of serious plays.

 In 1843, a group led by **Daniel Decatur Emmett**, known as the **Virginia Minstrels,** formed the first complete minstrel show. At their debut
before an enthusiastic audience in New York City, they appeared wearing

The Pleasures of Song

Singing Families

Minstrelsy

Figure 10.4

Scene from a minstrel show, with "Mr. Bones" on the left and "Mr. Tambo" on the right. (The Bettmann Archive, Inc.)

white trousers, striped calico shirts, and blue calico coats with tails. They sang, danced, joked, and told stories in a manner imitative of plantation blacks and citified northern blacks as they understood (or misunderstood) them.

The fiddle and banjo were important musical instruments in the minstrel show. Also invariably included were a **tambourine,** derived from an African percussion instrument, and a pair of **bones** (simple instruments commonly replaced in more recent times by a pair of linked castanets, which provide the timbre and rhythmic effects desired for various rural musics). The minstrel troupe also frequently included a small accordion-like instrument called a **concertina,** which has a number of buttons on each side that control the pitch. The concertina is played by alternately pushing the sides inward and pulling them outward, producing the wind that makes the sound.

Minstrel shows began with a rousing grand march, during which the players entered the stage and formed a semicircle facing the audience. "Mr. Tambo" and "Mr. Bones" (the tambourine and bones players) sat at opposite ends of the semicircle, exchanging hilarious comments that greatly entertained the audience between musical acts (fig. 10.4).

The very concept of a minstrel show is of course offensive by today's standards, but it was a highly popular form of entertainment in the pre- and even post-Civil War periods, offering a refreshing contrast to the sentimental parlor ballads characteristic of that period. Although derived from

African and European customs, minstrel songs and dances were as indigenous to the American experience as are the folk hymns of New England and the South. The best of the minstrel music—often referred to as America's first popular music—had an unself-conscious and infectious charm. After the Emancipation, blacks themselves participated in minstrel shows, forming their own companies and writing songs that remain favorites today. Among the best-known are "Carry Me Back to Ole Virginny," "In the Evening by the Moonlight," and "Oh, Dem Golden Slippers," all composed by **James A. Bland.**

E. P. Christy was a famous white minstrel composer and skit writer. His four-man **Christy Minstrels** show toured the American South and West, bringing theater (of a sort) to people who had never experienced it before. But by far the outstanding composer of minstrel and other popular songs of this period was **Stephen Foster.**

Stephen Foster was born into the genteel society of Pittsburgh, Pennsylvania. As a child, he heard his sisters sing and play the piano and other instruments, and soon he was picking out tunes himself.

STEPHEN FOSTER
(1826–1864)

However, music was not considered a respectable profession, and Stephen dutifully went to work as a bookkeeper while still in his teens. He jotted down some of the tuneful melodies with which his mind was filled and—to his amazement—had his first song ("Open thy Lattice, Love") published when he was just eighteen. Soon he was writing and publishing professionally.

Foster's early sentimental love songs suited the genteel taste of his family and their friends better than his own taste or talent. His personal favorites were the lovely plantation-like melodies reminiscent of the songs he heard blacks singing as they worked on the Pittsburgh riverfronts and, especially, the rollicking, comic songs of the minstrel shows.

Thus, Stephen Foster experienced a conflict between the music he felt he ought to write and the music he wrote and loved best. His sentimental songs about home ("My Old Kentucky Home" and "Old Folks at Home"), his songs about unfulfilled romantic love ("Beautiful Dreamer," "Come Where My Love Lies Dreaming"), and his settings of poems about the Civil War were well enough received. But his finest pieces were the nonsense songs such as "Oh! Susanna" (Optional Listening Example) and "De Camptown Races," some in black dialect, of which he was ashamed.

Foster was a man of paradox. His irresistible minstrel and plantation melodies set America, and soon much of the world, humming his tunes and singing his words about a life he had never experienced, since Foster was neither black nor from the South. It seems a bitter irony that a man so gifted was destroyed by his own inability to distinguish between genius and gentility. Unwilling even to acknowledge some of his best songs, Foster gave them away or allowed them to be pirated. He married in 1850, but his increasing emotional instability and heavy drinking caused his wife to leave him three years later. Stephen Foster died a pauper, alone and unrecognized, at the age of 38.

The Songs of Stephen Foster

Analysis of Foster's best songs reveals little that is innovative or even particularly interesting in their form, rhythm, or harmony. The songs are in simple strophic form, with much repetition of the melodic phrases within each verse. There is little rhythmic interest, except for occasional, but effective, syncopation. Most of the songs were written with simple guitar or piano accompaniments, primarily based upon the three primary chords of the tonal system—the tonic, dominant, and subdominant triads (see pages 7–8).

Foster wrote his songs during the time the sentimental parlor ballad was in vogue, and some of them may be described as such. But it is particularly difficult (and fortunately, unnecessary) to place many of Foster's songs within a particular category or genre. They are hardly art songs, since the texts are not of the quality associated with that form, but they *are* art in the sense that they are long-lived and representative of their composer's distinctive style. Many of Foster's melodies are folklike, but they are clearly composed. The songs are popular in the sense that they are enjoyed all over the world, but except for the rollicking minstrel songs, they have not been part of our usual concept of popular music. The songs vary widely in kind and quality, but the world is unarguably richer for having received the music of Stephen Foster.

CIVIL WAR SONGS

In 1860, several southern states seceded from the Union, and soon the country was plunged into the Civil War. At such times of social, political, and emotional turmoil, people consistently turn to the arts, at popular or at more serious levels, to express their anguish and ease their sorrow. Thus, it is not surprising that many songs were written about this tragic conflict.

Indeed, Civil War songs appeared in a rich variety of folklike, religious, comic, and serious styles. Some were lyrical and dramatic, suggesting their composers' fondness for Italian opera. Others had the flavor of Irish jigs or Highland bagpipe tunes, reflecting their composers' British heritage. Regional favorites, such as "Maryland, My Maryland" and "Marching through Georgia," stirred patriotic fervor and became widely popular during the troubled period.

The history of one of America's favorite songs, "I Wish I Was in Dixie's Land," is particularly curious. Written by a Northerner, Daniel Decatur Emmett (1815–1904), as a minstrel song and dance, it was then adopted by the Confederate states (to the composer's dismay) and became a favorite song of the South. "Dixie" (Optional Listening Example) was played by the Confederate band at the inauguration of Jefferson Davis as president of the Confederate States, but Abraham Lincoln liked the song so much, he reclaimed it for the North. In fact, versions were printed with words adapted to suit either the Union or Confederate cause, and the song continues to be universally enjoyed today.

SUMMARY

During the period from just before until shortly after the Civil War, American artists discovered ways to capture the clear and pure American light in paint. Their scenic landscapes revealed their love and admiration for an idealized nature and their pride in the beauty of their land. Painters also sometimes revealed, as did sculptors, poets, and writers of the period, a newly aroused social conscience and a concern for social reform.

Songs of many kinds were composed, performed, and widely enjoyed. Religious songs, sentimental ballads, songs of social protest, and glees were sung in parlors and concert halls, and were included in the performances of well-known singing families such as the Hutchinsons.

The most popular entertainment of the period was the minstrel show, in which white men blackened their skin and imitated the songs, dances, and dialect of stereotypical blacks. Stephen Foster was the finest composer of minstrel songs, though the genteel society preferred his love songs, Civil War songs, and sentimental ballads about home. A minstrel song by another northern composer, Daniel Decatur Emmett, is recognized today as the great song of the South.

TERMS TO REVIEW

reed organ (parlor organ, cabinet organ, cottage organ, melodeon) A keyboard instrument, popular in the nineteenth century for its relatively small size and price, the variety of sound produced by adjusting stops, and the small amount of maintenance it required.

stops Levers or buttons that allow the player to adjust the timbres produced by certain keyboard instruments.

glee A part-song with three or more lines of music, in chordal or homophonic texture, with the melody usually in the top voice.

minstrel show A performance in which white men perform music and comedy in imitation of stereotypical blacks.

tambourine A small drum with metal disks that jingle when the instrument is struck or shaken.

bones A folk percussion instrument consisting of a pair of castanets tied together and held in one hand.

concertina A kind of accordion or portable reed instrument. Melody and chords are achieved by depressing buttons or keys, and the wind is supplied by a folding bellows.

KEY FIGURES

Painters
Frederic Edwin Church
James McNeill Whistler

Sculptors
Hiram Powers
Thomas Crawford
Edmonia Lewis

Literary Figures
Harriet Beecher Stowe
John Greenleaf Whittier
James Russell Lowell
Sidney Lanier
Mark Twain

Performing Groups
Hutchinson Family
Virginia Minstrels
Christy Minstrels

Musicians
Thomas Dartmouth "Daddy" Rice
Daniel Decatur Emmett
James A. Bland
E. P. Christy
Stephen Foster

OPTIONAL LISTENING EXAMPLES*

Stephen Foster: "Oh! Susanna"

Daniel Decatur Emmett: "I Wish I Was in Dixie's Land"

*Guides for Optional Listening Examples are in the Instructor's Manual and may be copied and distributed to students.

THE ROMANTIC
VIRTUOSOS

Chapter 11

Romantics enjoy expressive extremes, and nineteenth-century Europeans were as thrilled by the sounds of a large symphony orchestra as by those of an intimate solo recital. Americans, who had more access to the latter experience than to the former, attended concerts in the same frame of mind with which they viewed a circus or minstrel show, and were particularly impressed by brilliant solo performers called **virtuosos.**

Technical virtuosity may indeed enhance a music performance, but a good musician has intellectual and expressive assets as well. Concert music was highly evolved by the mid-nineteenth century, and the best musical artists of the Romantic period exhibited the broad combination of talents that comprises true **musicianship.**

Although musicianship is a concept that defies strict analysis, certain qualities are essential, in some proportion or degree, to the consummate musician. These qualities, which are immeasurably enhanced by innate talent, acquired knowledge, and wide experience, are:

THE QUALITIES
OF
MUSICIANSHIP

1. Sensitivity to the *style* of the music. **Style** refers to the predominant collective characteristics of the arts of a given period, such as the Renaissance or the Baroque. Because these characteristics reflect the social, economic, and religious climates in which art is conceived, the art of one period is significantly different from that of another, and performance practices suitable for one style of music may be inappropriate for music of another period.

2. *Originality* of interpretation. Within the stylistic context of a particular piece, there may be any number of valid interpretations. Music lovers often collect recordings of a favorite piece of music by several different performers, appreciating each for what it offers, and even professional reviewers frequently disagree as to which recorded interpretation is "best." Live performances offer even greater opportunity to experience varied interpretations. The same performer may play the same piece differently on different occasions, depending on

such factors as the size of the room, quality of the instrument(s), temperature and humidity, character of the audience, and the performer's mood and state of health.

3. *Accuracy* of interpretation. There have been performers who sacrificed fidelity to the written **score,** as notated music is called, in favor of expression and were nonetheless widely admired, but they clearly represent an exception to the rule.

4. *Expressiveness,* or effective interpretation of the emotional content of a piece.

5. The *variety* of styles a performer interprets effectively.

6. *Virtuosity.* The brilliant performance of difficult passages of music is thrilling to see and hear. However, mere technical display that draws unseemly attention to itself is considered musically empty.

THE MID-CENTURY CONCERT

The romantic tendency to exalt the *individual* encouraged a kind of hero worship of the virtuoso performer, particularly in America, where concert audiences were inclined to expect dazzling displays of technique. They also preferred to hear familiar pieces, and a serious gap developed and widened between contemporary composers and the concert audience. American composers were further frustrated by the conspicuous lack of interest in American music on either side of the Atlantic.

On the other hand, the great nineteenth-century virtuosos benefited from the passion Americans conceived for their performances at the very time that Europeans had begun to tire of them. They flocked gratefully to America, where an adoring public was eager to applaud their showy performance techniques.

Among the best known and best remembered of the outstanding concert artists who toured America are a Swedish singer, a Norwegian violinist, and a pianist from—Louisiana.

The Swedish Nightingale

The United States tour of **Jenny Lind** (1820–1887) (fig. 11.1) was arranged by P. T. Barnum, much in the way that he promoted his famous circus acts. Lind's talent was prodigious, but she wisely confined her programs in this country to the kind of repertoire that would entertain an American audience: familiar arias from European opera and oratorio, with "Home, Sweet Home" and songs by Stephen Foster as encores.

Jenny Lind stayed in America for about two years. She traveled by steamer from New Orleans to Memphis, Nashville, and St. Louis, and she visited many other cities as well. The most successful virtuoso singer of her period, she thrilled Americans with her lovely voice, amazing vocal technique, and charming personality.

"Jenny Lind fever" spread quickly, and many who had never heard or been interested in concert music before became adoring admirers of "the

Figure 11.1
Jenny Lind. (The
Bettmann Archive, Inc.)

Swedish nightingale." Concert halls were built to accommodate her performances, and the way was prepared for other European performers to follow.

The Norwegian composer **Ole Bull** is best remembered as the outstanding violinist of his day. He made five long visits to the United States and married an American woman.

Ole Bull
(1810–1880)

A dedicated nationalist who believed art should represent the culture that produced it, Ole Bull encouraged Americans to develop a characteristic music of their own. While managing a fledgling opera company in New York City, he offered one thousand dollars to any American composer who would write an opera on an American subject. No one accepted the challenge, however, and the company soon collapsed.

Like Jenny Lind, Ole Bull accepted the limitations of his inexperienced American audience and performed little serious music. He entertained them instead with his virtuosic tricks, playing on all four strings of the violin at once or producing incredibly soft *pianissimos* that must have seemed to Romantic ears to come from another world. In one of his own compositions, he portrayed the American Revolution by alternating phrases of "Yankee Doodle" with "God Save the King." Original, flamboyant, hugely talented and entertaining, Ole Bull added a valued dimension to nineteenth-century America's music experience.

PIANO MUSIC

Largely due to the artistic demands of the famous composer and pianist **Ludwig van Beethoven** (1770–1827), the eighteenth-century fortepiano was replaced by the larger, stronger instrument called the pianoforte, or piano (see Listening Example 14, page 80). The keyboard of the newer instrument was extended in both directions, providing a larger range of high and low pitches. A steel frame made the piano capable of sustaining greater tension and more dramatic playing than Mozart and his Classical contemporaries had required or desired.

The piano, in fact, was virtually the ideal Romantic instrument. The damper and sustaining pedals allowed the player to sustain all or selected tones, achieving a **legato** or smooth and lyrical line. They also permitted the accumulation of sounds, so that long crescendoes could build to a tremendous climax. On the other hand, the soft pedal, by shifting the keyboard, allowed a player to achieve the most delicate and intimate effects.

Adding to the advantages of the wonderful instrument was the availability in America of some of the finest pianos manufactured. Jonas Chickering, William Knabe, and Henry Steinway all lived in America, and the pianos their companies produced could not be surpassed. Lowell Mason's son Henry cofounded the famous Mason and Hamlin piano company in 1854.

The varied concert programs of the day often included a virtuosic piano performance by a resident or visiting concert artist. Piano music was also popular in the home, and much "household" piano music was composed at a level of difficulty appropriate for the average young lady to master.

Among the outstanding pianists of the period was an American who amazed audiences on both sides of the Atlantic with his virtuosic performances and entertained them with his original piano compositions. This was **Louis Moreau Gottschalk** (fig. 11.2).

LOUIS MOREAU
GOTTSCHALK
(1829–1869)

Louis Moreau Gottschalk was of mixed cultural heritage. His father, who was English and Jewish, had been educated in Germany. Gottschalk's mother was descended from a wellborn French family that had immigrated to New Orleans from the West Indies at a time when slave uprisings had driven many white families to seek safety elsewhere. She was called a **Creole,** meaning someone born in this country of a foreign family. (Later the word "Creole" was applied to people of mixed racial heritage.) Gottschalk's first and strongest language was French, though he also spoke Spanish and English fluently.

New Orleans was a city teeming with a rich variety of cultural experiences. French, Spanish, Creole, and black mixed freely in a sophisticated atmosphere unlike that of any other city in Europe or America. From this fertile environment Gottschalk absorbed the musical sounds of each culture. Exotic Creole tunes based upon French folk and popular melodies inspired many of Gottschalk's compositions.

Gottschalk's sophisticated family had no genteel compunctions regarding professional musicians. Recognizing Louis's precocious talent and the lack of opportunities at home, they sent him to France at the age of

Figure 11.2

Louis Moreau Gottschalk at the piano. (The Bettmann Archive, Inc.)

thirteen to study music. He stayed abroad for eleven years and became a great favorite of aristocratic European society. His youthful compositions for piano were much admired, and the young American's virtuosity astonished the most sophisticated audiences. Even **Frederic Chopin** (1810–1849), the famous Polish "poet of the piano," predicted that Gottschalk would one day be the "king of pianists."

Having amazed and delighted concert audiences in Spain, France, and England, Gottschalk returned to America in 1853. His long stay abroad made him seem respectably foreign to Americans, whom Gottschalk thrilled with performances of his melodically simple but technically demanding piano pieces.

Gottschalk then spent several years in the West Indies, the tropical sounds and flavors of which are reflected in some of his later compositions. Returning to America in 1862, he found the country desperately at war. Though a southerner by birth, he sided firmly with the North and began an exhausting concert tour across America, contributing most of what he earned to the Union cause.

Thus, Gottschalk brought piano recitals to remote towns and small cities, often reaching people who had never heard concert music before. Criticized by an elite few for playing his own tuneful pieces instead of the great classical music of Beethoven, Chopin, and others, Gottschalk replied simply that he played what the audience wanted to hear. However, he also remarked late in his short life that he had noticed a marked improvement in the level of American taste.

Gottschalk never married, but he was adored by women, who screamed and swooned when he appeared. A scandal caused by accusations that were probably false nevertheless forced Gottschalk to leave the country in 1865. He traveled to South America, where he organized huge concerts involving hundreds of performers, much like the musical extravaganzas popular in Europe at the time. Gottschalk died in South America at the age of forty, apparently of yellow fever, though the exact cause of his death remains a mystery—as is fitting, perhaps, for this quintessential Romantic man.

Gottschalk's Music

Gottschalk composed songs, orchestral works, and even operas, but it is for his piano music that he is remembered. This includes marches and transcriptions of familiar opera arias, as well as many pieces in the forms described in the following sections.

Dance Pieces

The rhythms and forms of popular dances had long been used by composers to invigorate many kinds of concert music, and Gottschalk continued this tradition by writing several *waltzes* and *mazurkas* for the piano. The **waltz** is a dance in triple meter that was very popular in nineteenth-century ballrooms on both sides of the Atlantic. The **mazurka** is a Polish folk dance, also in triple meter, but of a more robust character than the graceful waltz. Of course Gottschalk's dance pieces, like the waltzes, mazurkas, and **polonaises** (another Polish dance) of Chopin, were not intended to be danced. Rather, they were concert pieces based upon the mood, style, tempo, form, and meter of a popular dance.

The dances to which Gottschalk referred for inspiration included some that were popular in the city where he grew up. These included the stirring **bamboula,** which Gottschalk subtitled "Danse des nègres," but which in New Orleans, at least, was apparently popular with whites and blacks alike. (Gottschalk's "La Bamboula" is an Optional Listening Example.)

Character Pieces A **character piece** is a piano piece based upon a particular mood or semi-programmatic idea. It is a one-movement composition, and is often in three-part or **ternary form (ABA).** The **B** section contrasts with **A** in mood or style, and sometimes in key, meter, and tempo as well. The second **A** section may be a literal or modified return of the first.

Character pieces suited the Romantic composer by affording a stable, yet flexible form based upon programmatic rather than intellectual concepts. This enabled composers to evoke a mood or sentiment unhampered by the demands of a complex formal design.

The following are some of the kinds of character pieces found in the repertoire of Romantic piano music:

1. **Études,** which are studies or exercises on a particular problem of pianistic technique, such as scales, broken chords or **arpeggios,** large chords, or rapidly repeated notes. Exercises used to build technique may be called études, but those written as character pieces are intended for concert or recital performance.

2. **Ballades,** in which the dramatic **A** section seems to represent heroic deeds, and the lyrical **B** section knightly love. The name comes from the poems on those subjects that are called "ballads" or "ballades."

3. **Nocturnes,** which evoke the sounds and the moods of night.

4. **Impromptus,** which have a rhapsodic, improvisatory character and often include highly virtuosic passages.

5. **Berceuses,** or lullabies.

Theme and Variations

Another popular form of piano music is known as **theme and variations.** The melody or *theme* that recurs throughout the piece provides unity, or organization, while each presentation of the theme is *varied* in some respect for purposes of variety or contrast. (An apt comparison may be made with the musical theme of a movie, which recurs throughout the film, arousing any number of conflicting emotions according to the way it is performed.)

Listening Example 19 is a well-known theme and variations by Louis Moreau Gottschalk.

LISTENING EXAMPLE 19
Theme and Variations

Composer   Louis Moreau Gottschalk

Title   "Le Bananier" ("The Banana Tree")

Form   Theme and variations

The theme, a Creole melody, begins with an ascending broken minor triad. Strong accents and irregular phrase lengths enhance the exotic effect of the tuneful melody.

The first section of the theme (**a**) is played by the right hand while the left hand plays an "obstinately" repeated rhythmic pattern called an **ostinato,** which marks the duple meter. Section **a** is repeated.

The second half of the theme (**b**), higher than **a** in range, begins with three repeated and accented notes. Section **b** is repeated.

a is heard in the higher range, accompanied by a new ostinato. Repeat.

b is delicately embellished by the right hand, accompanied by chords in the left.

A variation of **a** is played in a major key.

There is a section of new material that sounds improvisatory.

The major version of **a** is played by the left hand while the right hand performs dazzling runs.

b recurs briefly.

The delightful piece concludes with fragments of **a** in the left hand and rapid, virtuosic figures in the right.

SUMMARY

Because Romantics enjoyed expressive extremes, both large orchestral and intimate solo performances were appreciated during the nineteenth century. Americans, however, were particularly entertained by a solo voice or piano recital.

Several outstanding European performers toured throughout the United States, thrilling audiences with their dazzling virtuosic displays. America's own piano virtuoso, Louis Moreau Gottschalk, was popular on both sides of the Atlantic as a composer and performer. He introduced American audiences of the Civil War period to piano music, generally performing his own light but stirring compositions.

TERMS TO REVIEW

virtuoso   A performer who possesses dazzling technical brilliance.

musicianship   A combination of qualities, including sensitivity to style, accuracy, originality, expressiveness, and virtuosity.

style   The characteristic manner in which a composer uses the elements of music, formal design, and emotional expression.

score   A notated composition.

legato   Smooth, uninterrupted.

Creole   In nineteenth-century New Orleans, a person born in America of a family native to another country. Later the term was used for people of mixed racial heritage.

waltz   A ballroom dance in triple meter.

mazurka   A Polish folk dance of varying character, in triple meter.

polonaise   A stately, festive Polish folk dance, in triple meter.

bamboula   A dance in duple meter with strongly marked accents, particularly popular in nineteenth-century New Orleans.

character piece   A relatively short piano piece, often in ternary form, of a characteristic style or mood.

ternary form   Three-part form: ABA.

étude   A study of a virtuosic technique. An étude may be an exercise to build technique, or may be suitable for concert or recital performance.

arpeggio   The notes of a chord played successively in ascending order.

ballade   A character piece in dramatic or heroic style.

nocturne   A piece about the moods of night.

impromptu   A piece that sounds spontaneous or improvisatory in character.

berceuse   A lullaby.

theme and variations   An instrumental form in which a theme or melody recurs to provide unity, but in altered guises for variety.

ostinato   A repeated melodic and/or rhythmic pattern.

KEY FIGURES

Foreign Virtuosos
Jenny Lind
Ole Bull

European Composers
Ludwig van Beethoven
Frederic Chopin

American Pianist/Composer
Louis Moreau Gottschalk

OPTIONAL LISTENING EXAMPLE*

Louis Moreau Gottschalk: "La Bamboula"

SUGGESTIONS FOR FURTHER LISTENING

Louis Moreau Gottschalk: "The Banjo"
Frederic Chopin: Polonaise in A♭ Major, op. 53
Franz Liszt: *Totentanz*

---

*Guides for Optional Listening Examples are in the Instructor's Manual and may be copied and distributed to students.

SEEDS OF NATIONALISM

Chapter 12

At about the same time that American paintings began to reflect the natural splendors of the land, a few composers set out to capture the American spirit in music and to promote performances of American music. However, these early seeds of **nationalism** fell on dry ground, for audiences on both sides of the Atlantic largely ignored them. Americans were considered to have great mechanical and industrial capabilities but to be novices in matters of art. Thus, the artists who struggled to establish a characteristic American style faced formidable odds.

The dominant influence the early nationalists tried to resist was that of German Romanticism.

GERMAN
ROMANTICISM

The great German composers of the nineteenth century wrote pieces that were generous in length, with long, expansive melodies accompanied by rich and full harmonies. Extreme contrasts of dynamic level are also characteristic of their style. Many pieces were based upon programmatic ideas, and the emotional expression was often intense.

The German sound of various pieces increasingly dominated music in America, where audiences preferred to hear music by Handel, Haydn, Mozart, **Franz Schubert, Robert Schumann, Felix Mendelssohn,** and lesser-known German composers than music by composers of any other nationality. Americans also chose to study music with German teachers when possible, and the great wave of German immigration to this country in the middle of the nineteenth century allowed amateur and professional musicians alike to do so. Those who could afford it traveled to Germany to further their music education.

Europeans as well as Americans turned to Germany for inspiration and instruction in the arts through much of the nineteenth century. However, certain nations not bordering directly on Germany began to assert their artistic independence and to establish characteristic styles of their own during the second half of that period.

TOWARD
NATIONALISM
IN THE ARTS

The movement toward nationalism in the arts gained impetus in Russia, many of whose writers and composers chose Russian subjects and used characteristic Russian means of expression. The irregular rhythms of Russian folk tunes and the somewhat Asian melodies of the Russian Orthodox church affected the music of Russian operas, symphonies, ballets, and art songs. In a further move toward artistic independence, titles, texts, tempo markings, and other expression indications were written in the Russian language, avoiding the traditional Italian terms.

This trend was soon joined by artists in other European countries, particularly Bohemia (**Antonín Dvořák, Bedřich Smetana**), Norway (**Edvard Grieg**), and Finland (**Jean Sibelius**), as they, too, established strong national styles. Folk or folklike tunes and national dance rhythms had flavored music in earlier times, but now writers, painters, and musicians based entire works upon the colorful folk tales, legends, and religious music of their own experience. Suddenly the local peasant became more interesting than the generic nobleman. Artists also came to admire the distinctive styles of cultures other than their own, and many imitations of Italian, Russian, Bohemian, and other works were produced.

Late in the nineteenth century, nationalism became a significant political and cultural movement throughout western Europe. By then the ruling aristocracies of several nations had been overthrown, and popular states of various kinds were becoming established, rendering the development of political and stylistic identities an important cause in many nations.

Most Americans, however, were yet unready to defy the established wisdom that Germans knew best how to write music. Curiously, the first (and most eccentric) nationalistic "American" composer was actually a Bohemian, who avidly adopted America as his new homeland.

Forced by financial reverses to leave his home and family, **Anthony Philip Heinrich** arrived in the United States in 1810. He became music director of a popular theater in Philadelphia but, unable to make a good living there, moved on to Kentucky in 1817. For a while he lived among the Indians of that area, charmed with the natural beauty of the country and the music of his Native American friends.

In Kentucky, Heinrich lived alone in a log cabin, practicing his violin and composing romantic pieces based upon his own ideas and experiences. While there he also conducted what was apparently the first performance of a Beethoven symphony in this country. Profoundly struck by the beauty of the American wilderness, through parts of which he had traveled by foot, Heinrich wrote several programmatic works extolling the scenery of his adopted country. He expressed his appreciation for the natural wonders of America in such extravagantly titled orchestral pieces as "The War of the Elements and the Thundering of Niagara."

Returning north to pursue his career as a conductor and composer, Heinrich wrote piano pieces, songs, and chamber works. He became best known, however, for his orchestral compositions, many of which were based upon American subjects. Heinrich was the first American (he preferred to be known as an American composer) to write large orchestral pieces based upon Indian themes, to which he gave fanciful titles such as "Complaint of Logan the Mingo Chief, Last of His Race."

ANTHONY PHILIP
HEINRICH
(1781–1861)

George Catlin, *White Cloud, Head Chief of the Iowas.* Canvas, .580 × .710 (22⅞ × 28). (© 1992 National Gallery of Art, Washington, D.C., 1844/1845, Paul Mellon Collection.)

Heinrich was well known and admired in this country and abroad. He was acquainted with many of the outstanding figures of his age and reflected their influence in some of his compositions. "The Ornithological Combat of Kings: or, The Condor of the Andes," for example, expressed an interest he shared with his friend John James Audubon.

Most of Heinrich's works were programmatic, and several were in the form of the *program symphony.*

The Symphony

A **symphony** is an orchestral composition that has more than one section or **movement,** much as a book has several chapters or a play several acts. During the eighteenth century, the symphony became standardized as a four-movement orchestral composition, though since the Romantic period, composers have been flexible in the number of movements they choose to write. A concert audience usually waits to applaud until the complete symphony has been performed, since applause between movements interrupts the continuity of the piece.

Heinrich's **program symphonies** (symphonies based upon and organized according to an extra-musical idea) often quoted Indian themes. However, they were harmonized, according to Western tradition. Thus, he idealized and romanticized the Indian experience, much as James Fenimore Cooper in his novels and George Catlin in his paintings presented the Native American in an attractive but unrealistic light. Though not a great composer, Heinrich made significant contributions to the American music

Figure 12.1
Metropolitan Opera
House, circa 1900. (The
Bettmann Archive, Inc.)

experience by expressing American ideas, quoting Native American themes, and enthusiastically promoting the performance of music by himself and other American composers. His music is rarely performed today, but "Father Heinrich" is remembered and revered for his important contributions to our musical heritage.

Musical activity increased significantly across America as the nineteenth century approached its close. Some of our finest professional music schools, or **conservatories,** were established and several concert halls and opera houses were built during this period. New York City was the outstanding performance center, where the **Metropolitan Opera House,** built in 1882 (fig. 12.1), and **Carnegie Hall** (1891) attracted enthusiastic audiences. The famous Russian composer **Peter Ilich Tchaikovsky** appeared as guest of honor at the opening of Carnegie Hall.

    Thus, Americans had access to more concert music of a greater variety and finer quality than ever before. Choral and chamber societies presented programs not only on the East Coast, but also in cities further west such as Cincinnati and Chicago, and both serious and light operas became more and more popular.

A GROWING
AWARENESS

The Early
Orchestral
Experience

Few orchestras existed in America throughout the nineteenth century, although dedicated professional and amateur musicians endeavored to make the orchestral sound appealing to an American audience. In 1820, the Moravians founded a Philharmonic Society for the performance of orchestral music in Bethlehem, Pennsylvania. In Philadelphia, American and immigrant musicians organized a Musical Fund Society, which performed symphonic music and also choral music accompanied by an orchestra. The New York Philharmonic Society, the nation's oldest orchestra still in existence today, was founded in 1842.

A number of European ensembles played orchestral music in America, generally performing European works, of course. The first organization to give serious attention to orchestral music by American composers was a visiting orchestra under the direction of the celebrated French conductor **Louis Antoine Jullien.** A showman in the tradition of P. T. Barnum, Louis Gottschalk, or more recently, Liberace, Jullien wore white gloves when he conducted and used a jeweled baton. However flashy he might have appeared, he led his ensemble in fine performances of great orchestral music.

Jullien added American musicians to his orchestra during the year he spent in New York (1853) and, strongly prompted by the local press, included some American works in his programs. Among those who benefited from this opportunity was one of the most outspoken American nationalists of the period, **William Henry Fry.**

WILLIAM HENRY
FRY (1813–1864)

William Henry Fry first became known as a composer of operas. His *Leonora* was the first American opera to be produced in this country, but he had to pay for the production himself, for although Italian operas presented by European companies were popular in New Orleans and New York, even those enlightened cities had little interest in an opera by an American composer. In fact, although *Leonora* was written in the familiar Italian style with lyrical melodies, attractive harmonies, and the lavish staging expected of Romantic operas, it was not very well received. Later, while working for an American newspaper as a music correspondent in Paris, Fry was quite unsuccessful in arranging for a performance of his opera there.

Fry's next venture was to offer a series of public music appreciation lectures. Insisting that Americans should support the efforts of native composers, he exhorted American musical societies to perform American works, audiences to listen to them, and critics to review them objectively. He bitterly complained that the New York Philharmonic Society never commissioned, and seldom performed, any music by an American composer. At one lecture, Fry asserted that "the American composer should not allow the name of Beethoven or Handel or Mozart to prove an eternal bugbear to him," and he further declared, "It is time we had a Declaration of Independence in Art, and laid the foundation of an American School of Painting, Sculpture and Music."

William Henry Fry wrote four symphonies and several other orchestral works. His music is rarely heard today, because it has been surpassed in quality by many other American and European compositions. Nevertheless, Fry is respectfully and rightfully remembered for his efforts in support of American music.

The other well-known American composer of orchestral music from this period was **George Bristow,** a violinist who once resigned as a player for the New York Philharmonic Society in sympathy with Fry's complaint at their lack of support for American music. He rejoined the orchestra later, but continued to promote acceptance of American music.

Better trained than Fry, Bristow was a successful conductor, teacher, and church organist as well as a composer and violinist. (It is significant that Heinrich, Fry, and Bristow all supported themselves by means other than their meager earnings from the composition of music.) As the conductor of an orchestra known as the Harmonic Society for eleven years, Bristow tried to introduce American works and have them favorably reviewed. However, his own orchestral and choral works sound more German than American. He used an American Indian melody in his Symphony no. 4, but his Western harmonies, rhythms, and orchestral timbres negated achievement of a genuine Native American sound.

Bristow wrote the second American opera, ten years after Fry's *Leonora,* and it had a modestly successful run in New York. He based his opera on an American subject, Washington Irving's "Rip Van Winkle," but like Fry, he set his story to Italian-sounding music.

The individual who finally raised the level of orchestral performance and appreciation in America was a musician of German background, **Theodore Thomas.**

When Theodore Thomas arrived in America from Germany, at the age of ten, he already played the violin very well. He soon became a member of the New York Philharmonic Society and also played for various theater and opera orchestras.

It was Thomas's ambition, however, to be an orchestral conductor. He fully intended to raise the level of appreciation for orchestral music in America—and so he did.

Scornful of the casual rehearsal and concert procedures of the New York Philharmonic Society, Thomas formed his own ensemble, the New York Symphony Orchestra. He hired only the best musicians, rehearsed them rigorously, and presented public programs guaranteed to please an audience. His method was to subtly but systematically alter the balance between light, familiar pieces and more serious, challenging works as his listeners became more experienced.

Thomas understood that American audiences were accustomed to varied and entertaining programs, so he invited outstanding soloists to perform in his concerts. Virtuosic singers and pianists—including Gottschalk on at least one program—dazzled the listeners, who then dutifully received one movement of a more serious piece.

Cartoon depicting
Theodore Thomas
conducting in Central
Park. Reproduced from
*Theodore Thomas: A
Musical Autobiography,*
ed. George P. Upton
(1905; rpt., New York:
Da Capo Press, 1964).
Used by permission.

Thomas was also careful not to plan programs that were too long for his audience. In the summer he offered outdoor "garden concerts," where refreshments were served. He traveled widely with his orchestra, bringing symphonic music to people who had never heard it before and extending the season's employment for his musicians. The quality of his performances was always superb, and America gradually developed an enthusiastic appreciation for the thrilling orchestral sound.

Inevitably, German composers formed the core of Thomas's programs. He believed that Beethoven "expressed more than any other composer" and would be appreciated by experienced and inexperienced listeners alike. **Richard Wagner** (1813–1883) offered a modern sound and exciting, colorful orchestration guaranteed to provide a thrilling climax. Other famous German (or Austrian) composers represented on Thomas's programs included Mozart, Haydn, Schubert, Schumann, Mendelssohn, and **Johannes Brahms** (1833–1897).

Thomas performed the great music of other countries as well, and in time gave generous attention to outstanding American composers of the day. With the support of some Chicago businessmen, Thomas established the Theodore Thomas Orchestra in that city in 1891. He served as the conductor of this ensemble, later known as the Chicago Symphony Orchestra, until his death in 1905. By that time, several other American cities had formed orchestras, and smaller towns enjoyed short orchestral seasons as well. During the next several decades, Americans continued to form numerous school, civic, and professional orchestras and to absorb the great symphonic literature of the world. By the mid-twentieth century, America had become a veritable nation of symphony orchestras.

SUMMARY

The seeds of American nationalism were sown during the nineteenth century, though they hardly bore fruit before the twentieth century. Among the most ardent nationalists was a Bohemian, Anthony Philip Heinrich, who adopted the cause of American-sounding music and pursued it with originality and zeal.

William Henry Fry sought performances of operas and orchestral music composed by himself and other Americans, but had little success with the public or the press. George Bristow occasionally used Indian themes in his orchestral music. He wrote an opera on the American subject of "Rip Van Winkle," though the music sounds quite Italian. His nationalistic ideals notwithstanding, Bristow's choral and orchestral music reflects the strong German influence upon the music of his day.

After the Civil War, conservatories, concert halls, and opera houses were built in several American cities. Theodore Thomas presented orchestral programs that pleased audiences and gradually raised their level of appreciation for the great European orchestral music. He conscientiously and effectively prepared the American audience to enjoy the symphonic works of their own, as well as European, composers.

TERMS TO REVIEW

nationalism   A nineteenth-century movement in which artists of many nationalities sought to express the particular characteristics of their own cultures.

symphony   A multimovement orchestral composition.

movement   One section of a large composition such as a symphony. Each movement has a formal design and a degree of independence.

program symphony   A symphony organized according to programmatic concepts, as opposed to principles of abstract or absolute music.

conservatory   A professional music school.

Metropolitan Opera House   An important opera house in New York City.

Carnegie Hall   A recital and concert hall in New York City.

KEY FIGURES

European Nationalistic Composers
Antonín Dvořák
Bedřich Smetana
Edvard Grieg
Jean Sibelius

Early American Nationalistic Composers
Anthony Philip Heinrich
William Henry Fry
George Bristow

French Conductor
Louis Antoine Jullien

German Composers
Franz Schubert
Robert Schumann
Felix Mendelssohn
Richard Wagner
Johannes Brahms

Russian Composer
Peter Ilich Tchaikovsky

Orchestral Conductor
Theodore Thomas

OPTIONAL LISTENING EXAMPLE*

George Bristow: Fourth Symphony (Arcadian), op. 49, third movement ("Indian War Dance")

*Guides for Optional Listening Examples are in the Instructor's Manual and may be copied and distributed to students.

SUGGESTIONS FOR FURTHER LISTENING

William Henry Fry: excerpts from *Leonora*

George Bristow: Third Symphony in F# minor, op. 26
Overture to *Rip Van Winkle*

part 5

AMERICAN MUSIC COMES OF AGE

AMERICAN CONCERT MUSIC MATURES

Chapter 13

By the latter part of the nineteenth century, certain American composers were finally being afforded a respectful, if limited, hearing. They were producing impressive works in all of the large instrumental and vocal forms—symphonies, concertos, sonatas, operas, and choral works. The best of these are well-crafted, highly attractive compositions whose qualities we are only now beginning to fully appreciate. Some, in fact, had fallen into virtual obscurity before enterprising musicians in recent years began to perform and record them. Reviewers of recent recordings of some symphonic works from this period have expressed admiration for the quality of the music and regret that it has been virtually ignored for so long.

However, neither composers nor listeners of the late nineteenth-century period showed much interest in music that *sounded* American. Rather, concert music in America continued to be dominated by the German Romantic style.

In 1892, Mrs. Jeanette M. Thurber, one of the few Americans genuinely interested in establishing a nationalistic style of composition, invited an outstanding Bohemian nationalist to direct the National Conservatory of Music in New York City. This prestigious European composer was Antonín Dvořák (1841–1904).

DVOŘÁK IN AMERICA

While in this country, Dvořák listened to the music of blacks and Indians with the same fascination with which he had absorbed the folk music of his beloved Bohemia, expressing surprise and regret that Americans seemed relatively uninterested in these "native" sounds. When admiring "Negro" music, Dvořák did not always distinguish between the genuine spirituals sung by black pupils at the National Conservatory and minstrel songs, which were written and performed by whites; nor did he specifically recommend that American composers quote or imitate black or Indian effects. However, he strongly suggested that these musics offered unique and important sources of inspiration.

To illustrate his ideas of how American music should sound, and also to express appreciation for the scenic beauty of the land, Dvořák wrote his Symphony no. 9 ("From the New World") and two chamber pieces during his American stay. Each of these works includes melodies that seem to be based upon the scales of black or Indian music as Dvořák understood them. However, because he harmonized the melodies and orchestrated the music according to Western custom, these very attractive pieces have no significant American characteristics.

In less than three years, Dvořák became too homesick to remain abroad and returned to his homeland, having raised very little interest in American-sounding music. However, at least a few Americans reflected his influence by using black or Indian references in their music. Among them was one of Dvořák's pupils, a black composer named **Harry Thacker Burleigh** (1866–1949), whose singing of spirituals had inspired Dvořák's interest in that field. Burleigh wrote a large number of songs, piano pieces, and choral settings of spirituals that remain popular concert selections today.

Arthur Farwell (1872–1952) studied music in Germany, but upon his return to America decided that imitating German music was not appropriate for American composers. He expressed the intention of exalting in his music "the common inspirations of American life," by which he meant, somewhat surprisingly, the experiences of the American Indian.

ARTHUR FARWELL AND THE WA-WAN PRESS

Thereupon, Farwell imaginatively arranged some Indian tunes and composed several original pieces based upon Indian melodies. In his settings of Indian tunes titled *American Indian Melodies* (1900), he attempted to reflect the essence of the myths or legends upon which they were based, recognizing that Indian music signified more than art or entertainment.

Farwell's music was coolly received by audiences and routinely rejected by publishers. Realizing that other American composers faced the same difficulty in having their music published, Farwell established in 1901 the **Wa-Wan Press**, which was dedicated to American music. The Wa-Wan Press (the name is from a ceremony of the Omaha tribe) existed for only a decade, but it published several hundred compositions.

Unfortunately, the worthy intentions of composers interested in Native American music were generally overwhelmed by their thorough indoctrination into tonal concepts. In any case, the market for their music was minimal. Most of the important composers who finally proved that Americans could indeed write effective music in all the large forms not only studied in Germany but wrote most of their music in the firmly established German Romantic style.

The intellectual atmosphere of the Boston area nurtured significant developments in music, as well as in philosophy and literature. Thus, while New York City remained the center of music performance activity, New England produced most of the important American composers of the late nineteenth century. Members of the so-called **Second New England School** of composers shared a dedication to the principles of German music theory and a concern for quality and craftsmanship. Much of their music was comparable—in quality as well as style—to that of many of their European contemporaries.

THE SECOND NEW ENGLAND SCHOOL

The Second New England School composers contributed to every genre of concert music. Many of them were church musicians and organists who included organ **transcriptions** of opera arias and symphonic music in their recitals. Much of this literature was new to Americans, who had little access to opera or orchestral concerts. These composers also contributed a significant number of strong compositions for organ to the American music repertoire.

Choral music was another important area of accomplishment for the Second New England School composers. Several members of the school wrote religious choral works intended for concert performance, including cantatas, oratorios, and settings of the sung portions of the Roman Catholic **Mass.**

The oldest member and the leader of the Second New England School was **John Knowles Paine.**

John Knowles Paine (1839–1906)

As a young man, John Knowles Paine made the unusual decision for his day to become a professional musician. He studied organ with a German teacher in America and then went to Germany to polish his skills. While there he gave organ concerts, studied music theory and composition, and composed. Although a Protestant, he wrote a *Mass in D* for chorus, soloists, and orchestra—the first large composition by an American to be performed in Europe. (The work was better received there, in fact, than at a later American performance.) Paine based his composition on a well-known Mass by Beethoven, and neither intended nor achieved an American sound.

When Paine returned to America in 1861, he found the country at war. Eager to share his newly acquired expertise, he became the university organist at Harvard University, and—though music had never been considered a proper course of study at American universities—he offered free, noncredit lectures in music to Harvard students. To the surprise of the university administration, the lectures were very well received. In 1875 music was formally included in Harvard's curriculum, and Paine became the first American professor of music.

Paine wrote many kinds of music, including large symphonic works, songs, hymns, and an opera. His orchestral music is more significant than that of Heinrich, Fry, or Bristow, who are mainly remembered today for their valiant efforts to promote American music. Paine's Symphony no. 1 was first performed by Theodore Thomas's orchestra in 1876 and was much admired. It was, in fact, the first American symphony to be published— but it was published in Germany, and only after Paine's death.

Paine's keyboard music is also significant and attractive. His admiration for and mastery of the form called **fugue** illustrate his appreciation for strict formal design (Listening Example 20).

Fugue

A fugue is a polyphonic composition with three to five melodic lines or "voices." The form was conceived for keyboard music, but was soon applied as well to compositions for other instruments, including the singing voice.

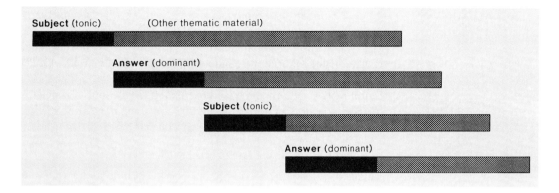

Figure 13.1

Diagram of the exposition of a four-voice fugue.

The **subject,** or principal theme, of a fugue is presented alone and then imitated by each of the other voices in turn. Entrances of the voices alternate between the tonic and dominant keys, with those in the dominant called the **answer** (fig. 13.1).

Whereas the imitation in a round or canon is literal, that in a fugue is merely similar, and each voice proceeds with independent material after entering. Therefore, although there are usually references to the subject and answer throughout a fugue, the form is quite flexible after the opening section, or **exposition,** is completed.

LISTENING EXAMPLE 20
Fugue

Composer   John Knowles Paine

Title   Fuga Giocosa, op. 41, no. 3

Form   Fugue

Key   G major

The subject, which is based upon an old baseball song "Over the Fence Is Out, Boys," includes a distinctive upward leap of an octave. It enters on the tonic note (G) and is soon answered at the level of the dominant (D). The third voice enters (tonic), and then the subject is tossed—like a baseball, perhaps—from one voice to another.

Paine explores several major and minor keys throughout the rest of the fugue. He sometimes treats the first four notes of the subject as a motive, repeating the figure sequentially. Occasional large chords provide effective contrast to the polyphonic texture, and the piece becomes increasingly virtuosic and dramatic. However, it is never pretentious and the end, like the beginning, is light and humorous.

**Other Members
of the School**

A large number of capable and prolific composers, many of them trained in Europe, were soon active in the New England area. Most found it necessary to acquire academic positions in order to make a living, since American audiences offered little support to American composers. Although very romantic in harmony and expression, these nineteenth- and early twentieth-century New Englanders have been called the **Boston Classicists** because of their concern for formal structure and their careful adherence to the rules of music theory taught by their German masters.

George Chadwick (1854–1931)

The music of **George Chadwick** has energy, humor, and a kind of audacity that gives a refreshing American flavor to some of his works. He sometimes used syncopated rhythms to set his English-language texts effectively. More creative and more original than Paine, Chadwick produced music that remains fresh and attractive today. For many years he was director of the prestigious New England Conservatory of Music, and he also, like Paine, taught a number of younger musicians who became important members of the Boston group.

Horatio Parker (1863–1919)

Like Paine and Chadwick, **Horatio Parker** was an organist who composed for "the king of instruments" and also for virtually every other vocal and instrumental medium. In 1894 he became the head of the new music department at Yale. He also formed the New Haven Symphony Orchestra, served as guest conductor for other ensembles, played for and directed a church service each week, and composed prolifically. His music, which clearly reflects his German training, was widely admired both here and in Europe. Parker's best-known work today is a sacred choral cantata called *Hora Novissima.*

Amy Cheney Beach (1867–1944)

Mrs. H. H. A. Beach, as **Amy Cheney Beach** preferred to be called, was a well-known pianist and composer—the only woman of the Boston group. She performed with Theodore Thomas's orchestra and other prestigious ensembles here and, after her husband's death, in Europe. Her own compositions were performed on both continents and were generally well received, but she could not escape the inevitable references to her sex in reviews of her work. Reviewers sometimes criticized her for trying to sound masculine, and praised her graceful melodies and more gentle symphonic passages as properly feminine in style. Although she handled the symphonic medium very capably, it is little wonder that Amy Cheney Beach composed more art songs (see Listening Example 21) than any other form, since they were readily accepted as fitting examples of feminine creativity.

Although the Second New England School composers proved that Americans could write effectively in all of the symphonic, choral, and solo genres, **Edward MacDowell**—too romantic to be called a classicist of any

---

LISTENING EXAMPLE 21
Art Song

Composer   Amy Cheney Beach

Title   "The Year's at the Spring"
This song is the setting of two verses by Robert Browning, from his poem *Pippa Passes*.

Meter   Triple

Accompaniment   The piano marks the triple division of the beats with rich chords that add interesting harmony and enhance the dramatic expression of the song.

Form   Modified strophic. The music of the second verse is similar, but not identical, to that of the first verse.

The first melodic phrase is repeated sequentially at higher levels of pitch at the beginning of each verse. Notice how this, together with an expressive crescendo, increases the dramatic intensity of the song. Key phrases ("God's in his Heaven," "all's right") are repeated for emphasis. The highest note is reserved for the word "right" toward the end of the song.

Text   *The year's at the spring,*
And day's at the morn;
Morning's at seven,
The hillside's dew pearled;

The lark's on the wing;
The snail's on the thorn;
God's in his heaven,
All's right with the world.

---

sort, and too individual to be included in a school of composers—became the first American to write concert music in a style distinctly his own.

In his teens, Edward MacDowell appeared equally talented in music and art, and he was sent to Paris to study both (fig. 13.2). Upon finally deciding to become a professional musician, he traveled to Germany, where he followed the prevailing custom of studying theory and composition. He was an accomplished pianist and concertized widely during his long stay in Europe. Some of his songs and piano pieces, written in the accepted German style, were published in Germany before he returned to America in 1888.

After several years of performing, composing, and teaching in the Boston area, MacDowell became the head of the new music department at Columbia University in New York City in 1896. There he was afforded the opportunity to implement his ideal of teaching music as related to the other arts. We have already noted that Romantics were often talented in a number of areas, and that relationships between the arts of music and literature

EDWARD
MACDOWELL
(1860–1908)

were of particular significance to them. MacDowell, the consummate Romantic, not only composed music and painted, but he also wrote poetry. He believed that the arts could only be understood as integrated subjects.

MacDowell insisted that American music should express the youthful, optimistic spirit of the country, and that quoting black or Indian themes was of no nationalistic significance. Nevertheless, he was unable to resist references to Indian music in several of his compositions. For example, he wrote a **suite** (an orchestral work consisting of several sections or semi-independent pieces) called *Indian Suite,* in which each section is based upon Indian lore or experience, and each uses Indian or Indianlike melodies. The harmonies and orchestral effects of MacDowell's *Indian Suite,* however, are entirely European.

MacDowell's piano pieces reflect his Romantic love of nature, painting in musical terms idyllic scenes of woodland lakes and hills. His famous set of character pieces titled *Woodland Sketches* includes one called "From an Indian Lodge," which imitates Indian sounds within a Western framework. Another of MacDowell's character pieces is described in Listening Example 22. However delicate, intimate, and modest they are, these piano

---

LISTENING EXAMPLE 22
Character Piece

Composer   Edward MacDowell

Title   "To a Wild Rose"

Key   A major

Form   Modified ternary (**ABA'**)

The first section includes two gentle phrases, each of which ends in a relaxed fashion on the tonic.

The slightly more agitated middle section (a breeze has risen?) rises in pitch and dynamic level and includes larger, richer chords. It ends on a suspenseful chord that functions as dominant, leading to the return of section **A.**

The return includes only the first phrase of **A.** The brief closing section begins with a gracefully falling pattern that includes a **chromatic** note (a tone that does not belong in the A major scale). The melody stretches briefly to a high tone, and then relaxes to a quiet finish.

This short, tranquil character piece, as unpretentious as the wild rose itself, perfectly captures the qualities of the lovely flower.

---

miniatures capture the very essence of the sounds and moods of nature as MacDowell loved it.

Although unable or unwilling to abandon German models entirely, MacDowell was the first American to write concert music with a distinctive style recognizably that of a particular composer. His vision of music as one of the integrated arts has also profoundly benefited the American experience. After his death, his widow established a summer colony on their estate at Peterboro, New Hampshire. Today artists, musicians, and literary figures are invited to spend uninterrupted summers working within their chosen fields at the **MacDowell Colony.**

SUMMARY

Although Dvořák encouraged Americans to develop a characteristic sound of their own, a nationalistic interest in American music developed slowly. A strong group of composers collectively known as the Second New England School produced the first significant American compositions in all of the large solo, choral, and symphonic forms. Their music, however, was primarily in the German Romantic style.

Edward MacDowell also studied the German style, but he developed a characteristic idiom of his own. His short piano pieces are particularly attractive. He believed in the integration of the arts, and the MacDowell Colony in Peterboro, New Hampshire, continues to invite artists in every discipline to spend summers working there.

TERMS TO REVIEW

Wa-Wan Press   A publishing company established by Arthur Farwell and dedicated to the publication of American music.

Second New England School   The first American composers to write significant works in all of the large concert forms. Sometimes referred to as the **Boston Classicists.**

transcription   An arrangement of a piece that was originally composed for a particular instrument or ensemble so that it may be played by a different instrument or combination of instruments.

Mass   A musical setting—for chorus, soloists, and orchestra—of portions of the Roman Catholic church service.

fugue   A polyphonic composition, originally for keyboard instruments, in which the imitative entrances of the voices alternate between tonic and dominant.

subject   The principal melodic theme of a fugue.

answer   The second presentation of the subject, at the dominant.

exposition   The first section of a fugue.

suite   An instrumental work composed of several dances or other semi-independent pieces.

MacDowell Colony   An artists' colony established on the estate of Edward MacDowell in Peterboro, New Hampshire.

KEY FIGURES

Black Composer/Arranger
Harry Thacker Burleigh

American Nationalistic Composer
Arthur Farwell

Important Second New England School Composers
John Knowles Paine
George Chadwick
Horatio Parker
Amy Cheney Beach

American Romantic Composer
Edward MacDowell

OPTIONAL LISTENING EXAMPLE*

Horatio Parker: Fugue in C minor

SUGGESTIONS FOR FURTHER LISTENING

Amy Cheney Beach: Symphony in E♭ (Gaelic), op. 32
　　Mass in E♭, op. 5

George Chadwick: "Tam O'Shanter"

Edward MacDowell: "Will o' the Wisp" and "To a Water Lily" from *Woodland Sketches*

John Knowles Paine: Second Symphony (In the Spring)
　　Fantasie uber "Ein' feste Burg"
　　Mass in D

*Guides for Optional Listening Examples are in the Instructor's Manual and may be copied and distributed to students.

THE GROWTH OF VERNACULAR TRADITIONS

Chapter 14

Vernacular music is a term used for the popular or common music language of a society, which of course requires no training or particular experience to enjoy. Folk songs, popular dances, and other vernacular forms evolve in a natural and unself-conscious manner, inevitably expressing characteristics of the culture that conceives them. Thus, while composers of art music struggled to achieve an American sound, popular music developed characteristic American traits in an effortless way. Popular songs, dances, and marches were invariably included in the programs of a new popular ensemble, the **concert band.**

The typical post-Civil War band concert included an entertaining variety of novelty pieces, marches, dance tunes, and arrangements of popular songs, with serious or concert music included in small quantities as well. Thus, at the same time that Theodore Thomas was *educating* listeners to appreciate orchestral music, concert bands were *entertaining* them with transcriptions of pieces from the orchestral and opera literature.

CONCERT BANDS

The addition of valves to trumpets, horns, and cornets early in the nineteenth century made it easier to play intricate melodies on those instruments, and they then assumed a more prominent role in the concert band. For a time, in fact, enthusiasm for the newly versatile brass instruments caused them to dominate the timbre of marching and concert bands. However, soon after the Civil War, two outstanding band directors established the balanced ensemble of woodwinds, brass, and percussion we are accustomed to hearing today.

Patrick Gilmore was among those who fled Ireland's desperate potato famine to make a new life in America. A virtuoso **cornet** player, he was appointed bandmaster of the Union army and became the most famous bandleader of the 1860s. He wrote several pieces, including the popular Civil War song "When Johnny Comes Marching Home Again" (Listening Example 23).

PATRICK SARSFIELD GILMORE (1829–1892)

After the war, Gilmore formed America's first concert band. He was a master entertainer who, like Gottschalk and Jullien, organized huge concerts in which thousands of performers participated. He brought European bands to perform in America and, through their influence and his own good

A concert band, circa 1875. (Culver Pictures, Inc.)

LISTENING EXAMPLE 23
Civil War Song

Title "When Johnny Comes Marching Home Again"

Tune The tune is that of an old Irish anti-war song, "Johnny I Hardly Know You," to which Patrick Gilmore set new words relating to the American Civil War experience.

Form Strophic

Scale The tune is based upon the minor scale. (In the first line, the word "home" occurs on the third tone of the scale, a half step lower than the third tone of the major scale.)

Meter Duple. (As will be explained in a subsequent section, the meter is *compound duple*, meaning that each beat is divided by three.)

---

taste, achieved an effective balance between brass and woodwind instruments in his ensemble. Gilmore's Grand Boston Band toured America, Canada, and several European countries, and was immensely popular.

The year Gilmore died, a young American formed his own band, which eventually surpassed in size, variety of repertoire, and quality of performance any previous wind ensemble. This talented young American was **John Philip Sousa.**

John Philip Sousa was a violinist who, like so many nineteenth-century American musicians, made a living for a while by directing a theater orchestra. Then, beginning in 1880, he served as director of the United States Marine Band under five presidents. He brought that prestigious ensemble to a peak of perfection, astonishing audiences with soft dynamic levels and other expressive effects previously thought possible only for the symphony orchestra. Later he formed his own Sousa Band, which earned a worldwide reputation.

    Sousa wrote many kinds of music, including songs, comic operas, operettas, and programmatic orchestral music. However, he is best remembered as the "march king." His marches are conventional in form and harmony and similar in most respects to many marches by European composers, but their wealth of melodic invention and their stirring spirit render them distinctively American and irresistibly attractive pieces.

JOHN PHILIP
SOUSA
(1854–1932)

MARCHES

Among the several kinds of marches are military marches, funeral marches, patriotic marches, and marches played as concert music. Marches differ widely in mood and tempo, but they are normally in duple meter, with a strongly marked beat, to correspond with the marching pattern LEFT-right-LEFT-right.

Meter

While meter always refers to the number of beats in a measure, meter is called *simple* or *compound* according to the manner in which the beats are divided.

1. **Simple meter** means that each of the beats in a measure is divided by *two*. For pieces in *simple duple meter* (for example, "Yankee Doodle" or Sousa's "The Stars and Stripes Forever"), we count the beats as **ONE**-and-**two**-and.

2. In **compound meter,** each beat is divided by *three*. For pieces in *compound duple meter* (such as "My Bonnie Lies over the Ocean," "When Johnny Comes Marching Home," or Sousa's "Washington Post March"), we count the beats as **ONE**-and-a-**two**-and-a or **ONE**-two-three-**four**-five-six.

A march may be in simple duple or compound duple meter. In either case, there is a strong beat (for the left foot) and a weak one (for the right), the difference between simple and duple meter lying only in the way each beat is divided.

Form

A march consists of a series of melodic sections called **strains.** Each strain is usually sixteen or thirty-two measures long and is repeated at least once. One of the strains, scored for fewer instruments, softer in dynamic level, and sweeter or more lyrical than the others, is called the **trio.**

There is also a section called the **break,** which is dramatic, highly rhythmic, and often percussive in style and timbre, providing effective contrast to the melodic strains.

A march may or may not have a short (four- or eight-measure) introduction.

Harmony

A march is usually tonal in harmony, with diatonic melody lines (that is, melodies using the notes of the major or minor scale) and conventional tonal chords. However, whereas tonal pieces normally end in the key in which they begin—the tonic—a march often ends with a repeat of the trio, which is usually in the subdominant key. The typical form of a march is illustrated in Listening Example 24.

Although Sousa's band played transcriptions of many of the same pieces as Theodore Thomas's orchestra, the two directors differed in their goals. Thomas intended to educate his listeners, while Sousa wanted to entertain them. Sousa therefore included a generous number of popular songs and dances in his programs as well as transcriptions of a popular new piano music called **ragtime.**

LISTENING EXAMPLE 24
March

Composer John Philip Sousa

Title "The Stars and Stripes Forever"

Meter Duple

Key E-flat major

Outline of the Form AABBCDCDC

    There is a four-measure *introduction*. (Counting the four measures of the short introduction will help you define the length of each strain.)

A The *first strain* (16 measures) begins with several repeated notes.

A The first strain is repeated.

B The *second strain* (16 measures) has a disjunct contour, including very high and low notes.

B The second strain is repeated.

C The third strain is the *trio*. Softer and more melodic than the others, it is also longer—32 measures. The key is the subdominant, or A-flat, major.

D There is a bold, dramatic *break*.

C The *trio* returns with a perky **countermelody** (different melody) in the piccolo that provides polyphonic or **contrapuntal** interest.

D There is another *break*.

C The march ends with the *trio* accompanied by a new countermelody in the trombones.

THE RISE
OF RAGTIME

The last decade of the nineteenth century is nicknamed the "Gay Nineties," and indeed it was a hectic and, at least superficially, carefree time. The mood was ripe for dance, and talented black pianists began to play a new, highly syncopated dance music in bars, brothels, and other places of entertainment. By 1897, the term "ragtime" was being used, and to "rag" a melody meant to syncopate it in the new way.

    Ragtime is a written piano music; that is, it is composed, not improvised, and it is intended for piano performance. The roots of ragtime lie in both white European and black African traditions, for the form and the harmony of ragtime are European concepts, but the rhythms are black.

Form

A rag, like a march, generally has a brief introduction, followed by several strains in the order **AABBCCDD** (each letter representing a new strain). One of the strains is usually a trio, which is often in the subdominant, and many rags—like some marches—end in this key. The pattern is not rigid; for example, the first strain may return, and many other variants of this basic march form are also used.

Harmony

Some of the early ragtime players were self-taught, but others had solid music training and brought their knowledge of European harmony to the popular piano style. Therefore, although early rags were clearly tonal, some included rather complex harmonies using chromatic tones.

Rhythm

The late minstrel shows were an important source of inspiration for the rhythms of the hot new piano style. After the Civil War, minstrelsy provided a lucrative source of income for black as well as white performers. Therefore, blacks formed their own lively shows, in which they syncopated or ragged banjo tunes and danced the high-stepping plantation dance called a **cakewalk.** This dance, which became a regular feature of the **finale,** or last scene, of a minstrel show, was based upon the syncopated figure *short-LONG-short.* (Because duration implies accent, we hear the long note as stronger than the short notes that surround it.)

This distinctive rhythm was used occasionally by many composers (for example, Gottschalk in "The Banjo" and other pieces; Stephen Foster in the chorus of "Oh! Susanna"; and Daniel Emmett in the chorus of "Dixie"). And it was used consistently by the ragtime pianist, whose left hand marked the regular duple meter while the right hand played the syncopated melody. Syncopation had occurred in Western music from the earliest times, but the spicy nature and consistent application of the new (black) syncopated effects were distinctive characteristics of the vigorous new vernacular music called ragtime.

Eubie Blake, who died at the age of one hundred in 1983, was one of the outstanding ragtime pianists. There were many others, but the acknowledged king of ragtime was **Scott Joplin** (fig. 14.1).

SCOTT JOPLIN
(1868–1917)

Music was a part of the Joplin family experience. Scott's father, a former slave, played the violin, and there were other instruments in the Joplin home as well. As a child, Scott studied piano with a German immigrant musician, who also provided basic studies in theory.

While still a teenager, Joplin left his home in Texarkana, Texas, and traveled east to Missouri, earning some money by playing the piano in dives and bars along the way. In Sedalia and later in St. Louis, the early center of ragtime creativity, Joplin addressed both white and black music markets, playing in black bars and saloons and writing sentimental songs and arrangements in the white popular style. A shy and gentle man, he liked composing and teaching better than playing in the rough environments where ragtime was popular. The huge commercial success of his "Maple Leaf Rag" (Listening Example 25), published in 1899, finally allowed him to concentrate on the activities he preferred.

Good rags are very easy to enjoy, but they may be difficult to perform. Joplin insisted that rags should be played as written, without improvised embellishment. He also stressed that they must never be played fast, for the strength and dignity of a great rag are trivialized by a dashing tempo.

LISTENING EXAMPLE 25

Ragtime

Composer   Scott Joplin

Title   "Maple Leaf Rag" (excerpt)

Key   A-flat major

Outline of the Form   AABBACCDD

A   The first strain (16 measures). The short-LONG-short cakewalk figure occurs in the second half of the first measure and recurs frequently throughout the piece. The first two measures are repeated. Notice the chromatic notes in the next two measures and the dramatic ascending figure that follows.

A   The first strain is repeated.

B   The second strain (16 measures) is rhythmically similar to the first, but higher in pitch. It begins with a chromatically descending melodic line and is marked **staccato,** meaning that it should be played in a crisp, detached manner.

B   The second strain is repeated.

(Your listening example tapers off here, but the rag follows the form outlined above, with **C** representing the trio, in the subdominant key. The last strain (**D**) returns to the tonic.)

Figure 14.1

Scott Joplin (1868–1917) was honored with a commemorative stamp by the U.S. Postal Service in 1983 as part of its Black Heritage series. (Copyright 1983 U.S. Postal Service.)

Joplin's early rags (including "Maple Leaf Rag" and the popular "The Entertainer") are irresistibly tuneful and entirely unpretentious, but some of his later rags (such as "Euphonic Sounds") sound more like European concert pieces than dance music.

Joplin also wrote at least two operas, one of which (***Treemonisha***) was published in 1911 in what is called a "piano score"—that is, without orchestration. Joplin wrote the words as well as the music of *Treemonisha;* the story illustrates Joplin's belief that blacks must acquire education in order to improve their social and economic situation. The opera includes some ragtime and other dance pieces, as well as more conventional operatic arias.

There was little interest in an opera by a black composer during Joplin's lifetime, and he was unable to have the work properly performed. However, it was scored for orchestral instruments by Gunther Schuller (see page 254) in the early 1970s, and it has been performed several times since then. Several recent productions of Joplin's opera, including one that was televised, have been well received.

THE INFLUENCE OF RAGTIME

Ragtime had a phenomenal effect upon many kinds of music, including social dances. Even before the Civil War, Americans had largely abandoned popular eighteenth-century country dances, preferring dances led by a caller and European couple dances such as the waltz and the energetic polka. After the rise of ragtime, however, an American dance called the **two-step** or **fox-trot,** with the frequent syncopations that delighted young dancers of that period, replaced all others in popularity. By the early twentieth century, many forms of American popular music reflected a strong black influence, and some of the most popular fox-trots were written by a black bandleader and composer, **James Reese Europe** (1881–1919).

Soon white composers were writing songs using ragtime rhythms, such as "Hello, My Baby!" by Joe Howard and "Waiting for the Robert E. Lee" by Lewis F. Muir. By 1914, thousands of rags had been published. Several European composers of the period reflected the influence of ragtime by writing syncopated concert pieces with "rag" or "ragtime" in their titles.

But by the end of World War I, ragtime had declined in popularity. Some composers were producing rags that were too complex for popular appeal. Also, in an effort to reach a broad audience, the popular music publishing industry, or **Tin Pan Alley,** diluted the very characteristics that made early rags exciting.

TIN PAN ALLEY

The American popular music publishing industry was known as Tin Pan Alley through the first half of the twentieth century. The industry centered in New York City, changing only its street location from time to time. The mythical street name referred to the sounds of many pianos playing at once, as house composers worked out new songs and **song pluggers** demonstrated songs by playing them for customers.

Even before the turn of the century, popular music had become an important business, and songs were written for the purpose of making money. Songs with piano accompaniment were printed in sheet music form and sold in amazing quantities. They were made popular by variety show and music theater performances, piano rolls, and the hardworking song pluggers. In the 1920s, the new recording industry began to assume some of this responsibility. Radio stations played popular recordings in the thirties, but it was yet another decade before radio became influential in determining the popularity of a song.

The Songs of Tin Pan Alley

Although early Tin Pan Alley composers wrote songs "to order," they nevertheless produced some wonderful tunes that are well remembered today. Many were waltzes, reflecting the popularity of European operettas (see pages 166–68) and other European music. "Take Me out to the Ball Game," "Casey Would Waltz with the Strawberry Blonde," and "East Side, West Side, All Around the Town" are waltz tunes that remain familiar today.

Other popular Tin Pan Alley songs had ragtime syncopations, black dialect, or other distinctively American characteristics. "Bill Bailey, Won't You Please Come Home?" is an example of this type of song.

Couple enjoying Tin Pan
Alley songs on piano rolls.
(Jane Kramer/EKM-
Nepenthe.)

Verse-Chorus Form

Early Tin Pan Alley songs usually told a story, which might be dramatic
and sentimental or light-hearted and humorous. They had three or more
verses, which included the narrative information, and a catchy **chorus,** which
was repeated after each verse. In theater performances or stage shows,
singers articulated the words of the verse carefully, sometimes half speaking
them, in fact. Then the audience would often join in singing the familiar
chorus.

By the 1920s, Tin Pan Alley composers were writing shorter verses
and fewer of them, for listeners clearly preferred the memorable choruses.
Early recordings could only contain three or four minutes of music on a
side, so they often omitted the verses of a popular song. Later, even when
there was time for a verse, performers often chose to repeat the familiar
chorus instead. Finally, many Tin Pan Alley composers simply wrote songs
without any verses at all.

Irving Berlin (fig. 14.2) was among the best known and most popular of all
American songwriters. He was born Israel Baline in Russia, but early in
his life became totally immersed in the popular music and music theater
scene in America. He worked on Tin Pan Alley as a song plugger and held
jobs as a singing waiter before he began writing songs for vaudeville and
other musical entertainment. "Alexander's Ragtime Band" (which is not
a rag!) was written for a vaudeville show in 1911, and it became his first
hit song.

IRVING BERLIN
(1888–1989)

Figure 14.2

Irving Berlin. (The Bettmann Archive, Inc.)

LISTENING EXAMPLE 26
Tin Pan Alley Song

Composer   Irving Berlin

Title   "Blue Skies"
   The song was included in a 1926 musical (*Betsy*) and was later used in several movies, including *Blue Skies* (1946) with Fred Astair and Bing Crosby.

Form   Strophic, verse-chorus. Each four-line verse is succeeded by the more tuneful eight-line chorus.

Meter   Duple. The lively piano accompaniment and interludes give the song a distinct ragtime flavor.

A self-taught musician, Berlin learned to play only on the black keys of the piano, which seems very strange to anyone who has studied the instrument. This meant that he was unable to play in more than one key. Normally, a composer uses different tonalities to match the range of a singer's voice or add variety to a piece of some length. Different keys also have different effects—some warm and rich, some cool and light—that seem to suit the character of particular songs. So Berlin had a trick piano built on which he could slide a board to **modulate,** or change the key in which he was playing.

Irving Berlin wrote about 1,500 songs, of which close to 1,000 are still in print. He was particularly attracted to the syncopated music of popular dances, and many of his songs have rollicking tunes and jolly rhythms. Several have become classics, including "White Christmas," "Always," "God Bless America," and "Blue Skies" (Listening Example 26).

A painter as well as a musician, Berlin passed his last years in quiet retirement. The world celebrated his hundredth birthday in 1988, but long before that, he was universally acknowledged as the elder statesman of American popular song.

SUMMARY

Before the turn of the twentieth century, several vernacular musics had achieved an American flavor. Concert bands included popular American songs and marches in their programs.

Patrick Gilmore's concert band was a balanced ensemble capable of performing transcriptions of orchestral and operatic literature as well as more popular pieces. John Philip Sousa, the "march king," brought the United States Marine Band and later his own Sousa Band to even higher levels of professionalism.

Ragtime is a written piano music that combines certain black rhythmic effects with European harmony and form. Syncopated melodies in the right hand are accompanied by a simple duple pattern in the left, in a form similar to that of a march. By the time of World War I, rags were widely published by Tin Pan Alley, and many popular Tin Pan Alley songs had the sound and spirit of ragtime.

TERMS TO REVIEW

concert band An instrumental ensemble including brass, woodwind, and percussion instruments.

cornet A brass instrument similar in shape to the trumpet, but smaller in size and more mellow (less brilliant) in timbre.

simple meter Each beat in a measure is divided in half.

compound meter Each beat in a measure is divided by three.

strain A melodic section in a rag, march, or other vernacular form of music.

trio A strain that is lighter in texture, softer in dynamic level, and more melodic than the others in a piece.

break A dramatic, unstable, strongly rhythmic section, as in a march.

countermelody A melody performed together with another melody.

contrapuntal Another term for *polyphonic*.

ragtime A written piano music, duple in meter and moderate in tempo. The left hand generally marks the beat while the right hand plays a syncopated melody.

cakewalk A plantation dance with syncopated melodies, including the short-LONG-short figure that became characteristic of ragtime.

finale In music theater, the final scene of an act or of the show.

staccato Short, detached.

Treemonisha An opera by Scott Joplin.

two-step or **fox-trot** An American dance derived from ragtime. The meter is duple, the rhythm syncopated, the tempo moderate.

Tin Pan Alley The popular music publishing industry from the late nineteenth through the first half of the twentieth centuries. Also, the street(s) in New York where the publishing houses were currently located.

song plugger A music store employee who played popular songs on the piano to demonstrate them for customers.

verse The section of a Tin Pan Alley song that tells the story.

chorus The refrain, or tuneful section repeated after each verse of a Tin Pan Alley song.

modulate To change key systematically, usually by using one or more tones common to both keys.

KEY FIGURES

Patrick Gilmore
John Philip Sousa
Eubie Blake
Scott Joplin
James Reese Europe
Irving Berlin

OPTIONAL LISTENING EXAMPLE*

Scott Joplin: "A Real Slow Drag"—the finale of *Treemonisha*

SUGGESTIONS FOR FURTHER LISTENING

Compound triple meter: Amy Cheney Beach, "The Year's at the Spring," Listening Example 21, p. 139

Recordings of Tin Pan Alley songs performed by Joan Morris and William Bolcom

*Guides to Optional Listening Examples are in the Instructor's Manual and may be copied and distributed to students.

REACTIONS TO
GERMAN ROMANTICISM

Chapter 15

We have seen that, well before the turn of the twentieth century, artists began to resist the domination of German Romanticism and to seek a mode of expression relevant to current taste and experience. The several new movements included some that were nationalistic in style and others that merely sought to break away from the German sound.

IMPRESSIONISM

As early as the 1860s, young French painters began to experiment with new techniques of painting, seeking to capture on their canvases the fleeting nature of the experiences of life. New, portable tubes of oil paints (an American invention) made it possible for the first time to complete a painting out-of-doors, and the young artists effectively caught the changing qualities of light and the hazy French atmosphere in their daring works.

For their subjects, the **Impressionists,** as they were called, chose everyday figures and events—peasants in the field, children playing in a park, workers on the streets of Paris, or young people dancing in a cafe. Their name came from the title of the first such painting to be exhibited and become known, **Claude Monet's** *Impression: Sunrise,* which critics ridiculed for its unorthodox techniques.

Impressionism had a strong influence on Americans, and several American painters adopted—or adapted to their own style—the new French techniques. Among them were **Theodore Robinson, John Twachtman,** and **Childe Hassam.** Another, **Mary Cassatt** (fig. 15.1), went to live in Paris, where she worked and studied with the outstanding Impressionists and formed a personal relationship with a French artist closely associated with this group, **Edgar Dégas.**

In a sense, Impressionism represents a kind of French nationalism, but its intent was more to avoid being German than to assert a French style. Impressionists exhibit many of the traits associated with Romanticism: love of nature, emphasis upon mood, flexibility of technique, sensuous use of color, and a highly subjective approach to art. But the heaviness and exaggeration of the impassioned late nineteenth-century German works were avoided in the emotionally cool Impressionistic style.

Figure 15.1
Mary Cassatt (1845–1926), *The Cup of Tea.* Oil on canvas, 36⅜ × 25¾ in. (The Metropolitan Museum of Art, from the collection of James Stillman. Gift of Dr. Ernest G. Stillman, 1922. [22.16.17].)

Claude Debussy (1862–1918) applied many of the Impressionists' ideas to his music, becoming the leading composer in that style. He considered sound, as the painters considered color, a quality with its own intrinsic value. He, like they, avoided obvious or expected effects; for that reason he extended tonal concepts to their very limits.

Impressionistic Music

Melody

The melodies of Impressionistic music are generally vague in contour. To enhance the ethereal, relaxed effect of their music, Impressionists often alter or avoid melodic intervals that imply predictable consequences. Characteristics of Impressionist melodies include the following:

1. Avoidance of the **leading tone,** as the next-to-the-last step of the major (and often the minor) scale is called. Just one-half step from tonic, the leading tone creates a strong sense of pull toward the tonic note. Impressionistic composers often lower the seventh tone to lessen this sense of direction and impending resolution.

2. Impressionists may alternately raise and lower the third step of the scale, creating ambiguity (a favorite quality of the Impressionists) between the major and minor modes.

3. Impressionists often use modal, pentatonic, or other nontonal scales to create lovely drifting or floating effects. The whole-tone

scale is of particular appeal to Impressionist composers because it has neither a dominant nor a leading tone, nor any half steps at all.

Harmony

Tonal relationships between subdominant, dominant, and tonic are generally avoided by Impressionists because of their predictability. Dissonances are gentle and are used for color rather than function, neither creating tension nor requiring resolution. Most harmonies in Impressionistic music are soft and sensuous dissonances, reminiscent of the unorthodox blend of colors in an Impressionistic painting.

Rhythm

Rhythms are free and flexible, with any number of beats per measure and no pattern of regularly recurring accents. Frequently changing meters preclude anticipation of a downbeat, allowing the music to flow gently forward.

Form

Forms, too, are relatively unstructured and are often suggested by a program or text. The Impressionist composer, like the painter, may use color as an element of form and—also like the painter—generally avoids intellectual concepts of proportion and balance.

CHARLES
TOMLINSON
GRIFFES
(1884–1920)

As a young musician, **Charles Griffes** left his native New York to study piano and composition in Germany, where he dutifully produced a number of songs and other works in the German Romantic style. However, he soon tired of familiar and overused effects and became strongly attracted by the work of the French Impressionist musicians.

Like many other young Western musicians of his day, Griffes expanded his musical palette to include certain Asian effects. Most composers adjusted Oriental techniques to fit Western concepts, but Griffes orchestrated his several pieces based upon Japanese themes in a delicate manner, preserving their Eastern flavor. Recognizing that Oriental music includes intervals other than those of the tonal scale, he used occasional **quarter tones,** lying halfway between a half step, which is normally considered the smallest interval in Western music. Griffes also restricted the harmonic combinations in his Oriental-based pieces to octaves, fifths, fourths, and seconds, avoiding the rich thirds and sixths of Western music.

The influence of nationalistic Russian works is also apparent in many of Griffes's compositions. Yet, from all these varied sources, he fashioned a sound uniquely his own.

Griffes wrote a number of art songs, later scoring some of them for orchestra, as he also did with some of his piano pieces. His chamber ensembles include certain unusual but effective combinations of instruments.

His best-known orchestral work is *The Pleasure Dome of Kubla Khan* (Optional Listening Example), which he originally conceived as a piano piece but later rewrote as a **tone poem.**

A tone poem or **symphonic poem** (the terms are used synonymously) is a one-movement programmatic orchestral piece that expresses in music instead of words a story, experience, or idea. It is often based upon a literary reference, such as a poem or play, and its form evolves from the story or scenes it depicts. The tone poem was considered by many Romantics an ideal means with which to meld literary and music interests.

Tone Poem

Although Griffes died very young, his late works began to show yet a new style of expression. His *Piano Sonata,* for example, published the year after his death, appears to follow a path that could have led entirely away from tonality. This strong, dissonant, emotionally powerful piece is intellectually, rather than programmatically, constructed.

Griffes's Late Works

In the *Sonata*'s pounding rhythms, Griffes reveals the same fascination with dramatic rhythmic effects heard in the music of a towering figure of twentieth-century music, **Igor Stravinsky.** Stravinsky's ballet *Le Sacre du Printemps* (*The Rite of Spring*), in the style that became known as **Primitivism,** caught the new century unaware and shocked the sensibilities of complacent audiences.

The Primitivists found modern culture too restrictive for a healthy life, and Impressionism too pretty and refined to express their views. They were particularly moved by the striking artworks that had been recently excavated from Africa and other non-Western areas, and they sought to capture some of the dramatic qualities of primitive art in their own works.

PRIMITIVISM

Best known of the Primitive painters was **Paul Gauguin** (1848–1903). He started as a businessman, became an amateur artist in the Impressionist style, and then suddenly abandoned home and family to live in Tahiti and the Marquesas Islands, where he painted vivid pictures of the colorful islands and their exotic inhabitants. A more recent example of Primitive style in painting is that of the American woman who became known as "Grandma Moses." Her highly attractive paintings on everyday, familiar subjects (see plate 5) are bright in color, clearly designed, and rather flat in terms of perspective.

There are few outstanding music compositions in the Primitive style, and Stravinsky's *The Rite of Spring* is the most familiar and most frequently cited work. Stravinsky did not remain committed to Primitivism, but this ballet made an indelible impression on musicians and audiences alike. Indeed, Stravinsky and certain other European composers had so profound an influence upon American composers that some understanding of their music is essential for comprehension of developments in twentieth-century American music.

IGOR
STRAVINSKY
(1882–1971)

Figure 15.2

Igor Stravinsky.
(Historical Pictures/Stock
Montage.)

ARNOLD
SCHOENBERG
(1874–1951)

The Twelve-Tone
Technique

Igor Stravinsky (fig. 15.2) was among the many talented Russian artists who fled their country after 1918, when the Russian Revolution effectively destroyed artistic freedom there. Like many others, he went to Paris, which became the international center of artistic activity in the 1920s.

Stravinsky's early works have a distinctive and very attractive Russian flavor. But it was his ballet *Le Sacre du Printemps* (*The Rite of Spring,* 1913) that captured worldwide attention. The story is of a primitive sacrificial ritual in which a young girl is abducted and finally dies, literally dancing herself to death; the music, like the story, is harsh and brutal. Notwithstanding its initial reception, the ballet soon became a favorite with a wide public, and neither European nor American composers could approach music in quite the traditional way after confronting the savage, pounding rhythms of *The Rite of Spring.*

Stravinsky and a number of other important European composers fled to America to escape the horrors of World War II. Many of them composed and taught here, and some spent the rest of their lives in this country, their influence significantly changing the course of American music.

Of this group, the composer with the most revolutionary ideas about music and its future was the Austrian **Arnold Schoenberg.**

The earliest works of Arnold Schoenberg (fig. 15.3) are in the late Romantic, sometimes called **post-Romantic** style. However, he soon abandoned soaring melodies, rich harmonies, and grand orchestrations to write **atonal,** or nontonal, works.

Schoenberg understood that relatively brief pieces—especially those with a text—may make musical sense without a tonal center, since other concepts—the text, or patterns of rhythm or timbre, for example—may provide the necessary unity. But listeners often find the loss of tonic almost as disturbing as the loss of gravity! Thus, to substitute for traditional methods of organization in pieces of some length and complexity, Schoenberg developed the **twelve-tone technique.**

In twelve-tone music, all twelve pitches of the chromatic scale are arranged into a series or **row,** each pitch being of equal importance. Because the ear tends to gravitate toward a repeated tone as a tonic (a concept Schoenberg wished to avoid), no tone in the row may be repeated out of order until all have been heard. Methodical use of the tone row provides all of the melodic and harmonic, or the linear and vertical, material of a twelve-tone composition.

Variety is achieved in twelve-tone music by using the tones in reverse order (the *retrograde* version of the row), in *inversion* (a mirror image), or in *retrograde inversion* (fig. 15.4). The tones of the row may be selected from any octave, causing the angular or disjunct melody lines characteristic of much twelve-tone music. This technique, called **octave displacement,** is something we have all probably experienced when singing a song (such as "The Star Spangled Banner"?) that includes some notes that lie too high

Figure 15.3

Arnold Schoenberg at the University of California. (Bettmann Newsphotos, Inc.)

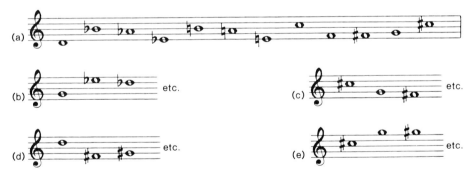

Figure 15.4

(*a*) A twelve-tone row. (*b*) The row transposed up a fourth. (*c*) The retrograde version (the row backwards). (*d*) The row inverted (upside down). (*e*) The retrograde inversion (backwards and upside down). (Courtesy of Frederick Carl Gurney.)

for our voices. We typically jump down an octave to sing those passages, returning to the original pitch levels when it becomes comfortable to do so.

Twelve-tone music is indeed tightly organized, but the scheme, applied rigidly, is too complex for the ear to recognize. Because of this, the effect may be of a relentless sameness or, conversely, of unrelieved chaos. Of course the intellectual conception of a piece does not preclude warmth and intensity of expression. Like Impressionism and Primitivism, twelve-tone music was a reaction against the overripe post-Romantic style, but it was not inherently anti-romantic itself, and some twelve-tone music is emotionally accessible and intensely moving. Neither is twelve-tone exclusively an atonal concept, for it may be adapted to produce tonal effects.

Although most composers have abandoned the twelve-tone technique today, it made an important impact on American music in the 1950s, and some composers continue to find it a valuable alternative to traditional systems of organizing music.

SUMMARY

Impressionism was an important late nineteenth-century art movement in France. It began as a style of painting, but the French composer Claude Debussy introduced vague contours, flexible forms and rhythms, and a sensuous feeling for color to music.

Charles Griffes added certain Asian effects, developing a sound distinctively his own. His search for a new style continued, however, and his last works reflect the influence of Stravinsky's pounding, asymmetrical rhythms. Near the end of his life, Griffes seemed to be considering the possible abandonment of tonality.

Arnold Schoenberg's twelve-tone technique, conceived as a method for organizing atonal music, ultimately had great influence on the course of Western music. According to this system, all twelve tones of the chromatic scale are of equal importance and are related only to each other, since there is no tonic. Twelve-tone technique has proved adaptable to the differing tastes and inclinations of several important American and European composers.

TERMS TO REVIEW

Impressionism   A style of art, and later music, that avoids definite statement in favor of suggestion and atmosphere.

leading tone   The seventh note of a major (or often minor) scale; so called because it is a half step that implies resolution to the nearby tonic.

quarter tones   Intervals half the size of a half step.

tone poem or **symphonic poem**   A one-movement programmatic orchestral composition.

Primitivism   A style of art and music that emphasizes the relaxed, sometimes savage experience of life in uncivilized societies.

post-Romanticism   A general term for several romantic styles that succeeded the dominance of German Romanticism.

atonal music   Music that has no tonic or tonal relationships.

twelve-tone technique   A method developed by Arnold Schoenberg to organize atonal music. All twelve notes of the chromatic scale are equal, and each must be used before any may be repeated.

row The pattern in which the twelve notes of the chromatic scale are arranged for a particular twelve-tone composition.

octave displacement The choice of a note of the same letter name from a distant octave.

KEY FIGURES

French Impressionist Painters
Claude Monet
Edgar Dégas

American Impressionist Painters
Theodore Robinson
John Twachtman
Childe Hassam
Mary Cassatt

American Primitivist Painter
Anna Mary Robertson ("Grandma Moses")

French Primitivist Painter
Paul Gauguin

French Impressionist Composer
Claude Debussy

American Impressionist Composer
Charles Griffes

Influential European Composers
Igor Stravinsky
Arnold Schoenberg

OPTIONAL LISTENING EXAMPLE*

Charles Griffes: *The Pleasure Dome of Kubla Khan*

SUGGESTIONS FOR FURTHER LISTENING

Charles Griffes: *The White Peacock Piano Sonata*

*Guides for Optional Listening Examples are in the Instructor's Manual and may be copied and distributed to students.

part 6

MUSICAL THEATER

PRECURSORS OF THE BROADWAY MUSICAL

Chapter 16

As prosperity returned to the nation after the Civil War years, theater became increasingly popular—musical theater especially. Most American musical shows had a variety format with little if any plot, but full-length musical shows imported from abroad were also very much enjoyed.

By the turn of the twentieth century, several kinds of musical shows vied for popularity with the Broadway audience.

BLACK MUSICAL THEATER

Although the minstrel show waned in popularity, black musicians continued to be an important influence on Broadway. A number of black musicians wrote songs for white shows, and several musicals in the first decade of this century were written, directed, and performed by blacks.

The earliest all-black musicals were closely related to minstrel shows, which had themselves become more black than white, but which perpetuated the stereotypical black characters. For example, the minstrel reference is apparent in the title of a distinctive black show that appeared in 1898: *Clorindy, or the Origin of the Cake-walk.* The composer, **Will Marion Cook** (1869–1944), was a concert violinist who had studied music at Oberlin College in Ohio, in Germany, and later with Dvořák at the National Conservatory of Music.

Cook also wrote the music for several other black shows that were popular during the first decade of this century, including *In Dahomey* (1903), the first all-black musical show to play in a major Broadway theater.

VAUDEVILLE

Vaudeville shows were similar in many ways to minstrel shows and often included blackface acts. However, each act of a vaudeville show was independent and involved different performers, whereas a minstrel troupe remained on stage throughout the show. Vaudeville also featured a much wider variety of entertainment, including circus stunts, jugglers, dog acts, comedy teams, songs, dances, and virtually anything to amaze and delight an eager but unsophisticated audience.

Comic scene from a
vaudeville show. (The
Bettmann Archive, Inc.)

Burlesque is a kind of satire in which something important is ridiculed or, conversely, something silly is treated with mock dignity for humorous effect. The burlesque shows of the late nineteenth century were strings of comic scenes of this type. However, striptease performances inserted between acts often drew more applause than the comedy scenes, so that burlesque finally degenerated from a rather risqué to a fairly crude form of entertainment.

    A rollicking remembrance of the best in burlesque titled *Sugar Babies* opened on Broadway in 1979. Mickey Rooney and Ann Miller sang and danced their way through an uproarious evening of nonsense that delighted Broadway audiences for more than a thousand performances and then toured until mid-1986.

BURLESQUE

A **revue** is a musical show whose scenes are related by a common theme rather than by a plot. The music may all be by one composer, or the song texts all by one lyricist, even though the songs are taken from several different shows. Alternatively, each scene of the revue may address the same topic, such as love through women's eyes or relations between the sexes, with the music taken from varied sources.

    The revues of the early twentieth century were lavishly staged spectacles featuring lovely costumes, extravagant sets, and—especially—beautiful girls. Shows titled "Follies" or "Scandals" or "Vanities" were staged

REVUES

every year from the early 1900s through the 1930s, providing generous job opportunities for composers, singers, dancers, stage and costume designers, and orchestra musicians.

By the thirties, social and political commentary was accepted even in the format of a musical entertainment. *Pins and Needles,* for example, was a very successful revue sponsored by the Garment Workers Union. Created and performed by amateurs, and basically a propaganda forum for the union, the show included some great songs and was a hit on Broadway.

Ziegfeld Follies

Most popular of all the revues were the **Ziegfeld Follies,** staged by **Florenz Ziegfeld** (1869–1932) nearly every year between 1907 and his death. (Three more Ziegfeld Follies were produced after that.) These shows, whose theme was the glorification of the American girl, were extravagantly staged and costumed. They included wonderful songs, such as "Shine On, Harvest Moon" from the *Follies* of 1908 and "A Pretty Girl Is Like a Melody," written by Irving Berlin for the *Follies* of 1919. (A musical biography of Florenz Ziegfeld, titled *Ziegfeld,* opened on Broadway in 1988 but was not very well received.)

Recent Revues

Unlike vaudeville and burlesque, the revue remains a popular form of entertainment. Many recent revues have been based upon the music of one composer, such as *Side by Side by Sondheim* (1977); *Eubie!* (1978), a collection of the rag- and jazz-based songs of Eubie Blake; *Ain't Misbehavin'* (1978), with songs by Fats Waller; and *Sophisticated Ladies* (1981), a dance extravaganza on the music of Duke Ellington. *Bubbling Brown Sugar* (1976) was an all-black revue featuring songs by several great black writers, including Eubie Blake, Fats Waller, and Duke Ellington.

Hair (1968) was billed as a rock musical but might better be called a revue, since the show has no integrated plot. *Hair* addressed concerns of the youth culture and counter-culture of the sixties—drugs, free love, racial prejudice, the burning of draft cards, the Viet Nam War, and more. In the notorious seminude scene, "police" ran through the audience as if raiding the show, prophetic of the audience involvement that has become characteristic of many contemporary musicals. The spectacular staging of *Hair* indicated another important trend in the modern musical theater.

Before the turn of the century, a form of music theater in which the elements of musical entertainment are connected by a plot became immensely popular on Broadway. This was the European *operetta,* which provided a vital stimulus for the American musical stage.

OPERETTA

An **operetta** (sometimes called a **light opera**) is a musical play in which the songs, dances, and instrumental pieces are closely integrated with the story. The music of the great operettas is of a quality and level of difficulty suitable for trained singers, but no effort or experience is required of the audience, who may expect to be thoroughly entertained.

Three national styles of operetta invaded America in the late nineteenth and early twentieth centuries. They became extremely popular and had important and lasting effects upon the development of an indigenous American music theater.

Opéra Bouffe

It is difficult to explain the popularity in America of French comic operas, called **opéras bouffes,** especially since they were often performed in the French language. However, the French have always provided visual spectacle in their theater, and the beautiful staging contributed to the charm of the opéras bouffes. There were also lilting melodies and lovely chorus and dance scenes that richly entertained an audience looking for something between an opera and a minstrel show.

The opéras bouffes of **Jacques Offenbach** (1819–1880) attracted especially enthusiastic, if limited, attention. Offenbach used mythology and other unlikely settings to disguise pointed social and political commentary in his delightful operettas, which continue to charm modern audiences in America and abroad.

Gilbert and Sullivan

In 1878, the British comic operetta *H.M.S. Pinafore,* with words by **William S. Gilbert** and music by **Arthur Sullivan,** was performed in Boston, San Francisco, Philadelphia, and finally New York City, breaking all previous records for the popularity of any musical show. Over the next several years, twelve New York theaters staged performances of *Pinafore,* and sometimes as many as three performances were offered simultaneously.

Of course, the fact that *Pinafore* is in English enhanced its popularity in the United States. Gilbert was a comic poet with a gift for puns and a completely irreverent approach to every subject. He ridiculed politics, manners, and every aspect of society, even the British Queen. His **patter songs,** in which the words come very rapidly, never fail to delight an audience and have served as models for composers of every kind of humorous musical entertainment.

Sullivan's music makes fun of opera, religious music, virtuosic singing, and every other serious aspect of music. His delightful tunes are unforgettable, and his simple harmonies and attractive orchestration provide a wonderful music experience. The hilarious stories, clever satire, outrageous puns, and above all, catchy melodies of **Gilbert and Sullivan operettas** make them virtually irresistible entertainment.

The Viennese Style

Last to become popular in the United States, but most influential of all upon the development of American musical theater, was the **Viennese operetta.** More romantic than comical, Viennese operettas featured exotic settings that lifted the audience from the real world to heights of delightful fantasy. The music, too, was Romantic in style, with memorable melodies, rich harmonies, and attractive orchestration. The complicated love stories, no matter how unlikely or contrived, always ended satisfactorily.

A scene from Gilbert and Sullivan's *H.M.S. Pinafore.* (Courtesy Opera News.)

The outstanding composer of Viennese operettas was **Johann Strauss, Jr.,** also known as the "waltz king." His lilting waltz tunes inspired Americans to include many waltzes in their own operettas and early musicals. *The Merry Widow* by **Franz Lehar** dominated the American musical theater stage from 1907 until World War I, replacing comic opera in the public's affections and precluding the success of the struggling new form of Broadway musical comedy for several years.

In the early years of the twentieth century, three musicians who had recently arrived from Europe became the first composers of **American operettas.**

AMERICAN OPERETTAS

Although based upon European traditions and written by composers who were born and trained abroad, the music of **Victor Herbert, Rudolf Friml,** and **Sigmund Romberg** was conceived for an American audience and is valued as a part of our American music heritage. Like their Viennese predecessors, American operettas had foreign or exotic settings and characters who were royal, noble, or secretly wealthy, and often in disguise. Although dated, in the sense that the stories and songs are representative of the late nineteenth and early twentieth centuries, these shows contain a wealth of enchanting music no less appealing today than it was a century ago.

Victor Herbert (1859–1924)

Victor Herbert was one of the most versatile musicians America has known. He was born in Ireland and studied music in Germany, finally coming to America when his wife was invited to sing with the Metropolitan Opera. A fine cellist, Herbert also conducted bands and orchestras and composed symphonic music and opera.

Herbert found that the operetta was the form of music theater that suited him best, and he wrote forty operettas in all. He could write any kind of music an occasion required, and his operettas include lovely waltzes, stirring marches, exciting ensemble scenes, and thrilling choruses. Some, including *The Red Mill,* became popular motion pictures. Others, such as *Babes in Toyland,* continue to be revived from time to time. Many contained songs that we remember and love today, although the show to which they belong has been forgotten.

Naughty Marietta, one of Victor Herbert's most popular shows, exemplifies the best in operetta. Set in exotic eighteenth-century New Orleans during the French occupation, the show gave every opportunity for extravagant staging and costumes. The music includes a rousing march, stirring choruses, romantic love songs, and one excellent example of the virtuosic style of singing called *coloratura* (Listening Example 27).

Rudolf Friml (1879–1972)

Rudolf Friml was a concert pianist from Bohemia, an area more recently known as Czechoslovakia. Although he had never composed for musical theater, he was asked to write the music for an operetta when a leading singer quarreled with Victor Herbert and refused to sing Herbert's music ever again. Perhaps to his own surprise, Friml's show was a great success, and he went on to write several more.

By the 1920s, as we shall see in chapter 17, musical comedies were vying for popularity with European and American operettas. Friml disapproved of the manner in which the new musical comedies interpolated songs that had no connection with the story. In his own operettas, he carefully integrated words and music, writing songs that would further, rather than interrupt, the drama.

Friml's most successful operetta was *Rose-Marie,* which had an extremely long run on Broadway. It was also performed for several years by four touring companies, becoming one of the most financially successful shows the Broadway theater has known.

Sigmund Romberg (1887–1951)

Sigmund Romberg came from Hungary, having studied music there and in Vienna. Thoroughly steeped in the Viennese waltz tradition, he readily absorbed ragtime and other American dance rhythms, and soon began writing dance tunes. An incredibly prolific composer, Romberg produced seventeen scores in three years for every kind of musical show on Broadway.

Romberg was the last of America's great composers of operetta. He was so successful that at one time two of his operettas were running simultaneously on Broadway. Among his best-known shows were *The Desert Song* and *The Student Prince,* which was made into a movie starring Mario Lanza in the fifties.

LISTENING EXAMPLE 27
Coloratura Style

Composer   Victor Herbert

Title   "Italian Street Song" from *Naughty Marietta*

Form   Verse/chorus

The verse is in the style of the Viennese waltz, in rapid tempo and *triple meter*. In it Marietta tells of her longing (in the Romantic way) for her home in Naples and her memory of happy times there.

The chorus is in *quadruple meter*. Marietta's friends accompany her by singing in the background, while she indulges in the showy vocal display called **coloratura** singing. Since words would only interfere with performing these technically difficult passages, Marietta sings this section with neutral or meaningless syllables.

Text   *Ah! my heart is back in Napoli,*
Dear Napoli, dear Napoli,
And I seem to hear again in dreams
Her revelry, her sweet revelry.

The mandolinas playing sweet,
The pleasant fall of dancing feet.
Oh! could I return, oh! joy complete!
Napoli, Napoli, Napoli!

(Chorus)   *Zing, zing, zizzy, zizzy, zing, zing,*
Boom, boom, aye.
Zing, zing, zizzy, zizzy, zing, zing,
Mandolinas play.
Zing, zing, zizzy, zizzy, zing, zing,
Boom, boom aye
La, la, la, ha, ha, ha,
Zing, boom aye.
La la, la, la, Ha, ha, ha,
Zing, zing aye. (etc.)

SUMMARY

After the Civil War, musical theater became increasingly popular in America. The minstrel show waned in popularity, but several other kinds of variety show flourished. Vaudeville shows included blackface acts and many other varieties of entertainment. Burlesque shows were a series of satirical comedy and striptease acts. Revues were elegant and sophisticated spectacles featuring lovely staging and costumes and beautiful girls.

Unlike these variety shows, the operetta had an integrated plot. The French opéras bouffes were visually stunning, and Gilbert and Sullivan operettas provided hilarious entertainment. Most influential of all upon the American music stage was the Viennese operetta, with its romantic stories and make-believe settings.

The first American operettas were written by Europeans who adapted the characteristics of the Viennese style to produce shows addressed to a Broadway audience. Victor Herbert, Rudolf Friml, and Sigmund Romberg are among the best loved and revered representatives of the Broadway musical experience.

TERMS TO REVIEW

vaudeville A show with acts of every variety, including blackface scenes, dogs, circus stunts, songs, and dance.

burlesque A variety show featuring satirical humor; later associated with striptease acts.

revue Originally, a lavishly staged and costumed show with no integrated plot. Later, a series of scenes united by a theme but without a plot.

Ziegfeld Follies Elegant revues produced by Florenz Ziegfeld nearly every year from 1907 to 1932 to glorify the American girl.

operetta (light opera) A form of music theater in which the music and dancing are closely integrated with the plot.

opéra bouffe A French style of operetta, featuring satirical humor and visual spectacle.

patter songs A feature of Gilbert and Sullivan operettas (and other forms of music theater) in which humorous words are sung very rapidly, with comic effect.

Gilbert and Sullivan operettas Comic English musicals (words by Gilbert, music by Sullivan).

Viennese operettas The style of operetta written by Johann Strauss, Jr., and other Viennese composers, featuring exotic settings and romantic plots.

American operettas Musical shows adapted from the Viennese style, written for the Broadway stage.

coloratura Brilliant vocal display, usually consisting of extremely high pitches sung with neutral syllables.

KEY FIGURES

Black Composer
Will Marion Cook

Theatrical Producer
Florenz Ziegfeld

French Composer of Operettas
Jacques Offenbach

English Comic Poet and Librettist
William S. Gilbert

English Composer
Arthur Sullivan

Viennese Composers of Operettas
Johann Strauss, Jr.
Franz Lehar

Composers of American Operettas
Victor Herbert
Rudolf Friml
Sigmund Romberg

SUGGESTIONS FOR FURTHER LISTENING

Rudolf Friml: excerpts from *Rose-Marie*

Sigmund Romberg: excerpts from *The Student Prince, The Desert Song,* and *Blossom Time*

THE BROADWAY MUSICAL

Chapter 17

Blessed with a wealth of European and American operettas, as well as variety shows ranging in style from crude burlesques to extravagant revues, the early twentieth-century Broadway audience hardly felt the need for a new form of music theater. Despite their early resistance, however, an exciting new genre that blended popular entertainment (as in vaudeville) with an integrated plot (as in operettas) emerged just after the turn of the century.

The earliest **musical comedies,** as the new musical shows were called, were gaudy, boisterous productions barely held together by a thin excuse of a story. Scenery was simply painted on backdrops, and there was little in the way of a stage set. However, large and talented casts provided zany entertainment that was irresistible, if unsophisticated, fun.

The eventual great success of the fledgling form was largely assured by the efforts of one brash Irish-American who never gave up—**George M. Cohan** (fig. 17.1).

GEORGE M.
COHAN
(1878–1942)

The parents of George M. Cohan were vaudeville performers, and George and his younger sister were virtually brought up on the vaudeville stage. In fact, by the time he was in his teens, George was providing most of the material for the family's acts. Completely self-taught, he made up the skits, composed the songs, wrote the lyrics, promoted the shows, and acted, sang, and danced in them. In effect, he simply created the musical comedy.

Cohan was a zealous patriot who truly Americanized the Broadway theater. His shows always had an American theme and were filled with jaunty, flag-waving songs. His first full-length show—usually considered the first real musical comedy—was *Little Johnny Jones* (1904), the story of an American jockey who goes to England to win the derby. The plot is thin and does not hold together very well, but the score is filled with tuneful, high-spirited songs, including "Give My Regards to Broadway" and "Yankee Doodle Boy." (Cohan liked to say, as in the latter song, that he was born on the Fourth of July, though his birthdate was actually July 3.)

Other Cohan shows also featured American heroes—a reformed gambler, a baseball player, a senator—and stirring songs. He stormed Broadway with show after show that, while not always good, always had catchy tunes. To his regret, he was replaced in popularity in the twenties by several more-talented composers, but James Cagney recreated Cohan's

Figure 17.1

George M. Cohan.
(Culver Pictures, Inc.)

life in the movie *Yankee Doodle Dandy* (1942). In 1968 a successful musical, *George M!,* brought the Cohan magic back to Broadway.

BLACK MUSICALS

As we have seen, the black influence on popular music was particularly strong in the early years of the twentieth century. But curiously, there was a period of about ten years, from just before until soon after the First World War, when interest in black musical theater waned, although the musical stage generally flourished throughout that time. As the war lessened Americans' enthusiasm for European products, we developed a new confidence in our own artistic talents.

Then in 1921, *Shuffle Along,* with music by Eubie Blake and words by **Noble Sissle,** became a Broadway hit. This was one of many shows that lie somewhere between a revue and a musical comedy. There was a loosely-integrated plot, but it was regularly interrupted by entertainment scenes. Whites laughed uproariously at the satire, much of which was directed at them, and they enthusiastically applauded the stunning chorus line, tap dancing, and singing of the black troupe. The cast included **Josephine Baker,** who later became a star in Paris theaters. William Grant Still (see page 223) played oboe in the orchestra. One of the songs from the show, "I'm Just Wild About Harry," was revived as a campaign song for Harry Truman years later.

The 1920s witnessed several other popular shows with all-black casts, although some, including two "Broadway operas" to be discussed in chapter 18, were written by white composers and lyricists. The landmark show of the decade was *Show Boat* by **Jerome Kern,** a white composer who addressed interracial relations with sympathy and sensitivity.

JEROME KERN (1885–1945)

Jerome Kern studied piano and composition in Europe, at first intending to become a composer of classical music. He was irresistibly drawn, however, to the popular music theater, and began writing songs for Broadway. His first songs were interpolated in British revues imported to Broadway. It was usual, in fact, to add or to substitute songs even in early Broadway musical comedies, since the songs had little if anything to do with the plot and could fit as well in one show as another. Many composers took advantage of the opportunity to write one or more songs for a show without having to be responsible for the entire score.

Kern also worked as a song plugger and a rehearsal pianist for Broadway theaters. He then began writing his own shows, collaborating on two of them with the famous English writer P. G. Wodehouse, and in 1927 he wrote *Show Boat*.

Show Boat

Show Boat was remarkable in several ways. Unlike earlier musical comedies, which were basically collections of songs and variety acts loosely held together by a thin plot, *Show Boat* was based upon a novel by an established literary figure, Edna Ferber. This revolutionary idea eventually became the norm, as many, if not most, later musicals were based upon literary works: *South Pacific* on a novel by James Michener; *Kiss Me Kate* and *West Side Story* on Shakespeare plays; *The King and I* on an autobiography; and *Cats* on poems by T. S. Eliot, to name just a few. *Show Boat* proved the feasibility of basing a Broadway musical upon a literary work.

Also, the story of *Show Boat* expressed sympathy for the situation of black people in America. It even included an interracial love story—astonishing at a time when audiences expected sheer entertainment from a musical show. Again, this was prophetic in the sense that social, political, and even religious messages have been included in many later musicals. No longer would the term "musical *comedy*" be appropriate for all musical Broadway shows.

Most important of all, Kern was a sophisticated composer who wrote music of the finest quality. His lovely melodies and interesting harmonies are as attractive today as they were more than half a century ago. Melodies associated with particular characters recur throughout *Show Boat,* providing musical and dramatic unity. The classic love song "Why Do I Love You?," the bluesy "Can't Help Lovin' Dat Man of Mine," and the moving "Ol' Man River" seem likely to remain classics in the American song repertoire.

The quality of the music and the serious nature of the plot have caused some to refer to *Show Boat* as an operetta. In fact, the differences between the various kinds of music theater are often indistinct and, as we shall see, have become largely meaningless in recent times.

THE GOLDEN AGE OF BROADWAY MUSICALS

Before the 1920s, many great songwriters made their living by writing individual songs, some of which might be included in a Broadway musical. **Irving Berlin** (see pages 151–52) became involved with the Broadway musical stage while in his teens, but he was at his best writing individual songs, and his shows often seemed more like revues than typical musical comedies. For example, Berlin's *Watch Your Step* (1914) had a thin plot, but it starred

Figure 17.2

George Gershwin (1898–1937). (The Bettmann Archive, Inc.)

the famous dance couple **Irene and Vernon Castle** and included an elegant tango as well as other popular dances of the day. The Castles' dancing and Berlin's great songs made the show a hit.

During the twenties and thirties, songwriters' incomes from sheet music sales declined. Most people had radios in their homes by then and found it easier and cheaper during that difficult period to listen to the radio than to buy sheet music and learn to read it. They continued to buy tickets to Broadway musicals, however, so Kern, Berlin, and the other great songwriters concentrated their talents on the Broadway stage, producing an unprecedented quantity of sparkling popular music.

After 1929, sound movies gave another significant boost to songwriters' incomes. Several Broadway musicals were made into sound films that could be shown in any town with a local movie house, and the great songs soon became familiar nationwide. Throughout the thirties and forties, Broadway's amazingly gifted composers and lyricists continued to evolve artistically, producing many shows of lasting quality and beauty.

George Gershwin (fig. 17.2) was born in Brooklyn, New York. While still a teenager, he worked as a song plugger on Tin Pan Alley, playing and singing new songs as requested by shoppers in the sheet music stores.

Gershwin soon began writing songs of his own, many with clever lyrics by his brother **Ira Gershwin** (1896–1983). Although he was not a jazz musician himself, George Gershwin's musical language has the sounds and the flavor of jazz, and his songs lend themselves particularly well to jazz interpretations. Like Irving Berlin, he also had a gift for creating delightful syncopated dance rhythms, and some of his shows included outstanding dance

George Gershwin (1898–1937)

sequences. *Lady Be Good!* (1924) had the wonderful song "Fascinating Rhythm" and featured the famous dance team of **Adele and Fred Astaire.** More surprising at a time when dramatic integrity was scarcely expected of Broadway musicals, *Of Thee I Sing,* which satirized the American election process and for which Gershwin wrote the music, won the Pulitzer prize for drama in 1931.

Cole Porter (1892–1964)

Cole Porter (fig. 17.3), another outstanding songwriter who also composed for the Broadway stage, produced some of the most memorable songs of the thirties and forties. He was a witty, sophisticated musician who wrote his own clever, and often quite risqué, lyrics. "Night and Day" and "Begin the Beguine" are two of Cole Porter's best-known songs. The movie version of *Kiss Me Kate* (1948), a show he based upon Shakespeare's play *The Taming of the Shrew,* has been seen and loved by millions.

Richard Rodgers (1902–1979)

In a sense, **Richard Rodgers** had two careers—both of them as a songwriter. He collaborated with one lyricist for many years, producing a number of extremely successful musicals. Then he wrote several new shows with a different lyricist, whose style and character differed markedly from that of the first. Rodgers effectively adapted the style of his music to suit the words his two lyricists provided.

Rodgers and Hart

The lyrics for Rodgers's first outstanding shows were written by **Lorenz Hart** (1895–1943), one of the most talented lyricists Broadway has known.

Their musical *On Your Toes* (1936) was choreographed by the famous **George Balanchine** (1894–1987) and was remarkable for the manner in which dance was integrated with the drama. The show's magnificent dance scene, "Slaughter on Tenth Avenue," was an integral part of the story and actually furthered the action of the plot.

Rodgers and Hart's *Pal Joey* (1940) also included a ballet scene, for the Broadway audience was developing a strong fondness for the classical dance style. However, *Pal Joey* was remarkable in another way. The main character was a sort of antihero—a two-timing gigolo who took advantage of the innocent to further his own selfish goals. In spite of the wonderful music ("Bewitched, Bothered, and Bewildered" is probably the best-known song of the show), the critics hardly knew how to receive it. The show was much more successful, in fact, when it was revived twelve years later.

Talented as he was, Larry Hart finally became impossible to work with, for Rodgers never knew when he would disappear on an alcoholic binge. Finally, Rodgers turned to **Oscar Hammerstein II** (1895–1960) to write the lyrics for a new show, *Oklahoma!*

Rodgers and Hammerstein

Oklahoma! was widely expected to fail because it had no opening extravaganza, no chorus line, and no interpolation of songs for the sheer sake of entertainment. Rodgers and Hammerstein believed that all the music and dance in a musical should enhance the plot, and they accomplished their ideal in *Oklahoma!*.

The show was not only a great success but, like *Show Boat,* it is considered a landmark in the history of the Broadway musical. The story was built upon believable characters and situations. The choreography was by **Agnes de Mille** (a niece of the movie director Cecil B. de Mille), who had a gift for the expressive story-dance. (She had choreographed Aaron Copland's ballet *Rodeo* shortly before *Oklahoma!* opened.) And the songs were simply irresistible. The carefree "Oh, What a Beautiful Mornin'," romantic "Surrey with a Fringe on Top" and "People Will Say We're in Love," comic "Everything's Up to Date in Kansas City" and "I Cain't Say No," and of course the rousing "Oklahoma!" were instant and lasting hits. Critics, audience, and composers alike realized that *Oklahoma!* had ushered in a new kind of music theater.

Hammerstein's words were more thoughtful and serious than Hart's, and Rodgers responded by writing a different kind of music. *Carousel* (1945), which like *Oklahoma!* was based upon a play, had elements of tragedy and included a "message" song, "You'll Never Walk Alone." "Hello, Young Lovers" from *The King and I* (1951) is another example of a song more serious than Rodgers and Hart would have produced. Like Jerome Kern's *Show Boat,* for which Hammerstein also wrote the lyrics, *South Pacific* (1949) addressed the sensitive subject of interracial marriage. Even *The Sound of Music* (1959), perhaps the frothiest of the Rodgers and Hammerstein shows, concerns real characters in difficult situations.

Lerner and Loewe

Another famous Broadway team were **Alan Jay Lerner** (1918–1986) and **Frederick Loewe** (1901–1988), who wrote the wonderful shows *Brigadoon, Paint Your Wagon, Gigi, Camelot,* and *My Fair Lady.* Lerner was an American, but Loewe was born in Vienna, Austria, and came to the United States in 1924. "I Could Have Danced All Night," "On the Street Where You Live," "I've Grown Accustomed to Her Face," and "If Ever I Would Leave You" are among the great songs from Lerner and Loewe musicals.

THE TREND TOWARD THE SERIOUS MUSICAL CONTINUES

Today, classical and popular art have again grown close together, as they were before the nineteenth century drew self-conscious distinctions between them. For example, **Frank Loesser** (b. 1910), a composer who had previously written such delightfully entertaining but traditional musicals as *Where's Charley?* and *Guys and Dolls,* produced in 1956 *Most Happy Fella,* which he referred to as "a musical with a lotta music," but which is often called a popular or Broadway opera. It was performed, in fact, by the New York City Opera in 1991, and many felt the show was more at home there than on the Broadway stage. *Fella* requires highly trained voices and a full orchestra, and like Rodgers and Hammerstein's *Carousel* and Gershwin's *Porgy and Bess* (see pages 187–88), it probes deeply the emotional lives of its characters. The show provides plenty of entertainment and generous comic relief, but it requires more of its performers and audience than did the conventional, earlier style of musical.

Leonard Bernstein (1918–1990)

Leonard Bernstein (fig. 17.4) was a pianist, conductor, and composer primarily associated with concert music. Yet he also made significant contributions to vernacular music and particularly to the Broadway musical stage. Bernstein's early musical *On the Town* (1944) was adapted from a ballet he had written earlier. The ballet's famous choreographer **Jerome Robbins** (b. 1918) participated in directing the new musical, for the dances were an integral part of the show.

Wonderful Town in 1953 and *Candide* in 1956 were also successful Bernstein shows, but his Broadway masterpiece was *West Side Story* (1957). The dance scenes of *West Side Story* were choreographed by Robbins, who effectively worked them into the drama. The show is a retelling of Shakespeare's *Romeo and Juliet,* although the setting is the streets of uptown New York City and this Juliet (Maria in the show) does not die at the end. The rough language, realistic characters, lyrical music, and stunning dance scenes had an overpowering effect on Broadway and have become familiar to untold numbers of people through the movie version.

One of the most effective kinds of music theater scene is the **ensemble,** in which several characters present their own points of view, each singing different words and music at the same time. The finale to Act I of *West Side Story* illustrates the musical and dramatic impact of an ensemble scene (Listening Example 28).

Figure 17.4

Leonard Bernstein
conducting the New York
Philharmonic. (© AP/
Wide World Photos.)

The lyrics to the songs in *West Side Story* were written by a young man who has since become famous as a composer in his own right—**Stephen Sondheim.**

Stephen Sondheim studied with Milton Babbitt (see pages 206–8), among others, intending to become a composer of concert music. However, like Jerome Kern, he was early drawn to Broadway. His first experiences with the musical theater involved writing lyrics, a technique he studied with the highly talented and experienced Oscar Hammerstein II.

Stephen Sondheim (b. 1930)

After his early collaboration with Leonard Bernstein, Sondheim wrote both the lyrics and the music for many shows, including *A Funny Thing Happened on the Way to the Forum* (1962), *Company* (1970), *Follies* (1971), *A Little Night Music* (1973), *Pacific Overtures* (1976), *Sweeney Todd* (1979), and *Sunday in the Park with George* (1985). *Funny Thing* and *Follies* were traditional musicals that proved Sondheim could write within the conventions as well as anyone. *Night Music* was an elegant show, admired by critics but faulted by audiences for not having enough "good tunes," although it included the lovely "Send in the Clowns."

However, *Company* was a new kind of musical, prophetic of many shows to come to Broadway in succeeding years. Its cast is small, the settings are modest, and it has no continuous plot. The show, which asserts the impossibility of a successful marriage (at least in upper-middle-class, educated New York society) raises questions and confronts issues without

---

LISTENING EXAMPLE 28
Music Theater Ensemble

Composer   Leonard Bernstein

Title   Finale from Act I of *West Side Story*

A gang of assorted Americans, the Jets, have challenged the rival Puerto Rican gang, the Sharks, to a rumble (fight) "tonight." As the finale begins, the Jets and Sharks, each gang singing in unison, make excited threats to destroy each other. Their fast, highly rhythmic song is punctuated by sharp accents in the orchestra.

Anita, girlfriend of the leader of the Sharks, enters, singing of her plans for "tonight" to the same music.

Then Tony, the young "Romeo" of the show who is also a leader of the Sharks, sings the love song "Tonight," wishing that the night would last forever and that he could spend forever with his beloved Maria. Although the underlying pulse of Tony's song is the same as the "rumble" music sung by the gangs and Anita, his soaring melody lines and emotional delivery provide a romantic contrast to the other music.

The gangs begin their threatening lines again, and as they continue, we hear Maria in the distance singing Tony's love song. Tony joins her, and finally Anita completes the ensemble, in which each element (the two gangs, Anita, and the lovers Tony and Maria) express independent and indeed conflicting plans for "tonight." The beautifully written, tightly integrated ensemble achieves an almost unbearable level of dramatic tension.

---

resolving them. This "concept musical" indicated important new directions that music theater would follow in the seventies and eighties.

Pacific Overtures succeeded several musicals by other American composers that also reflected a strong Oriental influence, including *South Pacific* (1949), *The King and I* (1951), *Kismet* (1953), *Teahouse of the August Moon* (1953), *Flower Drum Song* (1958), and *The World of Suzie Wong* (1958). But *Pacific Overtures*, which concerned Admiral Perry's opening of Japan to the West as seen from a Japanese perspective, was more serious than the other shows, and it followed Eastern techniques more literally than Broadway was prepared to receive. It also made the unwelcome suggestion that Americans had erred by imposing Western ways upon the reluctant Japanese. The use of an Asian cast, Oriental musical instruments, and elements of the stylized Japanese theater called **kabuki** provided fascinating and provocative theater, but the show was not popular with audiences.

Sweeney Todd (1979) startled the Broadway audience even more with its melodramatic subject and serious music. Subtitled *The Demon Barber of Fleet Street,* this grisly story of murder and cannibalism has been called

a Broadway opera. However, unlike Gershwin's *Porgy and Bess* and Thomson's *Four Saints in Three Acts* of half a century earlier (see chapter 18), *Sweeney Todd* was virtually unrelieved by conventional entertainment scenes. It has been critically acclaimed as Sondheim's masterpiece, but audiences generally find it dark and depressing.

In 1985, Sondheim won the Pulitzer prize for drama for *Sunday in the Park with George.* More sentimental and optimistic than most of Sondheim's work, this show describes the struggles and triumphs of the **pointillist** artist **Georges Seurat** (1859–1891) and later of his great-grandson, who became a modernist sculptor. In one scene, the actors stunningly portray the characters in Seurat's famous painting *Sunday Afternoon on the Island of La Grande Jatte* (fig. 17.5).

Several shows in the sixties and seventies were based upon rock music, but they do not seem to have established a discernible trend. *Grease* (1972) was a rollicking hit about the rock and roll era. *Hair,* more of a revue than a musical, seems unlikely to spawn imitations.

At least two important shows of that period were based on religious themes. *Jesus Christ Superstar,* a rock opera with music by Andrew Lloyd Webber and words by Tim Rice, was one of an impressive stream of English imports to the Broadway musical stage. It actually became famous as a record album before it was produced on stage, and it remains better known for its music than its story. More successful as a theater piece was *Godspell* (1971), with songs by Stephen Schwartz (b. 1948). In *Godspell*, a small cast interpreted the Gospel According to St. Matthew in a striking new way, singing Schwartz's simple, appealing songs, the best-known of which is "Day by Day."

THE VARIETY WIDENS

Several black musicals were produced in the seventies and eighties, including a black interpretation of *The Wizard of Oz* called *The Wiz*. An all-black version of *Guys and Dolls* appeared in 1976, and *Dream Girls*, featuring three black female singers and based upon the experience of The Supremes, had a successful run in 1981.

CURRENT TRENDS

Staging has become a more significant element of musical theater than ever before. While questions of economy encourage the production of small or *chamber* musicals, the more widely popular shows feature large casts and sets that are extravagant in design and breathtaking in effect. Some of the most lavishly staged musicals on Broadway today are foreign imports. Andrew Lloyd Webber's *Cats, Starlight Express,* and *Phantom of the Opera* offer elaborate staging and costumes, as do *Miss Saigon* and *Les Miserables* by the French composer Claude-Michel Schonberg.

Dance is also more important than ever in the Broadway musical. The loose plot of *A Chorus Line* (1975) concerns the manner in which a choreographer selects dancers, and much of that delightful show's entertainment—in both its live and movie versions—is derived from its wonderful dance sequences. (The 1978 movie *Saturday Night Fever* reflected in film the same sheer love of dance.) The musical *42nd Street* (1980) is an extravaganza of song and dance that continues to have successful runs around the country and abroad, and a recent revival of Rodgers and Hart's *On Your Toes* was very well received.

There is also increasing interest in **multimedia shows,** which combine music, dance, drama, and sophisticated special effects. Audience involvement, complex lighting techniques, tape recordings, films, slides, and video are often part of the music theater experience today. For example, roller skates race on ramps over the heads of the audience in *Starlight Express*, a chandelier makes a spectacular fall in *Phantom of the Opera*, and a helicopter lands on the stage in *Miss Saigon*.

The years 1991–1992 witnessed a curious development on Broadway, which enjoyed an explosion of talent on the musical stage, but in shows that were revivals of earlier hits or were based upon the music of earlier times. Frank Loesser's *Guys and Dolls* and *Most Happy Fella* were warmly received by both critics and audiences. A new show, *Jelly's Last Jam,* was fashioned from vintage Jelly Roll Morton jazz tunes, and *Crazy for You,* another successful new musical, used classic Gershwin tunes, some of which appeared originally in other shows. It is simply too soon to know whether this signals a healthy, indeed exciting, renewal of vitality or is evidence of fading creativity for the American musical stage. Certainly the talents of new choreographers, stage designers, and actors offer enormous hope for this indigenously American musical form.

The "Broadway musical" has become an international phenomenon, with unprecedented creative and technological sophistication and an apparently limitless variety of styles. Now Broadway audiences expect the ultimate mating of the arts that used to be considered the sole prerogative of opera. Many contemporary shows are entirely sung, using no spoken dialogue at all. Thus, Broadway has learned what opera lovers have always known—once caught up in the magic of music theater, reality is simply superseded by art, and the emotional and aesthetic rewards are grand.

SUMMARY

Early musical comedies combined elements of two kinds of music theater already popular on Broadway: operetta and variety shows. By writing several shows that had a story but included vaudeville's song, dance, and comedy routines, George M. Cohan was most influential in accustoming the Broadway audience to the new style.

Jerome Kern's *Show Boat* proved that a Broadway musical could be based upon a literary work and could address serious subjects effectively. *Oklahoma!* by Rodgers and Hammerstein successfully integrated all the entertainment scenes with the drama. Each of these shows had a profound effect upon the development of the Broadway musical stage.

The twenties and thirties are considered the Golden Age of the Broadway musical because so many outstanding shows were produced during those years. Since then, the musical theater has become more complex and more sophisticated. Leonard Bernstein and Stephen Sondheim are among several composers who applied both classical and popular interests in various ways to the musical stage. Dance continues to be a significant feature of many musicals, which today are often multimedia affairs combining technologically complex aural and visual effects.

TERMS TO REVIEW

musical comedy   A play with music, in which the elements of entertainment are connected by a plot.

ensemble   In music theater, a group of solo singers, each performing their own words and music at the same time.

kabuki   A highly stylized form of Japanese music drama.

pointillism   An art style related to Impressionism, in which tiny dots of pure color seem to blend when viewed from a distance.

multimedia shows   Performances including some combination of music, dance, film, slides, tape recordings, and other sound and visual techniques.

KEY FIGURES

Composers of Broadway Musicals
George M. Cohan
Jerome Kern
Irving Berlin
George Gershwin
Cole Porter
Richard Rodgers
Frederick Loewe
Frank Loesser
Leonard Bernstein
Stephen Sondheim

Lyricists
Noble Sissle
Ira Gershwin
Lorenz Hart
Oscar Hammerstein II
Alan Jay Lerner

Choreographers
George Balanchine
Agnes de Mille
Jerome Robbins

Dance Teams
Irene and Vernon Castle
Adele and Fred Astaire

Black Singer
Josephine Baker

Pointillist Painter
Georges Seurat

TWENTIETH-CENTURY AMERICAN OPERA

Chapter 18

Almost since operas began to be written, early in the seventeenth century, Italians have hummed favorite opera tunes while strolling down the street. Other Europeans as well have delighted in the emotional intensity and high drama or comedy of many wonderful operas in various styles.

Americans, on the other hand, until recently considered opera an elite and unlikely form of entertainment, and "American opera" was almost inconceivable. Fry's and Bristow's operas (see pages 128 and 129) were intentionally Italian-sounding. Other enthusiasts sought to attract an American audience by translating Italian, French, or German operas into English, but that did not necessarily make them accessible or meaningful to American listeners.

Yet, opera is the grandest of all the arts—combining singing, acting, orchestral music, drama, staging, costuming, dance, and lighting effects in a form infinitely greater than the sum of its parts. Therefore, it is surprising that it took so long for opera to assume the vital role in American music theater it finally enjoys.

Since World War II, a significant number of opera companies have been formed in America, and performances in the major opera houses around the country are regularly sold out. During the 1980s, films of two Italian operas by Giuseppe Verdi (1813–1901)—*La Traviata* and *Otello*—were commercially successful at popular movie theaters. Saturday afternoon broadcasts of Metropolitan Opera performances have been popular since 1931, and recently network television has been offering full-length live performances of great operas from many countries and periods.

Americans have discovered that there are as many kinds of opera as there are movies or books. It is true that, because of its complexity, opera requires more preparation on the part of the audience than any other form of art or entertainment, but the combined visual and musical effects offer unparalleled rewards.

OPERA

An **opera** is a drama that is sung instead of spoken. Like a play, it may be long or short, comic or serious, grand or modest—good or bad. Of course it is unnatural to sing everything rather than to speak, so the opera viewer must abandon, or suspend, rational thought to become immersed in the art—the magic—that is opera. This is not as difficult as it sounds, for even skeptical viewers quickly forget that the dialogue is being sung instead of spoken. As noted in chapter 17, many modern musicals use the same technique, and Broadway audiences have come to expect it. After all, it is the role of art to express human feelings at a level *beyond* the limits of ordinary communication. As our emotions become involved and the real world slips away—or gets out of the way—the most artificial aspects of art somehow become more real than reality.

In an opera, the exchange of dialogue occurs through **recitative** rather than speech. Recitative (from the same root as "recite") is a style of singing in which the words are expressed clearly and economically, so as to move the drama along. The melody of a recitative often resembles the inflection (rise and fall of pitch level) of the words as they would be spoken, and the rhythm and form are also based upon the text. As you might expect, there is little repetition of phrases, because the purpose is to further the action.

    One kind of recitative, called **dry recitative** (or *recitativo secco* in Italian), is accompanied by a keyboard instrument only or, in early operas, by a keyboard and another instrument that doubles the bass line. The more expressive **accompanied recitative** is accompanied by the orchestra.

Recitative

An **aria** is a dramatic soliloquy that is sung rather than spoken. The music is usually more melodic, and often more expressive, than that of a recitative, for the emphasis is upon the music rather than the text. Time is simply suspended as a character reflects upon and expresses the deepest feelings and emotions aroused by situations in the drama.

    It is in the arias that we expect to hear fully displayed the beauty and range of a singer's voice. Here the performer may indulge in soaring melodic lines and virtuosic singing, since the words are less important than the expression of emotion. There may, in fact, be considerable repetition of text ("I love you, I love you . . .") in order to enhance the emotional impact of an aria.

    An aria has metered rhythm and is organized according to musical principles of design. The most familiar aria *form* is called **da capo,** which means "from the beginning" and may be illustrated as **ABA.** The composer writes the first section, **A,** and a contrasting second section, **B,** indicating that the first section is then to be repeated "from the beginning." Here is further opportunity for vocal display, as a singer often adds improvised embellishments to the repetition of section **A.**

    The orchestral accompaniment to an aria may be far more than simple support for the vocal line. There is often an orchestral introduction, as well as orchestral interludes between sections or verses and a concluding orchestral passage. Throughout the piece, instruments in the orchestra may introduce or imitate the singer's melodic phrases, and sometimes the orchestra even plays a dramatic or psychological role, perhaps contradicting

Aria

the singer's words by making musical references to conflicting ideas. Instruments also provide sound effects, such as bird calls or storm sounds, that are independent of the singer's melodic line.

Ensembles

Ensemble scenes are among the most exciting in opera. A **chorus** is a large ensemble, with several voices singing each line of music. The members of an opera chorus generally represent characters in the drama, such as guests at a wedding or soldiers returning from battle.

A scene or act of an opera may end with an **ensemble finale,** each important character appearing individually and then joining others to form a solo ensemble—duet, trio, quartet, quintet, or even a larger group of soloists—to bring the scene to a musically and dramatically thrilling close.

OPERA IN AMERICA

Before the present century, the few existent American opera houses confined their repertoire almost entirely to foreign operas. French opera was well liked in New Orleans, where many people spoke French, and New York City had a small but enthusiastic audience for German and Italian operas. The works of William Henry Fry and George Frederic Bristow were isolated examples of American opera, and they were based upon the Italian style. No further American operas were presented for a long time.

During the first half of the twentieth century, however, several composers sought to establish an American national opera style by writing operas with American Indian settings. **Mary Carr Moore** (1873–1957) was among the more successful composers of operas on Indian themes. But the idea, though popular for a time, was short-lived. As we have seen, Scott Joplin was entirely unsuccessful in promoting *Treemonisha* during his lifetime, though it was well received on Broadway in 1975 and has been enjoyed elsewhere around the country since.

Curiously, two operas by white composers, each with an all-black cast and each performed in Broadway theaters rather than in opera houses, first brought American opera to a broad and appreciative audience.

VIRGIL THOMSON (1896–1989)

By the time he graduated from Harvard University, **Virgil Thomson** was convinced that concert music had become overly complex. He therefore imposed a refreshing simplicity upon his own compositions, which were often based upon the folk songs, hymns, and Civil War songs he had heard as a youngster in Missouri.

While continuing his music education in Paris with the extremely talented and influential Nadia Boulanger (see page 217), Thomson discovered that the French also found virtue in musical simplicity. Like him, they considered that the purpose of music was to amuse and entertain, rather than to improve, the listener. Thomson stayed in this congenial atmosphere for fifteen years, only driven home by the impending catastrophe of World War II.

Among Thomson's most stimulating experiences abroad was his collaboration with **Gertrude Stein** (1874–1946), an American writer who spent most of her life in Paris. Stein used words for their *sounds* rather than their *meanings,* producing attractive, often funny combinations of syllables, regardless of their sense or lack of it. Gertrude Stein wrote the words, or **libretto,** of *Four Saints in Three Acts,* the first American opera to appeal to the American public, and Virgil Thomson wrote the music.

Since Thomson's opera concerns fifteen saints and has four acts, it is immediately apparent that nothing about it is to be taken literally. Indeed, this highly attractive show makes little if any sense, but offers lavish and delightful entertainment to the eyes and ears.

Four Saints in Three Acts

The enchanting sets of the first performance, which took place in 1934 in New York City, were elegantly constructed of brightly colored cellophane—to the dismay of the city's fire department. Thomson's choice of an all-black cast seems curious, since the characters are (apparently) Spanish and have nothing to do with black culture. He simply admired the appearance and voices of the black singers. Although his concept may seem racist in today's more sensitive environment, Thomson's intentions were artistic and aesthetic, and he would have been astonished to have had his genuine esteem considered discriminatory.

The nonsensical libretto is somehow very appealing, and Thomson set it beautifully to music. It had been thought that American speech did not lend itself to musical settings, and this was the first time an American libretto was effectively and idiomatically set to an opera score. This, together with Thomson's folklike melodies and hymn tunes, the lovely choruses, colorful sets, and imaginative orchestration, won the appreciation of Broadway audiences accustomed to more frivolous entertainment.

The year that *Four Saints* opened on Broadway, **George Gershwin** (see pages 175–76) read a novel by Du Bose Heyward based upon the lives of real people who lived in a black tenement area in Charleston, North Carolina. Profoundly moved by the novel and by the play based upon it, Gershwin decided to write an opera on the subject.

GERSHWIN'S *PORGY AND BESS*

In preparation for writing his opera, Gershwin spent a summer in the Charleston area, where he listened to people talk and sing, and heard the street cries of the vegetable sellers, the work songs of the men, the lullabies women sang to their babies, and the shouts and hymns at church services. Then he returned to New York to write *Porgy and Bess,* which opened on Broadway a year after Thomson's opera—also with an all-black cast.

Porgy begins with an instrumental piece, usually called an **overture,** but simply called "Introduction" by Gershwin, who intended his show for a Broadway audience. Like a conventional opera overture, Gershwin's introduction sets the appropriate mood and includes some of the music to be heard later.

Figure 18.1

A scene from Gershwin's
Porgy and Bess.
(Courtesy of Opera
News.)

Porgy is a poor man, so crippled that he gets around only by goat cart. Bess, a "loose-living woman" from New York, falls deeply in love with Porgy and gives up her "big-city ways." Their story is tender and moving, with flashes of wit and humor and plenty of tense drama. A number of the songs (Gershwin also avoided the term "aria") became so popular that Americans were finally humming opera tunes on the streets.

In one of the most beautiful love duets ever written, Porgy and Bess eloquently express their devotion to one another (see figure 18.1 and Listening Example 29).

GIAN-CARLO MENOTTI (B. 1911)

Another composer who has written operas for a Broadway audience is an Italian who reversed the prevalent trend by coming to America to study music. **Gian-Carlo Menotti** was a child prodigy, having written two operas by the time he was thirteen. He came to America in 1928 to study at the Curtis Institute of Music in Philadelphia, Pennsylvania, where he became a close friend of another famous American composer, Samuel Barber (see pages 222–23).

In 1947, Menotti wrote a two-act thriller titled *The Medium,* which, because of its modest resources—five singers, one dance-mime role, and an orchestra of only fourteen players—may be called a **chamber opera.** (It is also quite brief, and Menotti intended it to be performed with another miniature opera of his, titled *The Telephone.*) The mood of *The Medium* is eerie, the melodies are memorable, and the libretto (which Menotti wrote

---

LISTENING EXAMPLE 29

Opera Duet

Composer George Gershwin

Title "Bess, You Is My Woman Now" from *Porgy and Bess*

Poignant falling figures in the strings introduce this beautiful duet. Porgy (*bass* voice) first declares his love for Bess and insists that she must "laugh an' sing an' dance for two instead of one," since he is unable to get around. Porgy's passionate melody is doubled in the strings, enhancing the emotional impact of the music. The verse has five lines of text, yet seems superbly balanced.

Bess (*soprano*) responds with her fervent declaration of love for Porgy, declaring she will go nowhere without him. Her melody is at first the same as Porgy's, but she soon soars to rapturous high notes, as if overwhelmed with love and joy.

Notice as they sing together that Bess generally carries the melody while Porgy's comments add contrapuntal interest and harmony. Also notice the orchestra's contributions, including melodic support, harmony, and independent "comments." You will hear expressively inflected "blue notes" (lying just under normal pitch—see pages 229–30) throughout, a characteristic derived from black performance practice and associated with blues, jazz, and many styles of black music.

---

himself) is dramatically effective. Not surprisingly, Broadway audiences found these performances moving and exciting.

Menotti's next major work was *The Consul,* which opened on Broadway in 1950. The story concerns the frustration and ultimate tragedy of a family who desperately try to escape from their country but are confronted with bureaucratic nonsense in response to their urgent pleas for assistance. The moving aria "To This We've Come" (Optional Listening Example) eloquently expresses the rage and despair of a woman prevented by bizarre circumstances from saving her doomed family.

The Consul

The Consul was written at the time of the Cold War, but neither the country nor the time is specified, allowing us to relate the events to our own knowledge, experience, or imagination. Because the characters and their desperate situation are realistic and entirely believable, the term **verismo**—usually reserved for nineteenth-century Italian operas based upon realistic stories—is sometimes applied to *The Consul.* The opera had a long, successful run on Broadway and won the Pulitzer prize and the Drama Critic's Award.

The next year (1951), Menotti was commissioned by the National Broadcasting Company (NBC) to write the first opera conceived especially for television. *Amahl and the Night Visitors* (fig. 18.2), based upon a painting

Amahl and the Night Visitors

Figure 18.2

A scene from Menotti's
*Amahl and the Night
Visitors.* (The Bettmann
Archive, Inc.)

Figure 18.2

A scene from Menotti's *Amahl and the Night Visitors.* (The Bettmann Archive, Inc.)

called *The Adoration of the Magi* by Hieronymus Bosch, has been performed at Christmastime every year since, often on TV but by amateurs in church and community settings as well. The simple, naive story and the lovely music consistently appeal to children and, as Menotti says, "those who like children."

Menotti has written several other operas, as well as symphonic and choral works. However, he is primarily a man of the theater, and his gifts for melody and drama seem to have been best expressed in his early operas written for the Broadway or television audience.

THE TREND TOWARD REALISM

Operas have traditionally dealt with fiction, fantasy, myth, or ancient history, but increasingly, opera composers have chosen topics from recent history and even from everyday life. As early as 1937, Marc Blitzstein addressed the traumas of the Great Depression in an opera about the struggle for labor rights called *The Cradle Will Rock.* Much of the music in this opera was popular in style, and the words reflected the ethnic speech of city streets. Douglas S. Moore wrote about American pioneer life in *The Devil and Daniel Webster* (1939), and in 1958, he wrote another opera, *The Ballad of Baby Doe,* set in the nineteenth century and including some of the music styles popular then. Aaron Copland's *The Tender Land,* about a midwest American farm family, was also written during the 1950s. A new opera by Ulysses Kay, *Between Liberty and Oppression* (1991), concerns the life of Frederick Douglass, a hero in black American history.

Figure 18.3

A scene from John
Adams's *Nixon in China.*
(© Andrew Popper/
Picture Group.)

Beginning in the 1980s, operas based upon recent or even current events began to appear. Philip Glass's *Satyagraha* (1980) tells of the early struggles of Mahatma Gandhi. *X,* by Anthony Davis (1986), concerns the black-nationalist leader Malcolm X. John Adams's first opera, *Nixon in China* (1987), describes President Nixon's visits to, and negotiations with, that country (fig. 18.3). In 1990, an opera called *Manson Family,* about the California mass murderer Charles Manson, was written by John Moran. And in 1991, John Adams presented a new opera, titled *The Death of Klinghoffer,* which is about the 1985 highjacking of the ship *Achille Lauro* and the murder of a wheelchair-bound American-Jewish passenger. Still another genre, science-fiction opera, has recently been approached by some composers.

Americans today are interested in all varieties of opera—old and new, domestic and foreign, funny and sad, short and long, simple and complex. Many American cities have an opera house and their own resident opera company, and virtually all Americans have access to live or taped performances on radio or television. Foreign operas are often performed in English translation, or alternatively, English surtitles are projected above the stage to avoid interfering with the visual presentation. Tightened budgets have put serious constraint upon the world of opera, because the complex presentations are exceedingly expensive to produce. But the American audience seems finally to have recognized opera as the marvelous form of entertainment it was always intended to be.

Further, as we saw in chapter 17, a distinct rapprochement between the musical and the opera has occurred in recent years. Many Broadway and London musicals are now sung throughout, and operas by Glass and Adams, for example, are closer to traditional Broadway productions than

AMERICAN MUSIC THEATER TODAY

to Italian or German operas. How, then, to distinguish between the various kinds of music theater? With difficulty, if at all! The old definitions of a *musical* as a play with occasional music, an *opera* as a musical drama with no spoken dialogue, and an *operetta* as something between the two extremes have become largely meaningless. Today's audiences both on Broadway and in the opera house are afforded grand entertainment on a lavish scale and of unprecedented variety and scope.

SUMMARY

An opera is a grand combination of literary, visual, and musical arts. Traditionally, dialogue was sung in recitative, but today some composers also include spoken words in their operas. Emotional reactions are expressed in solo arias, duets, and large or small ensembles.

In the 1920s, several American operas were enthusiastically received. Virgil Thomson's *Four Saints in Three Acts* and George Gershwin's *Porgy and Bess* were both successful on Broadway, as were Gian-Carlo Menotti's operas nearly three decades later. Thomson sought an elegant simplicity in music, Gershwin spoke in the spirit of jazz, and Menotti represents the Italian tradition of lyrical melodies and good theater.

Today's mainstream and progressive composers are producing a wealth of new American operas. In fact, operas of seemingly unlimited variety are enthusiastically viewed in American opera houses, theaters, and on TV, and are heard on radio and recordings.

TERMS TO REVIEW

opera   A drama that is sung, usually with orchestral accompaniment.

recitative   A declamatory setting of a text, with rhythms and inflections related to those of speech. Used in opera and other dramatic vocal works.

dry recitative (*recitativo secco*)   Recitative accompanied by a keyboard instrument.

accompanied recitative   Recitative accompanied by an orchestra.

aria   A songlike setting, musically expressive, accompanied by the orchestra.

da capo   "From the beginning." A three-part design. The composer writes the first section and a contrasting middle section of a da capo aria, and the performer repeats the first section with embellishments.

chorus   A large ensemble, with several voices on each part.

ensemble finale   An ensemble scene at the end of an act.

libretto   The words of an opera or other dramatic vocal work.

overture   In music theater, an introductory instrumental piece.

chamber opera   An opera for a small number of performers.

verismo   Realism in opera.

KEY FIGURES

Mary Carr Moore

Virgil Thomson

Gertrude Stein

George Gershwin

Gian-Carlo Menotti

OPTIONAL LISTENING EXAMPLE*

Gian-Carlo Menotti: "To This We've Come" from *The Consul*

*Guides for Optional Listening Examples are in the Instructor's Manual and may be copied and distributed to students.

part 7

REVOLUTION AND EVOLUTION

TOWARD THE FUTURE

Chapter 19

The twentieth century has produced an unprecedented diversity of music styles as new historical and cultural awareness has broadened our concepts of timbre, pitch, melody, harmony, and rhythm. Recent technology has also made important new resources available. With the energy, curiosity, and independence characteristic of the pioneer spirit, a number of American **experimentalists** have explored musical sound, extending the boundaries of its definition.

Three musical pioneers initated the experimental movement in America. One was a Connecticut Yankee who explored the manifold characteristics of sound. The second was a Californian who discovered new ways to use the piano. The third, a European, dreamed of new instruments that would create new sounds—and lived to see his dream come true.

CHARLES IVES (1874–1954)

The musical inventiveness of **Charles Ives** (fig. 19.1) began with his father, George, an amateur musician who taught his son to play several instruments and, more significantly, to be ever curious about music and musical sound. George Ives conducted sound experiments in the family barn, to the annoyance of his neighbors and the fascination of his son.

George Ives also taught Charles to value each piece of music for its own sake, a lesson his son took to heart. All his life, Ives considered Stephen Foster's music as worthy, in its own way, as was Bach's music, in its way. A good rag was as significant as a good hymn, and a fine march as important as a fine symphony. He felt that differentiating between *genres* of music in terms of quality was a form of musical snobbery, preferring instead to judge each *piece* on its own merits.

Ives went to Yale, where he studied music under Horatio Parker (see page 138), whom he respected, but whom he considered dogmatic and incapable of pursuing or appreciating new ideas. Convinced by his college experience that his broad musical concepts exceeded those of his contemporaries, and declaring that he did not intend his family "to starve on my dissonances," Ives devoted his professional life to his own highly successful insurance business. He then felt free to write music that pleased him, composing at night, on weekends, and during vacation time.

Figure 19.1

Charles Ives. (The Bettmann Archive, Inc.)

Ives was an inveterate romantic, who had strong literary interests and expressed himself effectively in words as well as music. He valued the *substance*, or the character, of music over its *manner*, or superficial beauty. For Ives, beauty was "like a drug that allows the ears to lie back in an easy chair." Ives scorned the word "nice," equating it with weak or genteel. He believed that music should be strong and challenging. For him, dissonant sounds were clean and virile, and people who feared them were musical cowards.

Philosophy of Music

Most of Ives's instrumental compositions are program pieces, frequently reflecting the New England environment he knew and loved. He admired the Transcendentalists (see page 86), sharing many of their ideas, and one of his most famous pieces, the *Concord Sonata,* is devoted to them. Each of the four movements of this substantial piano composition describes the ideas and character of one or more famous Transcendentalists: Ralph Waldo Emerson, Nathaniel Hawthorne, Amos Bronson and Louisa May Alcott, and Henry David Thoreau. Ives prefaced the work with *Four Essays Before a Sonata,* in which he explained in words the ideas expressed in the music.

Instrumental Compositions

One of Ives's best-known programmatic pieces is "General Putnam's Camp" from *Three Places in New England* (Optional Listening Example). This brash and exuberant piece, which depicts a small boy's fantasies as he enjoys a Fourth of July picnic held at a former Revolutionary War campsite, includes snatches of patriotic tunes that Ives altered in the most imaginative and sometimes amusing ways.

Ives also wrote about 150 songs, covering many subjects, with settings that range from simple to complex. He frequently based his songs (and instrumental pieces as well) on familiar tunes. In some cases, he quoted fragments, phrases, or complete melodies from American hymns, rags, marches, patriotic songs, Stephen Foster melodies, and the music of Bach and other composers, altering and/or juxtaposing them into complex layers of sound. "At the River" (Listening Example 30) turns a well-known tune into a new composition.

Songs

Always delighted by the irregular and charmed by the unconventional, Ives experimented with unusual tunings of musical instruments. In this way, he sometimes deliberately achieved the intriguing effect of youngsters playing their instruments slightly out of tune. While generally respecting the concept of tonality, he considered allegiance to one key at a time confining and occasionally indulged in **bitonality** (two keys at once) and **polytonality** (multiple simultaneous keys). His use of all twelve tones of the chromatic scale in some pieces foreshadowed the atonal music of other composers.

Other Characteristics of Ives's Music

Ives explored virtually every area of music. He conceived incredibly complex rhythmic relationships, and he frequently combined two or more simultaneous rhythmic patterns into exciting **polyrhythms.** Recognizing that

---

LISTENING EXAMPLE 30
Original Song Based on a Given Tune

Composer   Charles Ives

Title   "At the River"

Form   Verse-chorus

Tune and Text   By Robert Lowry

Accompaniment   The piano introduction sets a tentative, questioning mood. The piano then accompanies the familiar hymn tune with richly dissonant chords, adding competing melodic interest toward the end of the verse. A brief piano interlude occurs between verse and chorus.

Rhythm   Although the listener clearly feels the *quadruple meter* (four beats to the bar), the rhythm is quite free and flexible, contributing to the "questioning" quality of the piece.

Although Ives basically uses the original tune, he alters the end of the verse and the chorus with odd turns of phrase that also enhance the tentative mood.

---

there is a **continuum of pitches** between intervals, he availed himself of the **quarter tones** and **microtones** that lie between the half steps of a keyboard instrument.

The qualities of sound were a source of endless fascination for Ives, who made space a significant element in some of his compositions. He also valued a degree of spontaneity in music performance, anticipating what later became known as "chance music." These principles are illustrated in *The Unanswered Question* (Optional Listening Example), a programmatic piece in which a trumpet asks "The Perennial Question of Existence." A group of woodwinds, positioned at a distance from the trumpet, attempts to find "The Invisible Answer," while a string ensemble, located off-stage, plays slow, quiet, rather mysterious music, oblivious of the squabble taking place on stage. Six times "The Question" is posed, and six times the woodwinds' increasingly agitated replies are rejected. Finally, "The Question" is heard once more, remaining unanswered.

In his prefatory instructions for performing this piece, Ives indicated that "The Question" may be posed by any instrument that can play the trumpet's pitches, and the woodwinds may be all flutes or a combination of instruments. He also suggested that "The Answers" need not begin at the points he notated, but could as well come a bit early or late. Thus, *space* and *chance* play a small but significant role in this fascinating piece.

Ives's Place in History

Ill health prevented Ives from continuing his musical explorations after the 1920s, and it was twenty years later before his music was brought to public attention. His Third Symphony was written about 1904 but was first performed in 1947, when it won a Pulitzer prize, and other pieces have received similarly belated but impressive recognition. Ives has now entered the ranks

Figure 19.2

Henry Cowell. (Bettmann Newsphotos.)

of legendary figures in the history of American music, and many of his innovations have become part of the normal music experience. But the spark of his invention, the verve and the *nerve* of his style remain fresh and invigorating today.

HENRY COWELL (1897–1965)

By the time of the birth of **Henry Cowell,** the American frontier had been pushed all the way to the West Coast. Cowell (fig. 19.2) was born in San Francisco into an eclectic environment whose varied influences are reflected in his highly original compositions. Some of his programmatic pieces are based upon the Irish folklore he learned from his own Irish-American family. He was also introduced to Chinese music by childhood friends, beginning a lifelong interest in the music of the Orient. Further musical experience was afforded by an organist friend who allowed the budding young composer to attend his practice sessions, where Cowell absorbed the modal sounds of Roman Catholic church music.

Early Compositions

Cowell had decided to be a composer by the time he was eight years old. He taught himself to play the piano his own way, creating sounds he found interesting, and eventually using those sounds for imaginative programmatic purposes in his compositions. For example, while still in his teens, Cowell wrote a piano piece called "The Tides of Mananaun" (Listening Example 31). In this piece the performer used the flat of the hand or forearm to play large clusters of keys in the lower range of the piano, evoking the sounds of the rolling, roaring ocean tides. The result was extremely

---

LISTENING EXAMPLE 31
Tone Clusters

Composer   Henry Cowell

Title   "The Tides of Mananaun" (excerpt)

Form   This short piece is organized in an arch form, beginning very softly and low in pitch, rising to high levels of pitch dynamics, and tapering back to end much as it began.

Melody   Though based upon a minor scale, the melody has an archaic, modal flavor.

Accompaniment   The clusters in the bass form an ostinato accompaniment through much of the piece. At one point (just past the middle of the piece, and just before the tape excerpt ends), the outer tones (lowest and highest) of the clusters form rising scale passages that stand out dramatically against the melody played in octaves by the right hand.

---

dissonant, but it effectively suggested the unstable, ever-changing sounds he wished to achieve. Cowell believed that dissonant combinations evoked strong emotions, while consonance suggested simplicity; thus, he was astonished to learn later that people tend to hear dissonance and consonance as "bad" or "good" sounds.

Cowell and others later recognized **tone clusters** as simply a new kind of dissonant chord, built upon seconds rather than the thirds of conventional tonal harmony. Although they later became friends, Cowell did not know Charles Ives at the time he began using clusters, and it was only later that both men discovered they had "invented" the same idea at about the same time.

Piano Experiments

Cowell wrote many kinds of music, but he was particularly interested in the piano—probably because it was readily accessible. He desired to extend the range of sounds the piano could produce and discovered that he could do this by playing directly on the strings of the piano, as on any other string instrument.

Cowell wrote several pieces in which the piano strings are to be stroked, strummed, plucked, or struck, each technique producing an entirely different effect. He achieved even further variety of sounds by having the pianist either depress some of the keys while manipulating the strings or mute (stop) the strings with one hand while playing on the keyboard with the other. These ideas proved particularly fruitful, for they suggested the possibility of producing effective new sounds by playing other traditional instruments in nontraditional ways.

"The Banshee" (Listening Example 32) requires two performers, one seated at the piano and the other standing in the crook of the instrument.

LISTENING EXAMPLE 32
Piano Experiments

Composer   Henry Cowell

Title   "The Banshee" (excerpt)

Program   According to Irish folklore, a banshee is a ghost sent to conduct a dead soul to the other world. Uncomfortable in the mortal realm, the banshee howls in anguish while performing this arduous duty.

Techniques   One performer sits at the keyboard depressing the damper pedal while another stands in the crook of the piano and manipulates the strings. Specific techniques include:

1. sweeping the strings from the lowest note to a specified note with the flesh of the finger;
2. sweeping the strings up and back;
3. sweeping the length of one string with the flesh of a finger;
4. plucking the strings;
5. sweeping the strings with the back of a fingernail; and
6. sweeping the strings with the flat of the hand.

Sources of Inspiration

Listening Examples 31 and 32 reflect Cowell's interest in Irish folklore. He was also attracted to early American hymn and fuging tunes and wrote a set of instrumental pieces based upon them. Further, Cowell was among the first Americans to be fascinated with the music of central and eastern Asia. He had a gift for reflecting the sounds of Persia, Japan, and even Iceland in music that yet bore the distinction of his own style.

The music of the East encouraged Cowell to explore elements that he felt had been neglected by Western composers, who had concentrated primarily on *melody* and *harmony*. Cowell, and soon many other American and European composers, found that *timbre* and *rhythm* offered them many new and stimulating ideas.

The Expansion of Rhythmic Concepts

Cowell learned to divide rhythms by five, seven, or other numbers as well as by the conventional two, three, or four. Like Ives, he invented complex polyrhythms, difficult to notate and to perform. Cowell devised a new rhythmic notation in order to write down his sophisticated rhythmic concepts. He also developed, in collaboration with **Léon Thérémin** (inventor of an early electronic instrument that bears his name), a machine called the *rhythmicon,* which made it possible to reproduce rhythms of a complexity beyond the capacity of human performance. Of course the rhythmicon has since been replaced by computers and electronic instruments, but in its time, it allowed composers to extend their rhythmic creativity greatly.

Writings

Like Ives, Cowell wrote about his ideas and ideals, producing a book called *New Musical Resources* while still a college student. He deplored the manner in which American experimentalists were ignored by conventional publishers, and founded a quarterly journal, *New Music,* in which he published provocative works (and to which Ives apparently gave anonymous financial support). The term **new music,** in fact, came to mean music of an advanced or experimental nature.

Cowell also edited a collection of essays by important contemporary composers. He and his wife collaborated on a book about Charles Ives, with whom they became friends, and Cowell was among the first to bring Ives's music to public attention.

Writer, teacher, lecturer, editor, inventor, theorist, and composer, Henry Cowell contributed immeasurably to the cause of experimentalism and opened many doors to the future of American music. He traveled extensively, seeking instruction from others and also sharing his own ideas. He played his compositions to appreciative audiences in Europe, and he was the first American to give concerts in the Soviet Union (1928), thus arousing interest abroad in the new, experimental American music.

EDGARD VARÈSE
(1885–1965)

Edgard Varèse (fig. 19.3) was born in Paris but settled in New York City during World War I. Although educated in the European traditions and acquainted with many important composers of his day, Varèse was intensely interested in the music of the Americas. He organized a Pan-American Society and composed a piece titled "Amériques," which he said symbolized discovery, adventure, and the unknown.

Philosophy
of Music

Varèse was one of the first composers to think of music simply as "organized sound" and to believe that any sounds—including those called "noise"—could be used in a musical composition. He spoke of music as "sound masses moving in space." Varèse considered the potential forms of a composition, formed around a particular idea, as limitless as the external forms of a crystal formed around a grain of sand.

Early
Compositions

Like Ives and Cowell, Varèse was intrigued with the qualities of sound; but more than either of them, he craved sounds that had not yet been realized. For a time he composed for a wide array of mostly wind and percussion instruments, including many of indeterminate pitch. Among his "percussion instruments" were anvils and chains, rattles, woodblocks, and sleigh bells, as well as drums, cymbals, gongs, bells, and chimes. Varèse's *Ionisation,* an Optional Listening Example, was one of the first pieces for percussion instruments only.

Varèse also explored the extreme ranges of instruments for varied effects. He liked sustained, sliding sounds, called **glissandos,** and for these he used sirens, which soared dramatically through a broad continuum of pitches. Unlike keyboard instruments, on which the smallest interval is the half step, sirens allowed him to achieve varied "hues" of sound, just as painters achieve hues of color on their palettes.

Figure 19.3

Edgard Varèse. (The
Bettmann Archive, Inc.)

Efforts for New Music

Varèse shared Cowell's concern for the need to bring new music to attention. He founded a New Symphony Orchestra but had to give it up when the public rebelled at his progressive programming. (Among the works they resisted so vigorously were those by Claude Debussy and Béla Bartók, who have since become among the best-known and most-admired twentieth-century composers.) In 1921, Varèse founded the International Composers Guild, also to support new music.

A Career Interrupted

Having experimented boldly with all the available materials, Varèse stopped composing for about fifteen years, apparently waiting for new sounds to be invented. He predicted that one day new instruments would create sounds at a composer's will and that other machines would reproduce exactly what a composer intended, without relying upon a performer for interpretation. His predictions were indeed prophetic, for they accurately described many functions of the electronic synthesizer, electronic tape technique, and computers. When these became available, Varèse plunged enthusiastically into composing more new music.

SUMMARY

Just as earlier pioneers had defied geographical boundaries, some early twentieth-century Americans extended the horizons of music. They broke ground for succeeding generations of experimentalists by exploring and extending the concept of musical sound.

Charles Ives was curious about the properties of sound. He equated dissonance with strength and composed in a bold, complex, independent style. He scoffed at the musically timid and encouraged adventurous listening. Ives greatly extended the sounds and the meaning of music.

Henry Cowell introduced new piano techniques, proving that conventional music instruments could produce new timbres. He was among the first Western musicians to draw inspiration from the East. Cowell greatly extended the range of rhythmic complexity and actively supported the cause of new music.

Edgard Varèse came from Europe but became an American composer. He explored the sounds of nontraditional instruments and predicted the invention of instruments that would create new sounds and reproduce a composer's intentions with absolute accuracy.

TERMS TO REVIEW

experimentalist   A composer who challenges traditional concepts of musical sound.

bitonality   Two keys at the same time.

polytonality   Two or more keys at the same time.

polyrhythms   Two or more simultaneous rhythmic patterns.

continuum of pitches   The continuous series of pitches of a voice or instrument, including those that lie between half steps.

quarter tone   The interval halfway between a half step.

microtone   Any interval smaller than a half step.

tone cluster   A chord, usually of several tones, built upon seconds. Clusters are often played with the flat of the hand, the arm, or a board cut to a particular length.

new music   The term used for music of an experimental nature.

glissando   A slide from one tone to another, including the continuum of pitches within the interval.

KEY FIGURES

Charles Ives

Henry Cowell

Léon Thérémin

Edgard Varèse

OPTIONAL LISTENING EXAMPLES*

Charles Ives: "General Putnam's Camp" from *Three Places in New England* *The Unanswered Question*

Edgard Varèse: *Ionisation*

SUGGESTIONS FOR FURTHER LISTENING

Charles Ives: "Hallowe'en" (orchestral) "Serenity" (song)

Henry Cowell: *Hymns and Fuging Tunes*

*Guides for Optional Listening Examples are in the Instructor's Manual and may be copied and distributed to students.

Plate 5

Anna Mary Robertson ("Grandma Moses"), *Hoosick Falls, N.Y., in Winter,* oil, 19¾" × 23¾". Vivid colors, clear outlines, and pleasing design are among the characteristics of this refreshingly naive and thoroughly delightful primitive-style painting. (© The Phillips Collection, Washington, D.C.)

Plate 6

Jackson Pollock,
Number 1, 1948, oil on
canvas. Pollock's
imaginative works involve
interaction between
chance and the artist's
creative intent. His
Abstract-Expressionist
paintings are expressive of
the energy and rapid
tempo of American life in
the 1940s. (Collection,
The Museum of Modern
Art, New York,
Purchase.)

Plate 7

Edward Hopper, 1882–1967, *Nighthawks,* 1942. Oil on canvas, 76.2 cm × 144 cm. This lonely scene is characteristic of the isolation and despair experienced by many Americans during the Depression era. (Friends of American Art Collection, 1942.51, © 1989. The Art Institute of Chicago. All rights reserved.)

Plate 8

The Virtuoso, by David Adickes, 1983, 36′ tall. This whimsical sculpture, which stands in front of an office building in downtown Houston, is one of the countless works of art inspired by musical instruments. (Courtesy of David Adickes.)

A NEW WORLD OF MUSICAL SOUND

Chapter 20

From the time the tonal system of harmony became the governing influence on Western music—that is, from the early seventeenth century—*melodies* based upon the major or minor scale and accompanied by increasingly rich and dissonant *harmonies* were the predominant concern of most composers. Thus, melody and harmony have been the elements of music best understood and appreciated by Western audiences. However, we have already seen that *rhythm* and *timbre* have come increasingly to the fore during the present century.

During the nineteenth century, many composers became more rhythmically adventurous, some using *irregular meters* of five or seven beats in a measure. The Impressionists used *changing meters* in order to make their melodies flow smoothly, uninterrupted by regular accents. Primitivists used *irregular accents* for dramatic effect. And we have discussed the exciting *polyrhythms* and *polymeters,* often derived from the music of non-Western cultures, that were used by certain progressive composers in the early twentieth century.

INCREASED INTEREST IN RHYTHM AND TIMBRE

The range of musical timbres was also expanded during the Romantic period. The piano of that time, which was essentially the same as the modern instrument, was capable of producing a wider range of sonorities than the fortepiano of Mozart's day. Several woodwind and brass instruments had been technically improved, and some, including the trombone and tuba, were added to the symphony orchestra. Of course this necessitated adding string instruments to preserve the balance of orchestral sound, making orchestras very large during the late Romantic period. Impressionist composers treated the timbres, or colors, of musical sounds much as Impressionist painters treated colors on their canvases, valuing color for its own qualities rather than for traditional or functional purposes. Many Romantic composers had a great gift for orchestration, which they approached with unprecedented sensitivity and subjectivity, introducing new combinations of sounds and creating unusual timbres.

By the mid-twentieth century, rhythm and timbre had become the elements of primary interest for some composers. Experimentalists of that period carried forward the work begun earlier in the century by Ives, Cowell, and Varèse, altering traditional instruments, or playing them in new ways, in order to produce unusual sounds. Even the human voice was treated in an unorthodox manner, as singers or instrumentalists were required to produce whispers, shouts, groans, or other "vocal" effects. Some composers, of whom **Harry Partch** (1901–1974) is the best known, invented entirely new musical instruments. Important new technology also made it possible for experimentalists to produce original sounds and rhythms of unprecedented complexity.

Non-Western instruments offered a wealth of possibilities, and it has become quite usual for even traditional or mainstream composers to include non-Western instruments in their ensembles. Although the twentieth-century orchestra is generally smaller than the orchestra of the late Romantic period, it often includes a larger proportion of percussion instruments, which not only emphasize the rhythmic qualities of contemporary music but also add a wide range of exotic timbres.

Experimentalism is basically a romantic concept, in the sense that it denies traditional boundaries, explores new ground, and freely abandons established rules of composition. Because Americans are generally perceived as a romantic people—creative, inventive, independent, and accustomed to freedom and space—it is not surprising that they have been actively involved in, and in many instances have led, the experimental movement in music.

However, experimentalists in America and abroad have followed diverse paths, and it is not always possible to classify an experimental composer as a romantic or a classicist. Some have chosen an intellectual, highly controlled approach to their music, while others remain detached from their compositions, preferring to leave important decisions to the performers or to chance. And some composers of new music include elements of both romantic and classical styles in their work.

Concrete Music

During the 1940s, a number of composers working in Paris became fascinated with the myriad qualities of all kinds of sounds. Refusing to distinguish between musical and nonmusical sounds, they considered *any* sound potentially valid material for the composition of music. They used various techniques to manipulate sounds, creating a new kind of music called **musique concrète,** or in English, **concrete music.**

These composers recorded various sounds and altered them electronically, a process made all the more versatile with the invention of magnetic tape after World War II. They used the altered sounds to create compositions, rendering the music "concrete" in the sense that it could not be performed or interpreted, but existed only on tape.

Five processes are involved in the composition of concrete music:

1. *Selecting* the sounds to be taped. The sounds may include those of traditional instruments, such as a piano or voice; sounds of nature, such as raindrops or birdcalls; or sounds of machinery,

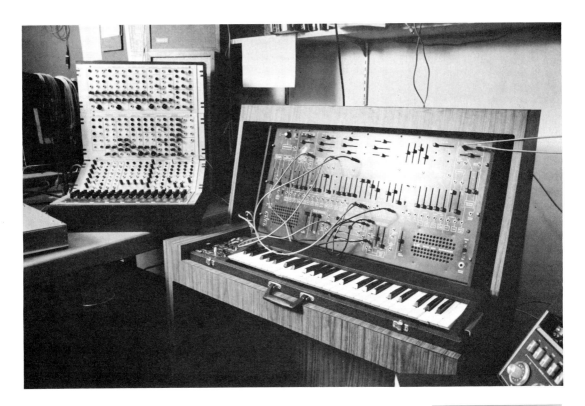

Figure 20.1

An electronic synthesizer.
(© John Maher/EKM-
Nepenthe.)

including a vacuum cleaner or jet plane. Any sound, in fact, may provide the raw material with which the composer works.

2. *Recording* the sounds. In order to alter the sounds and produce a work of art, the composer must have them on tape.

3. *Manipulating* the sounds. Sounds played backward, or faster or slower than normal, may become unrecognizable. Composers use these and other techniques to manipulate sounds as they please.

4. *Mixing* the sounds. This is the step in which the composer combines the sounds he or she has created, much as the traditional composer orchestrates a piece.

5. *Montage* is the process of "cutting and pasting" the tape to achieve the form of the completed composition.

The Electronic Synthesizer

About 1950, other composers also became interested in sounds for their intrinsic value. Desiring to realize sounds they imagined, but had been previously unable to achieve, they congregated in Germany to work with the new **electronic synthesizer** (fig. 20.1), an instrument of seemingly unlimited capabilities.

Composers achieve the *pitch* they desire on the synthesizer by plugging into **electronic oscillators.** ("Oscillation" is another word for "vibration.") A **fingerboard** allows players to slide through a range of pitches,

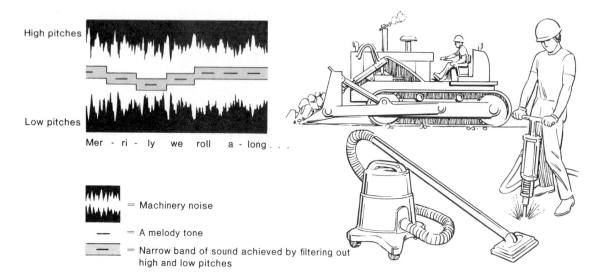

High pitches

Low pitches

Mer - ri - ly   we   roll   a - long . . .

= Machinery noise

— = A melody tone

= Narrow band of sound achieved by filtering out high and low pitches

Figure 20.2

On an electronic synthesizer, high and low pitches can be filtered out of machinery noise to produce a narrow band of sound or a melodic line.

unhampered by frets or keys. By plugging into other outlets on the synthesizer, they can alter the **shape of the sound wave,** thus determining the *timbre* of the sound to be produced. **Electronic filters** can select out high and low ranges of a broad sound, such as jet noise, producing a narrow band that may be used to produce a melody line of an interesting but nontraditional timbre (fig. 20.2).

The electronic synthesizer and other electronic techniques make it possible for composers to achieve sounds never heard before. Composers are also able to hear their compositions immediately, instead of waiting for very long periods before live performances can be arranged, and if the results please them, they can be saved on tape. Computers aid composers in the process of notating music, rendering it faster, more accurate, and more efficient. Computers also allow the use of tempos too fast and rhythmic combinations too complex for humans to accomplish live. Nontonal intervals that are very difficult for musicians to hear and reproduce accurately can be achieved at will. In other words, electronic techniques allow composers total control over the performance of their work.

Milton Babbitt is a primary exponent of the virtues of electronic music.

MILTON BABBITT
(B. 1916)

As a student at New York University, Milton Babbitt (fig. 20.3) discovered that using Schoenberg's twelve-tone technique allowed him to achieve the mathematical precision he desired in his musical compositions. He was also one of the earliest enthusiasts of electronic music techniques.

Babbitt was teaching music at Princeton when he was appointed one of the four codirectors who established the first electronic synthesizer in America (1959). The project was sponsored by Princeton and Columbia Universities, and the huge synthesizer was located at Columbia in New

Figure 20.3

Milton Babbitt. (Courtesy of Milton Babbitt.)

York City. It was several years later before synthesizers were available to composers in other parts of the country.

Babbitt is among the contemporary composers who find rhythm and timbre more interesting to work with than melody and harmony. Electronic techniques allow him to compose the exotic sounds and complex rhythms he desires. A brilliant man who composes difficult music, Babbitt has no patience with mistakes or misinterpretations by performers. Therefore, he prefers to write pieces that exist only on tape and for which there is no score, knowing they will always be heard as he intended. "Ensembles for Synthesizer" (Listening Example 33) is an early classic of this kind of electronic music.

Milton Babbitt was a leader in the movement to apply Schoenberg's concept of an orderly series of pitches (the twelve-tone technique) to other aspects of composition. For example, he arranges patterns of rhythms and durations, as well as tones, into series that are then systematically repeated throughout a composition. In some pieces, the various series are mathematically related to each other; in others, they are independent.

This extension of twelve-tone technique is called **total serialism, serialization,** or **serial technique.** Together with the resources of the electronic synthesizer, computers, and magnetic tape technique, total serialism allows Babbitt to achieve the highly ordered and logical music he prefers.

Although the rationales of total serialism and concrete music are clearly aesthetic as well as intellectual, some experimentalists reacted against the strict control imposed by these techniques of composition. Among them was the leading experimentalist of the 1950s and 1960s, who had

Serialism

LISTENING EXAMPLE 33
Concrete Music

Composer   Milton Babbitt

Title   "Ensembles for Synthesizer" (excerpt)

Form   This piece is a mosaic of tiny fragments (ensembles), each distinguished by a characteristic timbre, range of pitch, rhythmic pattern, dynamic level, and texture.

Timbres   Babbitt programmed the synthesizer to produce various metallic, wooden, and mysterious airy sounds, with occasional references to the sound of an electronic organ.

Rhythms   The rhythmic patterns are varied and complex, and are sometimes played at extremely rapid tempos, requiring electronic performance techniques.

Pitches   All twelve tones are used, though not according to Schoenberg's row technique. The ranges of pitch level are extreme.

Because this music is conceived and constructed differently from traditional compositions, it must also be approached differently by the listener. Concentration on and appreciation of the highly sensuous sounds and the fascinating rhythmic techniques yield intense listening pleasure.

---

sampled and abandoned both the twelve-tone and magnetic tape methods. Like Varèse, he wrote some music for percussion ensembles, and like Cowell, he extended the timbres of the piano. The name of this soulmate of Charles Ives, who tried everything that was available and invented what was not, is **John Cage.**

**JOHN CAGE
(1912–1992)**

Because Cage (fig. 20.4) studied music theory and composition with Arnold Schoenberg and Henry Cowell, it is not surprising that he took an unorthodox approach to writing music. Some of his early works were systematically organized according to the twelve-tone technique, but Cage soon decided that even that system was too rooted in the past to offer a viable path for the music of the future.

As a young composer, Cage also experimented with magnetic tape techniques as they became available, producing the first American example of concrete music, titled *Imaginary Landscape no. 5,* in 1951–52. But tape technique also soon ceased to intrigue or satisfy him.

Cage was the son of an inventor, and he consistently addressed his musical dilemmas with an inventor's ingenuity and creativity. Like Cowell, Cage was born on the West Coast and, again like Cowell, he felt less tied to the European traditions adhered to by many German-trained composers in New England and New York. He became profoundly interested in

Figure 20.4

John Cage. (© Steve Kagan/Photo Researchers, Inc.)

Oriental philosophies, religions, and music styles and soon turned from traditional instruments to those that would produce an intriguing variety of sounds similar to those of the music of the East. Because he wished to use pitches that are not in the Western chromatic scale, such unusual "instruments" as cowbells, automobile brake drums, and anvils, combined with Japanese temple bells, Chinese gongs, and other exotic non-Western percussion instruments, attracted him and met his early purposes.

Gamelan Music

Cage discovered that an elegant Indonesian percussion ensemble called a **gamelan** produced many of the sounds and pitches he desired. The gamelan is an orchestra, in the sense that it is a combination of instruments from various families. Unlike the Western string orchestra, however, the gamelan consists primarily of percussion instruments (fig. 20.5). These include **metallophones,** which are sets of metal keys suspended over a bronze or wooden frame and struck with a mallet; tuned gongs of various sizes, usually arranged in a semicircle; and drums. The gamelan also includes a few wind and string instruments that play sustained pitches and add color to the sound. Listening Example 34 gives a brief indication of the delicate and varied sounds of gamelan music.

Cage included a gamelan in some of his early compositions. But the ensemble, which is visually as well as aurally stunning, is too expensive to be widely available (though gamelans are becoming increasingly familiar in the West). Therefore, Cage invented a method of altering the grand piano in order to approximate many of the sounds of a gamelan.

Figure 20.5

An Indonesian gamelan.
(© George Holton/Photo
Researchers, Inc.)

LISTENING EXAMPLE 34
Balinese Gamelan Music

Title   Kebjar Hudjan Mas

Form   The metallic timbres of gongs and metallophones dominate the
beginning of the piece, before the full gamelan joins them. Notice the
expressive changes in tempo and dynamic level, as the piece evolves
slowly over relentless ostinatos that provide stability and seem to
anchor the composition.

The Prepared Piano

In 1938, Cage was the piano accompanist for the famous choreographer
Merce Cunningham, with whom he continued to collaborate on many projects throughout his life. Challenged by Cunningham's dance company to
extend the range of timbres in their performance music without exceeding
the limits of their budget, Cage discovered that the grand piano could be
altered or "prepared" so as to change the timbres and pitches it produced.
By applying pieces of wood, metal, and rubber to the strings of the piano,
he slowed the rate at which the strings vibrated, slightly changing the pitch
as well as the quality of the sound. His new, or modified, instrument is
called the **prepared piano.**

Most keys on a piano keyboard control three strings each. Therefore,
nuts, bolts, screws, bamboo strips, or other materials may be placed on one
of the strings, between any two, or touching all three. When the hammers
strike the prepared strings, timbres and tones similar to those of a gamelan

---

LISTENING EXAMPLE 35
Prepared Piano

Composer   John Cage

Title   *The Perilous Night* (excerpt)

Preparation   At the beginning of the score, Cage indicated the precise manner in which the piano should be prepared. Nuts, bolts, washers, strips of bamboo, and pieces of weatherstripping are to be placed at measured points between specific strings, creating a variety of wooden, metallic, and indeterminate sounds.

Form   Suite. There are six pieces of various character, though all have a muted, delicate effect due to the dampened piano strings.

Excerpt   The brief taped excerpt is the second piece of the suite. *Ostinatos* and *repeated notes* are characteristic of this piece (and other pieces in the suite), as they are of music for the gamelan. There is a strong feeling of *pulse*, but *accents* are irregular, with no definition of meter. *Pitches* lie between those of the Western scale. The *rapid tempo* of this busy little piece slows slightly at the end.

(An outline of the complete suite is included in the Instructor's Manual as an Optional Listening Example.)

---

or a Western percussion ensemble are achieved. A composer indicates precisely which strings of which keys are to be prepared, what foreign materials are to be used, and at what distance from the soundboard they are to be placed.

A wide variety of sounds and pitches may be achieved in this way, all on a readily available instrument and at the control of an individual performer. The pianist may also strike the wooden parts and metal braces of the instrument with the hand or an implement, producing even more varied sound effects. Many musicians were impressed with Cage's several independent compositions for prepared piano (see Listening Example 35), and soon other composers were also writing pieces in which a few, or many, strings were to be prepared.

Silence

We have seen that composers notate rests, or periods of silence, as carefully as they notate pitches (see table P1.1, page 2). But Cage discovered that, while specific sounds may cease, there are always *other* sounds that continue; thus, true silence is never achieved. Traditionalists would argue that the continuing sounds are "noise" as opposed to "music," but Cage denied the distinction. He considered *all* sounds worthy of attention, and he encouraged us to be aware and appreciative of them. In fact, he flatly stated that "silence" is an absurd concept that simply does not exist.

To demonstrate his theory that silence cannot be achieved, Cage placed himself in a soundproof chamber, as silent as technicians could make it;

Figure 20.6

Untitled, a mobile by the American sculptor Alexander Calder, 1976. Aluminum and steel, 9.103 × 23.155 (358½ × 912). (Gift of the Collectors Committee, © 1992 National Gallery of Art, Washington, D.C., 1976.)

still he found that his own bloodstream and nervous system produced clearly audible sounds. He wrote a book titled *Silence* (1961), and he composed the notorious "4′33″" ("Four Minutes Thirty-Three Seconds") for "any instrument or combination of instruments." The score indicates three movements, but the only marking for each of them is **tacet,** the term musicians use to mean "be silent." In other words, nothing at all is sounded! According to Cage, however, the audience has "a profound listening experience" for the duration of the famous non-composition.

RANDOM EFFECTS IN THE ARTS

During the 1950s and 1960s, artists in many fields were attracted to the concept of leaving significant details of their works to chance. For example, the **Abstract Expressionist** painters, led by **Jackson Pollock** (1912–1956), developed various techniques in order to achieve random effects. Pollock sprayed paints on a large surface, carefully choosing colors, direction, and density, but allowing chance to determine much of the result. The sculptor **Alexander Calder** (1898–1976) created figures that move through space, constantly changing in effect as the balance between space and object is altered (fig. 20.6).

Some musicians, too, turned directly away from the taut control of twelve-tone and magnetic tape techniques to *chance.* They were represented in the world of vernacular music by free jazz musicians (see page 255), among others, while John Cage led the movement toward chance in the concert world. Cage found the lack of spontaneity possible in performing twelve-tone and concrete music profoundly dissatisfying, and his primary interest for many years was in **chance** or **aleatoric** music.

Chance Music

Aleatory is music in which significant aspects of each performance are left to chance by the composer. Improvisation is one form of such **indeterminate music** (another term for chance or aleatoric music), requiring performers to make certain melodic, rhythmic, and harmonic decisions. But aleatory is a much broader concept than this.

Alea is the Latin word for dice, and throwing dice is one way that various aspects of an aleatoric piece—for example, melodic or metric patterns, or the number of repetitions of a phrase or section—may be determined. Other imaginative techniques used by composers of chance music include: graphic notation that may be interpreted in many different ways; making performance decisions based upon the Chinese *Book of Chance,* called *I Ching* (pronounced "E Jing"); scores that may be read backward, forward, or upside down; and circular scores that may be read clockwise or counterclockwise. The range of possibilities is limited only by the limits of a composer's imagination.

The degree of indeterminacy ranges from minimal, as in Ives's *Unanswered Question,* to **random** music, in which almost all of the composition changes from one performance to another. Cage's *Imaginary Landscape no. 4* (1951) is such a piece. It is "scored" for twelve radios, indicating specific positions on the radio dials, dynamic levels, durations, and even the degree of abruptness with which each sound begins and ends. But of course the material being broadcast will be different at each performance.

The meaning of music is being reexamined in our time, and respected opinions on the subject vary. Some would argue that Cage's *Imaginary Landscape no. 4* is random *sound* as opposed to *music.* Others believe that the piece is clearly "organized sound" and therefore meets the broad definition of music. Still others insist that the *quality* of the sounds determines whether a composition is music or simply a listening experience.

Other Composers of Chance Music

During the 1950s, three composers based in New York City became closely associated with John Cage, sharing many of his ideas and developing related ideas of their own. They sought to achieve objectivity in their music by refusing to specify details in the traditional way. In other words, they allowed their music to "come into its own."

Morton Feldman (1926–1987) sometimes used graphic notation to indicate his general intentions, leaving specific pitches and their durations to the determination of the performers. In one piece, he indicated the notes but specified no rhythms, intending them to evolve within a general tempo established by the conductor at the beginning of a performance.

Feldman is among the experimentalists whose imaginative scores are sometimes works of visual art. Feldman's *Projection 2,* for example, is a series of rectangles that indicate periods of time. Small triangles within the rectangles suggest when to play and how long tones should endure, and the vertical placement of the triangles gives a general idea of approximate pitch levels.

Earle Brown (b. 1926), another associate of Cage's, reflected in his music the mobility of Alexander Calder's sculptures and the spontaneity of Jackson Pollock's paintings. He said that he composed some pieces so rapidly and spontaneously that they represented "performances" rather than

Figure 20.7

Excerpt from the score for *December 1952* from *FOLIO* by Earle Brown. (Copyright © 1953 [Renewed] Associated Music Publishers, Inc. International copyright secured. All rights reserved. Used by permission.)

"compositions." He, too, developed new graphic notations. *December 1952* (fig. 20.7) is written on one page as a series of vertical and horizontal lines that indicate only in a general way the direction, dynamic level, duration, and pitch of the sounds.

The third New York associate of John Cage was **Christian Wolff** (b. 1934) who, like Feldman, wished to "set sounds free," and like Cage, was interested in silence as well as sound. His tones sometimes seem suspended in air, surrounded by space that lets them "breathe." Wolff has written some chamber pieces for which neither the instrumentation nor the duration of the tones (which *are* notated) is specified. The score for *1, 2, or 3 People* illustrates the artistic nature of his original notation.

SUMMARY

Whereas melody and harmony were the elements of primary interest through the seventeenth, eighteenth, and nineteenth centuries, many twentieth-century composers have devoted more attention to rhythm and timbre. The modern orchestra is smaller than that of the post-Romantic period but often includes a wide array of percussion instruments that emphasize the complex rhythms of modern music while adding exotic colors to the sound.

Experimentalists have continued to explore the world of musical sound, greatly extending its concepts. Those who prefer music that is highly organized, such as Milton Babbitt, may use the twelve-tone or even the total serial technique. Concrete music allows composers complete control over their compositions, which are taped under their direction and never performed live.

John Cage moved in the opposite direction, toward minimal influence over performances of his music. Composers of aleatoric music require performers not only to interpret their music, but to share in its creation.

TERMS TO REVIEW

musique concrète or **concrete music**   Music that has been created by manipulating taped sounds. Any sounds may be selected for this purpose.

electronic synthesizer   An electronic sound generator capable of producing, imitating, and altering sounds.

electronic oscillators   The means by which pitch is determined on the synthesizer.

shape of the sound wave   As the shape of the sound wave is altered, the timbre of the sound changes.

electronic filters   High and low pitches may be filtered from a wide band of sound to produce a narrow band, which may then be used to perform a melody.

fingerboard   A board on the synthesizer that is uninterrupted by keys or frets, allowing a player to slide through a continuum of pitches.

total serialism Also called **serialization** or **serial technique.**   Application of the twelve-tone technique to other aspects of a composition, which may also be arranged into series and repeated systematically.

gamelan   An Indonesian percussion ensemble.

metallophone   A percussion instrument consisting of metal keys suspended over a bronze or wooden frame and struck with a mallet.

prepared piano   A grand piano on which some or all of the strings have been "prepared" by placing foreign materials on them to alter pitch, timbre, and dynamic level.

tacet   "Be silent." The word is used by composers to indicate that certain voices or instruments should not sound.

Abstract Expressionism   A mid-twentieth-century art style in which painters allowed chance to determine aspects of their work.

aleatoric music   Sometimes referred to as **chance** or **indeterminate** music, aleatory is music in which the composer has left significant decisions to the performer or to chance. An extreme example is called **random** music.

KEY FIGURES

Experimentalists
Harry Partch
Milton Babbitt
John Cage
Morton Feldman
Earle Brown
Christian Wolff

Abstract Expressionist Painter
Jackson Pollock

Experimental Sculptor
Alexander Calder

OPTIONAL LISTENING EXAMPLES*

John Cage: *Aria and Fontana Mix* (aleatory) *The Perilous Night* (complete)

SUGGESTIONS FOR FURTHER LISTENING

Harry Partch: "The Letter: A Depression Message from a Hobo Friend" (1943) "Plectra and Percussion Dances" (1949–1952)

Milton Babbitt: *Three Compositions for Piano* (serialism)

John Cage: *Sonatas and Interludes* (prepared piano)

*Guides for Optional Listening Examples are in the Instructor's Manual and may be copied and distributed to students.

THE AMERICAN
MAINSTREAM

Chapter 21

During the 1920s, as Stravinsky and Schoenberg astonished listeners with their innovative techniques and Ives and Cowell challenged the very concept of musical sound, several talented young Americans set out to make their living as professional composers of concert music. They intended to write music that was not radically different from the masterpieces of the European musical heritage but that sounded distinctively American. Several were successful, becoming the first Americans to survive as professional composers without depending upon an academic or other income-producing position. Their compositions and those of their like-minded younger colleagues constitute the mainstream of American concert music.

THE PARIS
SCENE

Most of the eager young composers of the 1920s and 1930s found it necessary to study in Europe, for America did not yet offer comparably advanced music training. However, they turned not to Germany, but to France, which became the world center of artistic creativity after World War I. Writers, artists, and musicians from all over the world met in Paris, where they shared ideas that were disparate but fresh and invigorating, stimulating each other to reach new heights of creativity.

Stravinsky was in Paris at this time, fascinating and puzzling musicians with his unorthodox rhythmic techniques. Also influential were the group of French composers collectively called **Les Six** ("The Six"). These five men and one woman shared little in the way of stylistic ideals, but they collectively ridiculed the profundity of the German Romantic style. As a protest against a too-serious approach to art, they based some of their compositions upon music of the dance halls, including (to American amazement) the hot new style called jazz.

The young Americans found their study in France a liberating experience, for the French attitude toward music was far less dogmatic than that of the Germans. Giving them particular encouragement was a young French organist, composer, and highly gifted teacher who offered superb instruction to this and several successive generations of composers. She was **Nadia Boulanger.**

Figure 21.1

Nadia Boulanger.
(Courtesy of Milton
Babbitt.)

NADIA BOULANGER (1887–1979)

Mlle Nadia Boulanger (fig. 21.1) brilliantly taught skills and technique without inflicting style upon her students. She recognized each young composer's distinctive talents and the ways each might reach his or her best potential. Among her many assets was the unique ability to interpret her friend Igor Stravinsky's rhythmic concepts to eager but puzzled young musicians.

The first young American to study with Boulanger was **Aaron Copland.**

AARON COPLAND (1900–1990)

Aaron Copland (fig. 21.2) was born in Brooklyn, New York, to a family that was not particularly interested in music; yet he decided while still in his teens to become a composer of serious music. To this end, Copland spent three years during his early twenties studying in Paris with Nadia Boulanger.

The Jazz Influence

Until recently, it was generally acknowledged that Europeans preceded Americans in recognizing jazz as a source of inspiration and material for concert music. Although some musicologists now dispute that view, Aaron Copland was certainly incredulous when Nadia Boulanger suggested he use jazz techniques to achieve an American sound. However, several of Copland's early pieces indeed reflect the rhythms, melodies, harmonies, and timbres of jazz (see chapter 22). Among these early works are a suite for small orchestra titled "Music for the Theater" (1925—the year after Gershwin's *Rhapsody in Blue*) and a **concerto** for piano and orchestra completed the next year.

Figure 21.2

Aaron Copland.
(American Symphony
Orchestra League.)

Considering jazz emotionally limited, Copland soon sought inspiration in other American sounds, including cowboy songs and early American hymns. He became an avid proponent of American music, by which he meant music from both north and south of the Mexican border. His delightful tone poem *El salón México*, first performed in 1937 in Mexico City, effectively captures the flavors and spirit of Mexican folk and popular music, and it remains among the favorite Copland works today.

The Copland-Sessions Concerts

Copland was actively involved in the energetic movement to develop an audience interested in hearing music by American composers. From 1928 to 1931, he and another prominent American composer, **Roger Sessions** (1896–1985), organized and supported a series of programs at which American concert music was performed. Their efforts brought important new American compositions to public attention and critical review at a time before musicians could rely upon recorded music to reach a wide audience. Thus, the **Copland-Sessions concerts** were of inestimable value in encouraging the development of American music.

The Depression Years

The music Copland wrote just before and after the stock market crashed in 1929 is rather difficult, austere, and uncompromising, though beautifully written and stunning in effect when performed well. Many feel, in fact, that the *Piano Variations* (1929) is his finest composition.

Certainly the Great Depression affected the development of an American repertoire, as it affected every phase of American life. People simply were not able to address new subjects and cultivate new tastes at a time when their energies were absorbed by private and public tragedies. Copland was profoundly sympathetic with the conservative attitude of the shocked and saddened American public. He urgently wished to communicate with the public through his music at that difficult time, and most of his works from the Depression period, and from the years of World War II, are readily accessible and are reflective of Copland's great interest in all of America.

Appreciating the need for useful or functional music, Copland diligently provided scores for radio, films, schools, amateur musicians, and ballet companies. In 1942, he stirred the wartime audience's patriotic spirit with "Lincoln Portrait," which quotes fragments of Stephen Foster songs and American folk tunes and includes the narration of some of Abraham Lincoln's speeches.

Useful Music

A festive fanfare, also written in 1942, is one of Copland's most famous works. A **fanfare** is a rather short and dramatic piece for brass instruments, usually performed in celebration of a royal or state occasion. Copland's wartime piece, however, was titled "Fanfare for the Common Man." Its dramatic theme is based upon a rising motive introduced by a solo trumpet, variously treated by combinations of brass instruments, and forcefully punctuated by percussion. Copland's "Fanfare" (an Optional Listening Example) is frequently played today at events of national significance, such as the Olympic Games, and to highlight announcements of dramatic accomplishments by Americans.

As we saw in connection with the Broadway musical stage, Americans developed a strong and continuing interest in performances of ballet and modern dance in the 1930s and 1940s. Since then, we have nurtured a broad range of styles and talents in the field of dance. Among Copland's best-known works are his dance compositions, which are usually called ballets.

Music for Dance

Classical Ballet

Classical ballet is a formal, stylized dance form in which certain steps, gestures, and positions, together with mime, are used to describe characters and dramatize a story. Particularly characteristic of classical ballet are the female dancers' positions **en pointe,** or on the points of their toes. (Ballet evolved in the seventeenth-century French court of Louis XIV, and the language of classical ballet remains French today.)

Modern Dance

Copland's ballets, however, are really examples of **modern dance,** in which the steps and gestures are more varied and less stylized than in classical ballet. The costumes of modern dance are simpler than those of classical ballet, and the dancers perform barefoot.

Choreography

The movements of the dancers on the stage are determined by a **choreographer,** who may set steps to existing music or to music composed especially

Figure 21.3

A scene from
Appalachian Spring
(Graham, 1944). Erick
Hawkins, Martha Graham
and Company. (© Arnold
Eagle.)

for a particular dance. Choreography used to be handed down by tradition only, but methods of notation have been developed—some of them quite recently—that make it possible to preserve a choreographer's ideas accurately. Videotape provides another effective tool for this purpose.

Copland's Ballets

Copland wrote the music for two very effective dance performances, *Billy the Kid* and *Rodeo,* using his own versions of traditional American tunes and cowboy songs to establish the appropriate western flavor. Then the famous choreographer **Martha Graham** (1893–1991) commissioned him to write some music for her. Although Miss Graham performed and choreographed in the style called modern dance, Copland—who had no story in mind as he wrote the music—titled his work simply "Ballet for Martha."

When she heard Copland's music, which includes country fiddling and an early American hymn tune, Martha Graham was reminded of a poem titled "The Bridge" by the American poet **Hart Crane** (1899–1932). This long poem includes one section, "The Dance," in which the phrase, "O Appalachian Spring!" occurs. Thus, *Appalachian Spring* became the name of Copland's dance piece. A year later, in 1945, Copland extracted the most musically significant portions of *Appalachian Spring* (fig. 21.3) and composed an orchestral suite that has become one of his best-known works.

The story of the ballet (though not of Hart Crane's poem) concerns a young pioneer bride-to-be and her fiancé. As the performance begins, they stand in front of their newly built farmhouse, solemnly anticipating the joys and responsibilities of married life. A revivalist preacher exhorts the young

LISTENING EXAMPLE 36

Music from the Dance

Composer   Aaron Copland

Title   Variations on "Simple Gifts" from *Appalachian Spring*

Theme   The folklike hymn tune titled "Simple Gifts," which forms the theme of this section of *Appalachian Spring*, was composed in 1848 by a Shaker named Joseph Brackett. (The Shakers were an offshoot of the Quaker religious sect.) The theme, which is introduced by a solo clarinet over a very simple accompaniment, has two parts: The first begins with a rising inflection, and the second with a descending phrase.

Variation 1   The melody is played in a higher range by an oboe with a slightly faster tempo.

Variation 2   Violas play the theme at half its former tempo (a technique called **augmentation**), punctuated with an ostinato in the harp and piano. The violins and cellos then play phrases of the theme in imitative polyphonic texture.

Variation 3   After a brief transition, trumpets and trombones state the theme at twice the former speed (**diminution**), accompanied by rapid figures in the strings.

Variation 4   Slower and quieter, this variation gives the second part of the theme to the woodwinds.

Variation 5   The full orchestra plays the last variation, which is stately, majestic, slow in tempo, and fortissimo in volume.

couple and members of his flock to follow the ways of the Lord, while an older woman advises and comforts the young bride.

The most famous section of the ballet music is a set of variations on a well-known American hymn tune (Listening Example 36).

In the 1950s, Copland wrote two sets of *Old American Songs* and an opera with an American setting called *The Tender Land* (mentioned in chapter 18). He also surprised many people by writing several works based upon the principles of Schoenberg's twelve-tone technique. However, at that time many composers considered this system the logical extension of the trend toward increasing chromaticism that was apparent in twentieth-century music.

In fact, throughout his career, Copland demonstrated an unusual variety of tastes and talents, never becoming committed to a consistent trend or direction. Among his large body of works are choral pieces, film scores (including *Our Town,* 1940, *The Red Pony,* 1948, and *The Heiress,* 1949), chamber music, large orchestral works, the opera, and other ballets or dance pieces. He also wrote several very readable books about music.

Copland's Later Works

OTHER
MAINSTREAM
COMPOSERS

Beginning in the 1920s, many American composers followed Copland to Paris to study with Nadia Boulanger. Most were basically **traditionalists** who sought progress of an evolutionary kind. Some were **neoclassicists,** who wrote music for small ensembles and organized their compositions according to Baroque or Classical forms, though their music was distinctively of the twentieth century. For example, their ensembles, unlike the homogenous string or wind groups of the eighteenth and nineteenth centuries, often included members of different families of instruments—a trio for flute, violin, and piano, for instance. The disparate timbres allowed each instrument to be clearly heard, greatly increasing the independence of each musical line.

Many Americans have been inclined more toward a romantic than a classical style of composition. **Neoromantic** composers, of whom **Samuel Barber** (fig. 21.4) is an outstanding example, use twentieth-century harmonies and performance techniques to produce lyrical, warmly expressive music.

**Samuel Barber
(1910–1981)**

Among Samuel Barber's best-known works are several beautiful art songs. One is "Knoxville: Summer of 1915" for soprano and orchestra (Optional Listening Example), a setting of a portion of the prologue to James Agee's novel *A Death in the Family*. Barber worked within the traditional tonal system, using more dissonance and chromaticism than composers of earlier times but imbuing his compositions with warm emotional expression. Even his instrumental works have lyrical, songlike melodies that render them among the most accessible and appreciated compositions of this century.

In 1936, Barber arranged the adagio movement of one of his string quartets for a larger group of string instruments. As an independent composition in this more sensuous guise, *Adagio for Strings* has become very familiar to the American public. It has been suggested that the long, asymmetrical, rhythmically relaxed melody, clearly unfettered by preconceived rules and measurements, is characteristically American.

The *Adagio* is a quietly solemn piece that acknowledges the reality of sadness but offers comfort and rest. It was played during the radio announcement of Franklin Delano Roosevelt's death in 1945 and has frequently been performed at solemn state occasions since. It was heard in its entirety at the end of the poignant 1980 film *The Elephant Man,* and it was the musical theme of *Platoon* (Best Picture of the Year, 1986). Emotionally expressive, yet unpretentious, Barber's *Adagio for Strings* (an Optional Listening Example) has become one of the best-loved pieces in the American repertoire.

As a child, **William Grant Still** showed both interest and talent for music, studying violin and listening avidly to his stepfather's opera recordings. But as a black, he found it difficult to be taken seriously as a musician.

William Grant Still (1895–1978)

Nevertheless, Still won a scholarship to the prestigious Oberlin Conservatory of Music in Ohio, and after earning his degree, he continued his studies with the evolutionary composer George Chadwick and the revolutionary Edgard Varèse. For several years, he played in dance bands and variety shows and worked for a popular music publishing company, before becoming definitively involved with concert music. During his long and successful career, he wrote several operas and ballets, some film scores, and many songs and choral pieces.

Still's racial heritage was mixed, and he had personal interest in American Indian and Spanish-American music. However, he identified with black Americans, and it was their experience he primarily wanted to express. The main theme of the first movement of his *Afro-American Symphony* (Optional Listening Example) is a lovely blues melody, and he gave a prominent role to the banjo in the lively second movement of the same symphony. Still was the first black composer to have a symphony played by a major symphony orchestra; the first to conduct a major symphony orchestra; and the first to have an opera produced by a major American company. He received many prestigious awards and several honorary doctorate degrees.

William Schuman was a rather conservative composer with strong nationalistic interests. A Pulitzer prize winner, Schuman was at one time president of the Juilliard School of Music and also of the Lincoln Center for the Performing Arts, both in New York City. Schuman wrote a number of dramatic one-movement programmatic orchestral pieces called *concert overtures.*

William Schuman (1910–1992)

LISTENING EXAMPLE 37

Concert Overture

Composer   William Schuman

Title   "Chester" Overture

Form   Less formal in design than a piece for orchestra might be, this symphonic band overture is a fantasy (though Schuman resisted the term) on Billings's famous tune.

It begins slowly and quietly with the melody in the woodwinds. Cymbals crash, and with a sudden change of key, a stately second verse is played by the brass. Drum rolls and dramatic crescendoes enhance the drama.

The second verse dies away, the tempo changes abruptly to fast, and the tune returns. The treatment is less literal than at first and becomes even more imaginative as Schuman explores keys, timbres, harmonies, tempos, and moods. Fragments of the tune are recognizable throughout. Toward the end, the melody returns intact, but with new harmonization, and the piece comes to a stirring conclusion.

Concert Overture

The term overture usually indicates an introduction to a longer work, such as an opera, oratorio, or Broadway musical. However, **concert overtures** are independent works that have the dramatic characteristics of a music theater overture, making them effective opening pieces for a band or orchestra concert. Like a tone poem, a concert overture is a one-movement programmatic orchestral work. However, most concert overtures are shorter than most tone poems, and the form of a concert overture is more likely to have an intellectual as well as a programmatic basis.

Several of Schuman's concert overtures, including *American Festival Overture* and *William Billings Overture,* are based upon American tunes. His three-movement orchestral work *New England Triptych* includes sections on two tunes we have studied, both by William Billings: "When Jesus Wept" and "Chester." Schuman subsequently arranged the movement titled "Chester" as an overture for symphonic band (Listening Example 37).

By the 1950s, Americans had unprecedented access to many kinds of concert music. Long-playing records (LPs) were available, radio stations offered many hours of concert music a week, and television networks programmed live performances. Several art centers were built during the fifties, including New York City's Lincoln Center for the Performing Arts, which has large and small concert halls, an opera house (the new Metropolitan), and rooms for theater and dance performance. Important music conservatories in several American cities offered music training of the highest quality. All of this music activity stimulated large numbers of American composers to write concert music.

SUMMARY

The first American musicians to become professional composers independent of other sources of income came to maturity in the 1920s. Most of them studied in Paris with Nadia Boulanger.

Some of Copland's early works were based upon jazz, and he continued to use nationalistic effects in later compositions as well. Copland sought to please his audience during the trying years of the thirties and forties by writing orchestral, vocal, and dance compositions with tuneful melodies and catchy rhythms. He was actively involved in building an audience for American music. Some of his later works, however, in which he applied Schoenberg's twelve-tone technique, have yet to become part of the familiar American repertoire.

Other mainstream composers include Samuel Barber, whose music is melodically lyrical and warmly expressive; William Grant Still, who expressed the black American's experience in his music; and William Schuman, who has written a number of pieces based on early American tunes.

The modern American mainstream of music continues to be varied and changing, but its new modes of expression are rooted in the past. Mainstream composers, in fact, are traditionalists who continue the evolution of music in a logical, orderly manner, expressing their ideas in contemporary, yet familiar terms.

TERMS TO REVIEW

Les Six Six French composers who shared a dislike for German Romanticism and found popular music a source of inspiration for their works. They were Georges Auric, Louis Durey, Arthur Honegger, Darius Milhaud, Francis Poulenc, and Germaine Tailleferre.

concerto A multimovement (usually three-movement) work for orchestra plus solo instrument.

Copland-Sessions concerts A series of concerts sponsored by Aaron Copland and Roger Sessions from 1928 to 1931 for the purpose of promoting music by American composers.

fanfare A brief, dramatic piece for brass instruments, with the character of an announcement or celebration.

classical ballet A formal, stylized dance form that evolved in seventeenth-century France.

en pointe The female dancer's technique of dancing on the tips of her toes.

modern dance A contemporary American dance form, less stylized than classical ballet.

choreography The steps and movements of dancers.

augmentation A rhythmic variation in which note values are doubled, making a theme twice as slow as it was originally.

diminution A rhythmic variation in which note values are halved, making a theme twice as fast as it was originally.

traditionalist A composer who makes no radical departures from the styles and conceptions of earlier music.

neoclassicist A twentieth-century composer whose music is classical in style.

neoromantic A twentieth-century composer whose music is romantic in style.

concert overture A one-movement programmatic orchestral composition, often inspired by literature and dramatic in style. The organization is generally intellectual as well as programmatic.

KEY FIGURES

Composer and Teacher
Nadia Boulanger

Choreographer
Martha Graham

American Poet
Hart Crane

American Mainstream Composers

Aaron Copland
Roger Sessions
Samuel Barber
William Grant Still
William Schuman

OPTIONAL LISTENING EXAMPLES*

Aaron Copland: "Fanfare for the Common Man"

Samuel Barber: "Knoxville: Summer of 1915"
Adagio for Strings

William Grant Still: *Afro-American Symphony*, First Movement

*Guides for Optional Listening Examples are in the Instructor's Manual and may be copied and distributed to students.

SUGGESTIONS FOR FURTHER LISTENING

Aaron Copland: Music for the Theatre
Piano Variations
El salón México
Concerto for Piano and Orchestra
"Billy the Kid" Suite
Third Symphony

Samuel Barber: Piano Concerto

William Schuman: *American Festival Overture*
William Billings Overture
New England Triptych

part 8

JAZZ

THE BIRTH OF
A NEW VERNACULAR

Chapter 22

Americans danced into the twentieth century, and their dance fever lasted for more than forty years. Turn-of-the-century saloons and dance halls rang with the sounds of ragtime, the two-step, and various Latin dances soon to become even more popular. Thus, fast tempos, syncopated rhythms, and dance band timbres replaced the sedate ballroom dances played by string orchestras of an earlier time.

As dance rhythms became more complex, solo instrumental lines more independent, and timbres more varied, Americans discovered that the new music was exciting to hear as well as to dance to. By 1917, they were calling it **jazz.**

JAZZ

Jazz includes many styles that differ widely in mood, instrumentation, tempo, and artistic intent. Jazz musicians are expected to improvise, but the degree of improvisation varies from one kind of jazz to another. Conceived as dance music, and long considered a kind of popular or vernacular music, jazz has become a sophisticated art form that has interacted in significant ways with the music of the concert hall.

The roots of jazz are rich and varied. White, European sources include marches, hymns, and popular dances of many kinds, while Creole and Caribbean influences also affected the new music. But the stirring, hot rhythms of jazz, its dramatic percussive effects, and many of its vocal and instrumental performance techniques were derived from black Africa.

Among the earliest manifestations of the music that came to be called jazz was the *blues.*

THE BLUES

The **blues** is a solo folklike song, distinctive in character and form, that was invented by blacks and has had inestimable influence upon the development of not only jazz but every genre of American music.

The Rise of the Blues

The blues evolved some time after the Civil War, as many newly emancipated blacks found their lives more difficult than ever. Away from the familiar plantation environment, they were often lonely and in desperate need

The origin of the blues. (North Wind Picture Archives.)

of money. Some were migrants, some were in prison, and some had back-breaking and unrewarding jobs, such as digging ditches or laying railroad lines. In their new distress, they sometimes expanded shouts and hollers into simple solo songs laden with emotional content. In effect, they were singing the blues.

Soon the blues became a form of entertainment, sung around camp-fires or in the poorest living quarters in the evening. Any available instrument might accompany the voice, perhaps even competing with the vocal line by adding additional melodic interest. Still later, the blues were sung in places of commercial entertainment—saloons, bars, honky-tonks—usually accompanied by a guitar, harmonica, or (later) a piano. Eventually, songs called "urban blues" were recorded by professional blues singers and were thus disseminated to a wide and increasingly appreciative public.

Texts

The texts of the early, rural blues addressed every aspect of life. Some concerned work. More were about love—unrequited, betrayed, or somehow gone wrong. Blues singers expressed their troubles in a straightforward manner, with a lack of sentimentality and a wry or whimsical humor that lessened the sadness while increasing the poignancy of the tale of woe.

Melody

Blues singers, and later instrumentalists, typically adopted the African custom of treating the *third, seventh,* sometimes the *fifth,* and less often the *sixth* degrees of the scale as neutral, or ambiguous, tones. In fact, the pitches in the so-called **blues scale** are wonderfully flexible and may be expressively inflected (lowered, or sometimes slightly raised) to produce fluid melodic lines. These "bent," "tired," or "worried" notes are the **blue notes** of the jazz musician. Vocal and instrumental scoops and slides, or *glissandos,* also derived from black African singing styles, were effectively used in the performance of blues melodies, some of which, as already mentioned, were simply derived from familiar field hollers.

Form

At first, a blues stanza probably consisted of one line of text sung three times. But in time, it became the custom to sing the first line twice and add a conclusion or response, in the form **AAB:**

Hard times here, worse times down the road.
Hard times here, worse times down the road.
Wish my man was here to share the load.

Because there were *three* lines per stanza, and each stanza had *four* bars, or measures, the form was called the **twelve-bar blues.** Of course, not all blues follow this pattern, any more than all symphonies have four movements, but it became established as the classic form of the blues.

Harmony

A simple harmonic pattern including only the tonic, subdominant, and dominant chords emerged as the basic harmonic framework for the twelve-bar blues. Although the chords of the pattern are the most basic chords in tonal harmony, the order in which they occur in the last line of a twelve-bar blues is distinctive—that is, IV may go through V to I, but V does not normally "regress" to IV (review figure P1.7, page 8).

Line 1.	*I*
Line 2.	*IV - I*
Line 3.	*V - IV - I*

Improvisation

There was ample opportunity for improvisation within the simple framework of the blues. For example:

1. Each line of text took about two-and-a-half bars to complete, leaving a measure-and-a-half of thinking time for the singer. This interval might be filled with half-spoken, half-sung nonsense syllables, later called **scatting** or **scat singing,** or by improvisation on accompanying instruments.
2. Since the second line of text was a repeat of the first, the singer had additional thinking time to plan the last line.
3. The basic harmonic pattern allowed ample harmonic variety, since the simple chords supported, without getting in the way of, creative ideas.
4. Melodies could be embellished and colored by scoops, slides, and blue notes.
5. Vocal and instrumental timbres were limited only by a performer's imagination and the availability of musical instruments.

6. The possibilities for subtle rhythmic adjustments over the steady beat were virtually unlimited.

Robert Johnson's "Hellhound on My Trail" (Optional Listening Example) effectively illustrates many characteristics of the twelve-bar blues.

It was only a matter of time before the professional publishing and recording industries recognized the commercial potential of the blues. Published blues first appeared about 1912, and by the 1920s, so-called blues **race records** (the unfortunate term for recordings intended for a black audience) were being mass produced.

While the best-known singers of rural blues were men, the outstanding singers on the commercial, or **urban blues** recordings were women, including **Gertrude "Ma" Rainey** (1886–1939) and **Bessie Smith** (1894–1937). Bessie Smith was among several blues singers who wrote some of the songs they recorded. The great blues singers made some of their finest recordings with the outstanding jazz musicians of the day, and close connections were established between jazz and urban blues. A folk or popular heritage, regular beat, subtle rhythmic variations, versatile blue notes, and fluent improvisation were inherent qualities of both the blues and jazz traditions.

As the blues entered the popular music stream, the form was inevitably adapted to appeal to a broader audience. Some or even most of the stanzas of an urban blues were in the twelve-bar form, but one or more stanzas were in the conventional four- or eight-line (sixteen- or thirty-two-bar) form. Because urban blues were intended for performance by professional blues singers, their forms could be more complex and their harmonies more sophisticated than those of the rural blues. Blues pieces began to be published in sheet music form. White composers started to write blues, and the word "blues" appeared in the titles of many pieces, including some that were not blues at all.

The self-styled "father of the blues" was a black bandleader and composer named **W. C. Handy.**

URBAN BLUES

W. C. Handy (fig. 22.1) hardly invented the blues, but he led them into the world of commercial popular music. As a young man, Handy learned to play a cornet and (to his Methodist father's dismay) joined a minstrel troupe. He then formed his own dance band, which played in Memphis for a while, moving on to Chicago and finally to New York. There he began writing and publishing urban blues.

The best-known of all urban blues is Handy's *St. Louis Blues* (Optional Listening Example).

W. C. HANDY (1873–1958)

While the blues, both rural and urban, continued to develop, some ragtime pianists began to adapt the blues to their instrument.

JAZZ PIANO

Figure 22.1

W. C. Handy (at left) with Duke Ellington. (Frank Driggs Collection.)

Boogie-Woogie

Some time before 1920, certain ragtime pianists carried the twelve-bar structure and simple harmonic progressions of the blues to the piano, introducing a new piano music called **boogie-woogie, boogie,** or the **piano blues.** While *ragtime* was conceived as a written music, and is therefore viewed as a kind of precursor of jazz, *boogie* pianists were jazz musicians who improvised freely.

As with ragtime, the boogie pianist plays a syncopated melody in the right hand. But the boogie melody is accompanied in the left hand by a characteristic ostinato called **eight-to-the-bar,** because it subdivides the four beats of a measure into eight pulses, usually in the pattern *LONG-short-LONG-short-LONG-short-LONG-short.* The resulting cross rhythms make boogie an exciting music, more complex than ragtime, that quickly became a popular new music to dance and listen to.

Other Jazz Piano Styles

Several jazz pianists developed other styles that were also influential in the transition from ragtime to jazz.

Jelly Roll Morton (1890–1941) combined ragtime and boogie techniques to produce his own inimitable jazz piano style. His rhythms were looser and his melodies less embellished than those of ragtime.

Earl Hines (1903–1983) played with a swinging, flexible style usually associated with band instruments rather than the piano.

James P. Johnson (1894–1955) is known as "the father of **stride piano,**" a style in which the left hand alternates low bass notes (on *one* and *three*) with mid-range chords (on *two* and *four*), while the right hand plays an improvised melody. Because stride piano was more dissonant, more loosely structured, more strictly improvisational, and more highly syncopated than other jazz piano styles of the 1920s, Johnson is recognized as a particularly significant figure in the transition from ragtime to jazz.

Fats Waller (1904–1943) studied with James P. Johnson and developed his own legendary jazz piano style. He went on to become one of the great jazz entertainers and a composer of hundreds of tunes.

Adaptation of the blues to other instruments besides the piano was a vital step in the evolution of jazz.

EARLY JAZZ COMBOS

After the Civil War, music instruments left over from military bands were readily and cheaply available, and black musicians in the New Orleans area began to play them in their own style. They formed brass bands and played for parades, concerts, and even funerals, performing solemn music as the funeral party approached the cemetery and ragging familiar tunes on the way back to the city. In time, their instrumental techniques became more individual, the tempos faster, the mood high-powered and intense. Some of these musicians read music, but most did not. In any case, they improvised freely and were in fact playing jazz.

Soon small bands or **combos** of black musicians were playing for indoor entertainment. Their hot new dance music combined the steady beat and stirring tempo of European march and dance tunes with the subtle and complex syncopations of black African and Caribbean effects. Familiar popular music in New Orleans included French, Spanish, Creole, and black tunes; serious and comic opera; and airs from marching, dance, and concert bands. This rich cultural climate generously nourished the exciting new vernacular music, and the notorious Storyville red-light district of gambling saloons, bordellos, and dance halls offered ample job opportunities for jazz musicians. Thus, it is not surprising that New Orleans produced some astonishingly talented jazz musicians who soon attracted others to their city, making it the first important center of jazz.

New Orleans-Style Jazz

Most **New Orleans-style jazz** combos contained three to eight people playing clarinet, cornet, trombone, and drums. Later, the trumpet replaced the cornet, and a saxophone was added to the ensemble. The rhythm section was expanded to include string instruments—banjo, guitar, and perhaps a string bass—as well as drums.

Having selected a tune (a hymn, rag, march, popular song, or blues) and agreed upon the harmonic patterns to be repeated throughout, the musicians would begin improvising. The cornet handled the tune; the clarinet wove countermelodies around it; the trombone provided supporting harmonies; and drums marked the beat. Early New Orleans performances were basically collective improvisations played in this manner. As the soloists became more experienced, they took turns improvising complex melodies while the other musicians provided rhythmic and harmonic support.

By the 1920s, many of the outstanding jazz artists had moved from New Orleans to Chicago, which became the new performing and recording

Members of a jazz combo.
(© Washington Post.
Reprinted by permission
of the D.C. Public
Library.)

center for jazz. Chicago's larger population, thriving speakeasies, and better recording opportunities soon attracted jazz musicians from all over the country. Among those who moved north from New Orleans were a cornetist and bandleader, **Joe "King" Oliver** (1885–1938), and an outstanding member of his band, **Louis Armstrong.**

**Louis Armstrong
(1900–1971)**

Louis Armstrong (fig. 22.2) survived a violent childhood in New Orleans to become a gentle, kindly, good-natured person and an incredibly talented musician. He played the cornet in King Oliver's band as a boy, and in the early 1920s followed Oliver to Chicago. There Armstrong formed his own band (The Hot Five, later The Hot Seven) and began making important jazz recordings, including "Hotter Than That" (Listening Example 38).

Switching to the trumpet, Armstrong developed previously inconceivable virtuosic techniques for that instrument. Even more significant were his original and highly creative solo improvisations. Armstrong's solos were

---

LISTENING EXAMPLE 38
New Orleans-Style Jazz

Composer **Lillian Hardin Armstrong.** Lil Hardin, who became Louis Armstrong's wife, was an outstanding jazz pianist. She performed regularly with the Hot Five, the group who recorded this and many other early Armstrong hits.

Title "Hotter Than That" (excerpt)

Instruments Cornet, trombone, clarinet, piano, banjo, guitar. Notice how the cornet, trombone, and clarinet take turns improvising, while the other instruments provide a rhythmic accompaniment. Armstrong's cornet solos dominate, of course. In his scat singing, he "plays" his voice like another instrument, revealing a seemingly limitless range of creative and expressive techniques.

Figure 22.2

Louis Armstrong. (© UPI/Bettmann Newsphotos.)

beautifully expressive as well as technically brilliant, and the emotional range of his playing was extraordinarily wide, greatly expanding the concept of what jazz was all about.

Armstrong also sang—in a manner of speaking. That is, he scatted in an amazingly creative, often humorous, and always expressive way. Known as "Satchmo" (for Satchel Mouth), he won devoted converts to jazz, and especially to his own music, from around the world.

In Chicago, many young white musicians were enchanted with the sounds of the New Orleans combos, and in the sincerest form of flattery, set out to imitate them. **Dixieland** was the term later applied to this white imitation of New Orleans jazz, and in time it was applied generally to all jazz in the early style.

Meanwhile, the general public ignored, or deplored, New Orleans and Dixieland-style jazz. The mood was too wild, the volume too loud, the timbres too raucous, the rhythms too hot to satisfy a general audience. Besides, the atmosphere of the small, mob-controlled clubs where jazz was being played was distasteful to the white, middle-aged, middle class. **Paul Whiteman** (1890–1967) offered a tame but attractive substitute, called **sweet jazz,** that temporarily pleased them better.

Dixieland

Paul Whiteman was a classically trained violinist and violist who adored jazz but could not emulate the uninhibited improvisations of the jazz musicians he admired. Therefore, in the early 1920s, he formed a dance band that performed jazzy **arrangements** of popular and even classical melodies. Most of the notes were written out, providing the stability required by musicians dependent upon a score. The jazzy timbres and syncopated rhythms suggested the flavor of jazz, but the musicians were required to improvise little if at all.

SWEET JAZZ

The original Dixieland Jazz Band. (Frank Driggs Collection.)

A number of other leaders joined the sweet jazz bandwagon, and talented arrangers and orchestrators learned to create pieces for them that *sounded* improvised. Because the musicians had scores to follow, arrangements could be played by larger ensembles, providing a more sensuous sound than that of a New Orleans combo. Melodies could even be played by two or more instruments in unison, making them easy to identify and follow.

Sweet jazz was not really jazz at all, but it marked an important step in bringing jazz to public favor. It also introduced the art of the arranger, which was to become even more significant in the era of the big band.

SYMPHONIC JAZZ

Paul Whiteman was also involved in a different effort to make jazz respectable in the public mind: In 1924, he took jazz to Carnegie Hall. For that event, Whiteman commissioned George Gershwin to write a piece combining the qualities of symphonic music and jazz, and Gershwin produced his lovely *Rhapsody in Blue* (Optional Listening Example). This **symphonic jazz** composition involved no improvisation whatever, confusing some American critics who were not sure on which grounds to attack it, but the public greeted it with enthusiasm. Darius Milhaud (pronounced *Me-o'*), a member of the French group of composers known as Les Six (see page 216), had written a ballet based upon jazz called *La Création du Monde* the year before. He and other Europeans took symphonic jazz to their hearts and created several works in the symphonic jazz idiom.

Gershwin continued to be interested in concert as well as popular music. He wrote a *Second Rhapsody,* a tone poem titled *An American in Paris, Three Preludes* for piano, an overture (*Cuban Overture*), and a piano concerto (*Concerto in F*), each of which reflects the jazz implications that were an inherent part of Gershwin's music vocabulary. He also wrote the most popular of all American operas, *Porgy and Bess* (see pages 187–88). Tragically, George Gershwin died of a brain tumor at the age of thirty-nine.

Sweet and symphonic jazz remained in fashion through the late twenties, soothing audiences of the Great Depression years, while *real* jazz (hot, mostly black) went underground. In the 1930s, however, jazz finally found a popular audience. "Big-band" music came into its own, for Americans were ready to swing.

SUMMARY

When black musicians combined the forms, harmonies, and timbres of white popular musics with Creole, Caribbean, and black African rhythmic and melodic techniques, they produced a hot new music for dancing—and later for listening—called jazz.

The blues was an early manifestation of jazz that began as a black folk song style, but evolved to a sophisticated form of popular music. Boogie-woogie transferred the form and harmonic structure of the blues to the piano.

New Orleans nurtured the first important black combos, which developed a highly improvisatory style of jazz. Later, in Chicago, white Dixieland bands imitated the New Orleans sound. White as well as black youngsters danced to jazz, but the white, middle-aged general public preferred sweet and symphonic jazz during the turbulent depression years. While not really jazz at all, these genres introduced the art of the arranger and helped prepare America to swing with the big bands of the 1930s.

TERMS TO REVIEW

jazz A means of performing music. There are many moods and styles, but improvisation is an inherent characteristic of jazz.

blues A black vocal folk music.

blues scale A seven-note scale in which the third and seventh, and sometimes the fifth and sixth, notes are expressively lowered.

blue notes Flexible notes, usually slightly under normal pitch.

twelve-bar blues The classic form of the blues, consisting of three-line stanzas with four bars or measures in each line.

scatting or **scat singing** Improvising on nonsense or neutral syllables.

race records The term used before 1949 by the popular music industry for recordings intended for a black audience.

urban blues Blues pieces written for publication and professional performance.

boogie-woogie (or **piano blues**) A popular piano style with the form and harmony of the blues, but a faster tempo and a dance beat.

eight-to-the-bar The ostinato that accompanies a boogie. Each of the four counts in a measure is divided into a long and short beat.

stride piano A jazz piano style in which the left hand alternates low bass notes (on *one* and *three*) with mid-range chords (on *two* and *four*).

combo A small jazz ensemble.

New Orleans-style jazz Virtuosic improvisation by members of a jazz combo on a given melody.

Dixieland A white imitation of New Orleans-style jazz.

sweet jazz Music with the sound and flavor of jazz, but arranged so that playing it requires little improvisation.

arrangement In jazz, a written musical score that includes most or all of the notes to be played.

symphonic jazz Concert music that has some of the sounds of jazz.

KEY FIGURES

Gertrude "Ma" Rainey

Bessie Smith

W. C. Handy

Jelly Roll Morton

Earl Hines

James P. Johnson

Fats Waller

Joe "King" Oliver

Louis Armstrong

Lillian Hardin Armstrong

Paul Whiteman

OPTIONAL LISTENING EXAMPLES*

W. C. Handy: *St. Louis Blues*

George Gershwin: *Concerto in F*
Rhapsody in Blue

Robert Johnson: "Hellhound on my Trail"

SUGGESTIONS FOR FURTHER LISTENING

Examples of blues, boogie, and Dixieland
included in *The Smithsonian Collection of*
Classic Jazz

George Gershwin: *An American in Paris*

*Guides for Optional Listening Examples are in the
Instructor's Manual and may be copied and distributed
to students.

BIG BANDS AND BEBOP

Chapter 23

During the 1920s, while the white middle class was listening to sweet and symphonic jazz, certain black musicians added instruments to their small jazz combos and began to play in the style that became known as *big band* jazz. The "big bands" were not very big, but even a group of seven or eight players needed to follow some kind of structured arrangement. So instead of the collective improvisation of the early small combos, big bands relied upon arrangements that were either written down or thoroughly worked out in rehearsals.

Jelly Roll Morton was one of the first bandleaders to provide arrangements for his band, beginning in the mid-twenties. But even more influential on later jazz bands were the arrangements of Fletcher Henderson. He and other skilled arrangers made the larger groups *sound* as if they were improvising; in fact, they left room for improvisation within appropriate limits. Because many arrangements were based upon New Orleans originals, listeners perceived much the same sound as New Orleans and Dixieland jazz offered. However, the larger combos, more sensuous orchestration, and more structured atmosphere made the new sound more intelligible to a wide audience.

Jazz reached a peak of popularity in the mid-1930s. The time was right, with the Depression receding and involvement in World War II yet to come. Recordings and radio programs had made the sounds of sweet jazz widely familiar, preparing the audience for more adventurous listening. Even the atmosphere in which real jazz was now performed was congenial to the public; for after Prohibition ended, in 1933, popular dancing took place in large, cheerful halls rather than in the small, illegal speakeasies of the twenties. Jazz was suddenly both respectable and fun.

THE THIRTIES

Popular music was still segregated by the makers of race records and the managers of commercial radio stations, but black music inevitably became more familiar to and more popular with a widening audience. Whites considered it fashionable to travel to **Harlem,** a black neighborhood in uptown New York City, to hear the finest jazz musicians in the world **jam,** or improvise together. And even people who hardly understood the complex music were intoxicated with its nearly indefinable trait called *swing*.

Swing

Like many art terms, **swing** has several meanings. Some are rather technical: for example, **swing eighths** are strings of eighth notes performed in uneven rhythm, alternating long and short notes of subjective rather than measured length. This contributes to the flexible give-and-take, or expressive rubato, within the steady jazz beat.

Swing also refers to a mood, a lilt, a magical effect that great jazz musicians achieve. When every element of a jazz performance comes together and works, the music swings.

In the thirties, the most popular swinging music was that of the big bands, whose music also came to be called swing.

Big Band Swing

By 1935, thanks to the efforts of skillful arrangers, groups of twelve to eighteen players were performing the hot rhythms and hard-driven styles of the jazz pioneers. These **big bands** were comprised of three sections of instruments:

1. Brass (trumpets, trombones)
2. Woodwinds called **reeds,** in which the player causes small flexible pieces of cane to vibrate (saxophones, sometimes also a clarinet)
3. Rhythm (a guitar and/or double bass, piano, drums)

Sweet jazz had conditioned the timid ears of the public to a larger, lusher sound than that of New Orleans-style combos, and they flocked to hear the big bands play. By 1935, big band music resounded from radios, recordings, juke boxes, and dance halls all over the country. The new sound films were another important means of disseminating the intoxicating music.

Most of the big band musicians had more formal music training than most of the jazz pioneers had experienced. Thus, big band harmonies were more adventurous than those of early jazz, and the pieces were more structured. Much of the music was written out, or at least extensively rehearsed before performance. Solo improvisations were still hot, but they were brief, for the band played together much of the time.

Black and White Interaction

The swing bands experienced the stimulating interaction between black and white musicians that has characterized the development of jazz. Outstanding black arrangers of big band music included **Benny Carter** (b. 1907) and **Fletcher Henderson** (1897–1952), and the greatest composer/arranger of all was Duke Ellington (see pages 248–50). Tommy and Jimmy Dorsey, Artie Shaw, and Glenn Miller were among the best-known white bandleaders.

Figure 23.1

Legendary jazz clarinetist Benny Goodman in performance. (Culver Pictures, Inc.)

The king of swing was a white clarinetist and bandleader, **Benny Goodman** (1909–1986) (see fig. 23.1), who brought big band music to national attention through his many recordings and radio programs. Some of Goodman's outstanding soloists were black, for Goodman chose his musicians strictly according to their ability. Many of his band's best arrangements were by Fletcher Henderson, and in fact, it was Goodman's band that made many of Henderson's arrangements extremely popular. Both Goodman and Henderson had received classical music training, and both insisted on disciplined musicianship from their band members. The fact that Goodman's band became more popular than Henderson's was a source of some bitterness by the end of the decade.

Goodman later divided his playing and recording between big bands and various smaller ensembles, but big bands remained highly popular well into the forties. **Count Basie** (1904–1984) (Listening Example 39) became one of the most popular big band arrangers and leaders. A new generation of young Americans, who had not known the early styles, were delighted by swing, and many older people enjoyed it as well. The repertoire, after all, was familiar, for the big bands, like the earlier combos, based their music upon marches, hymns, and the made-to-order songs of Tin Pan Alley, whose formula had altered only slightly from the 1890s.

LISTENING EXAMPLE 39

Big Band Swing

Composers   Count Basie, Lester Young

Title   "Taxi War Dance" (excerpt)

Instruments   Four trumpets, three trombones, three saxophones, piano (Basie), guitar, double bass, drums

Basie introduces a rolling figure in the lower piano range. He continues as trumpets make brief, emphatic comments, accompanied by trombones and drums.

Lester Young begins his relaxed, swinging saxophone improvisation, which he extends and develops.

The trumpet figure returns, and then we hear a trombone solo accompanied by the rhythm section.

The trombones play a four-note motive (a distinctive rise, then a fall, in pitch), answered by the trumpets. This figure recurs several times, interspersed between solo passages for the other instruments, as the piece continues.

FROM BAND TO
VOCAL MUSIC

Although early jazz was primarily an instrumental concept, it had important reciprocal relationships with popular song. For example, many songs of the twenties and thirties were jazz flavored; the jazz combos of the twenties improvised on the melodies, or sometimes the harmonies, of popular songs; and the big bands of the thirties and forties played arrangements of old and new songs from Tin Pan Alley.

Nevertheless, big band music was primarily instrumental. The band arrangements were often quite complex, emphasizing rhythm and swing rather than tune. In fact, the source tune was sometimes quite obscure, or even absent, and the arrangements were held together by repeated rhythmic patterns called **riffs,** which also effectively heightened the intensity of the mood.

At some point in the thirties, the bands began to work closely with vocalists, and the style of big band music changed as the bands began to accompany singers, alternating instrumental and vocal choruses. Great instrumental soloists vied for popularity with outstanding vocalists such as **Ella Fitzgerald,** who was famous for her scat singing. Crooners, too—especially **Rudy Vallee** and **Bing Crosby**—became more and more popular as the technology of microphones and recording engineers allowed their more intimate, personal styles to project.

In time, crowds came primarily to hear Crosby, **Frank Sinatra,** and other popular singers, for whom the bands provided support. The lush string sound returned to favor, and by the mid-forties, singers accompanied by orchestral ensembles replaced the big swing bands in the public's affections.

Certain black jazz musicians reacted against the big band style as well, disliking the polished performances of written and rehearsed music, and resenting the broad popularity of a music that had once belonged to an exclusive few. The 1980s were to experience a strong revival of big band popularity, but for some decades before that, the style was out of favor.

In the search for new directions in jazz, some musicians turned to other cultures for inspiration.

OTHER REACTIONS AGAINST BIG BAND SWING

Like many other kinds of music in the forties and later, jazz reflected the influence of foreign musics. **Salsa,** for example, invaded New York from Cuba in the 1940s, and its popularity spread throughout the country in later years. The term, in fact, is sometimes used generically to denote all African-Latin popular styles.

Salsa

Salsa, indeed, was dance band music, but its instrumentation, rhythms, and general flavor were unlike the big band sound. The timbres were primarily those of voices and trumpets, or alternatively, flutes and violins. The rhythms, which were quite complex, were those of African-American dances, and were later affected by Puerto Rican and South American elements as well.

Of even greater influence on the future of jazz was a sophisticated new style called *bebop*.

In the early 1940s, a tight, difficult, and virtuosic new instrumental music called **bebop** emerged. Its inventors' intent was to return to the ideals of early jazz, including improvisation, virtuosity, and close interaction between soloist and combo. Yet bebop, or bop, is generally considered the first modern jazz.

Bebop

Like much of the concert music of the forties and later, bebop was music for a small ensemble of virtuoso performers. Each instrumental line was stark, clear, and technically demanding, and the melodies were angular—moving by leaps instead of steps—and unpredictable. Rather than following prearranged or familiar harmonic progressions, bop musicians challenged each other to chart new harmonic paths and make them work. Their chords were large and richly dissonant, startling to ears accustomed to tame and forever-pleasant sounds. In fact, the best bebop musicians achieved a revolutionary sound that effectively changed the course of jazz.

The typical bebop combo consisted of trumpet and saxophone, double bass, piano, and percussion. The melody instruments (trumpet and sax) sometimes began a composition by playing a pop, blues, or original melody in unison. Then they alternated with increasingly complex improvisations, supported by the other players. The double bass marked the beat, sometimes taking melodic responsibility as well, in a pattern inherited from the swing era and called the **walking bass.** The piano and percussion supplied unexpected and irregular accents.

Figure 23.2

Charlie Parker. (The Bettmann Archive, Inc.)

A saxophonist who died tragically young and a trumpet player who remains active today were among the innovators and outstanding exponents of bebop.

Charlie "Bird" Parker (1920–1955)

As a youngster in the important jazz center Kansas City, Missouri, **Charlie Parker** (fig. 23.2) absorbed the sounds of **Lester Young,** Count Basie, and other musicians. Later he moved to New York where he jammed in Harlem clubs with pianist **Thelonious Monk** (1920–1982) and trumpeter **Dizzy Gillespie,** inspiring and inspired by them to develop the new style of jazz.

Parker was not only an amazing saxophone virtuoso, but he introduced new rhythmic, melodic, and improvisational techniques that simply lifted jazz to a new plane. His tone was dry and biting and his melodies jagged in contour. He was a knowledgeable musician who sometimes quoted fragments of popular and classical compositions, moving rapidly from the familiar teasers to soaring flights of melodic virtuosity. Parker often performed with a fast tempo and an unrelenting emotional intensity that left the weak behind but offered the adventurous listener glorious new insights to jazz.

Parker has been called quite simply the most influential of all jazz musicians. Addicted to drugs and alcohol, he was ill for much of his short life and died when he was only thirty-four. In 1988, the movie *Bird* brought the story of Charlie Parker to popular attention.

LISTENING EXAMPLE 40
Bebop

Arranger Dizzy Gillespie

Title "Shaw 'Nuff" (excerpt). The piece was named for Gillespie's arranger and booking agent, Billy Shaw.

Harmony The improvisations are upon the chord patterns—not the tune—of the Gershwin song "I Got Rhythm."

Tempo Incredibly fast; beyond the ability of most jazz musicians, at least of the 1940s.

Instruments "Shaw 'Nuff" was recorded by Dizzy Gillespie's All Star Quintet: Gillespie, trumpet; Charlie Parker, sax; Al Haig, piano; Curly Russell, bass; and Sid Catlett, drums.

After a quiet beginning, a stunning break by Haig leads to an amazing unison passage by Gillespie and Parker, playing as one. The recorded excerpt includes virtuosic solos by the sax, trumpet, and piano. (There is another tight unison passage for trumpet and sax, and the piece ends quietly, as it began.)

The unprecedented energy and complexity of "Shaw 'Nuff" distinguished it as belonging to the new style, bebop.

Dizzy Gillespie, too, improvised rhythms of a complexity unprecedented in Western culture. He reached notes no one knew the trumpet could play and devised harmonic changes that challenged the rules of harmony. More important, his music was stirring and beautiful, as illustrated by "Shaw 'Nuff" (Listening Example 40), one of his best-known compositions.

John "Dizzy" Gillespie (b. 1917)

Gillespie liked African-Cuban rhythms and sounds and included them in some of his music. He has remained an active performer, perhaps less zealous than Parker and apparently comfortable with a variety of jazz styles and techniques. Despite some bouts with ill health in 1992, his famous balloon cheeks are highly visible today as he appears on television programs and in concerts around the world.

At the very time that Parker and Gillespie were leading the bebop revolution, a recording artists' strike caused a ban on commercial recordings of popular music that lasted for about two years. Although popularity was never a primary goal of the bebop musicians, their style might have attracted a wider audience if the public had been able to experience its evolution. Instead, the first bebop recordings, produced when the strike finally ended in 1944, were so sophisticated and complex that they left even the jazz audience nonplussed. People tend not to like what they do not understand, and there were many who did not understand bebop.

However, bebop is an important music that challenged and stimulated talented musicians and conscientious listeners, ushering in the age of modern jazz. Because bebop was meant for listening rather than dancing, it had significant implications for musicians interested in establishing relationships between concert music and jazz.

SUMMARY

In the mid-1930s, jazz reached its peak of popularity, which lasted for about a decade. Big bands played arranged rather than improvised versions of blues and pop tunes. Their harmonies were more adventurous and their pieces more structured than in earlier jazz styles. Also, the performers were more highly trained.

In the forties, the interest of the general audience and many serious jazz musicians turned away from big bands as singers replaced the instrumentally oriented big bands in popularity. Charlie Parker and Dizzy Gillespie led a musicians' rebellion against the commercialism and popularity of big band swing, establishing a new style of jazz called bebop. Music for listening, not dancing, bebop ushered in the age of modern jazz.

TERMS TO REVIEW

Harlem   A black neighborhood in uptown New York City that became an important center for jazz.

jam   To improvise together informally.

swing   A term with many meanings, including: (a) a mood of lilting spontaneity, or (b) a danceable music played by the big bands in the thirties and forties.

swing eighths   A series of eighth notes played in uneven rhythm.

big bands   Popular dance ensembles of the thirties and forties, consisting of twelve to eighteen players. The bands had brass, reed, and rhythm sections.

reeds   Wind instruments in which the player causes small, flexible pieces of material called reeds to vibrate. Clarinets and saxophones are single-reed instruments; oboes and bassoons have double reeds.

riff   A repeated rhythmic pattern that provides unity in a jazz composition.

salsa   A popular Cuban dance band music with rhythms derived from African-American dances.

bebop   A complex, highly improvised jazz style, largely developed by Charlie Parker and Dizzy Gillespie.

walking bass   A steadily moving pattern in the plucked string bass that has melodic as well as rhythmic implications.

KEY FIGURES

Benny Carter

Fletcher Henderson

Benny Goodman

Count Basie

Ella Fitzgerald

Rudy Vallee

Bing Crosby

Frank Sinatra

Charlie "Bird" Parker

Lester Young

Thelonious Monk

Dizzy Gillespie

JAZZ AS CONCERT MUSIC

Chapter 24

Although rooted in folk and popular styles, jazz never entered the popular music mainstream. It reached an enthusiastic segment of the popular music audience, of course, but it belongs to America's art music tradition as well.

Folk and popular musics have enriched concert music since the earliest days. Popular dances enlivened the music of the Renaissance, Baroque, and Classical periods, and many nineteenth-century composers tapped the resources of their indigenous folk and popular arts. Now, when popular music is more varied and sophisticated than ever, it is natural that contemporary musicians should also avail themselves of its riches, and jazz has become a particularly fertile source of inspiration.

VERNACULAR CONTRIBUTIONS TO CONCERT MUSIC

Almost from the start, some European composers included the distinctive rhythms, timbres, and performance techniques of jazz in their concert music. Darius Milhaud, Igor Stravinsky, Béla Bartók, and Maurice Ravel were among those who used these jazz techniques in some of their compositions and wrote pieces for particular jazz virtuosos.

Certain American composers, too, were stimulated by jazz. Charles Ives was as impressed by good jazz as by any other music, classical or popular, and we have seen that Aaron Copland based some of his most successful early pieces upon the new popular music. Milton Babbitt has also been seriously interested in jazz.

Conversely, a number of Americans writing music in the vernacular tradition have applied their knowledge of classical techniques to popular pieces. Many composers have simply refused to distinguish between classical and popular musics in terms of quality or preference. The march king John Philip Sousa composed operettas and symphonic works; Scott Joplin, the king of ragtime, wrote operas; and George Gershwin wrote an opera and several symphonic pieces as well as many Broadway show tunes.

CLASSICAL CONTRIBUTIONS TO THE VERNACULAR

Because the essence of jazz is improvisation, musicians who wished to combine classical and jazz techniques faced a new challenge; they had to create a balance between what was written, what was improvised by the soloists, and what an ensemble achieved collectively.

THE NEW CHALLENGE: CLASSICAL AND JAZZ

There were precedents for requiring performers in the classical tradition to improvise:

1. During the Baroque period, composers wrote the melody and bass lines of a composition, and a lute or keyboard player filled in the harmonies by playing the chords implied by the bass, which was sometimes figured (see pages 94–95).

2. In the early Classical period, soloists improvised one or more cadenzas in a solo concerto.

3. Church organists have often been expected to improvise music that connects one part of a service, or one verse of a hymn, to another.

In all of these cases, however, soloists have improvised within established guidelines and within a particular style of music. Jazz as classical music was a new concept, and musicians involved in its evolution faced new situations.

The symphonic jazz of the twenties was simply concert music with some of the flavors of jazz; and the big band arrangements approached the concept of composed music, but were hardly original compositions. However, by the 1940s, jazz composers were doing more than arranging familiar tunes—they were writing original jazz compositions. At that point, jazz entered the world of art music.

JAZZ AS CLASSICAL MUSIC

As we saw in chapter 23, jazz in the forties was steadily becoming more serious, dissonant, intellectual, and complex. Just as classical musicians had borrowed jazz techniques for their purposes, some jazz musicians were influenced by contemporary classical music. Jazz was no longer only for dancing and entertainment. It was also for *listening,* and had become, in fact, a kind of classical, or concert, music.

By the early 1950s, jazz was frequently performed in concert, especially on college campuses or at huge jazz festivals. Black and white jazz musicians, and their listeners as well, took a more intellectual approach to jazz. Jazz criticism, too, became a recognized field. Today jazz composers collaborate with poets, choreographers, and classical musicians to produce serious works.

One of the earliest and most important jazz composers was **Duke Ellington** (fig. 24.1).

EDWARD KENNEDY "DUKE" ELLINGTON (1899–1974)

Duke Ellington was born in Washington, D. C. He went to New York as a young man and soon formed his own band. He began to arrange music in a distinctive style, and then to compose jazz compositions, writing for unusual combinations of instruments. Ellington was a jazz pianist, but it has been said that his real instrument was the band or orchestra, for he explored the jazz ensemble's range of sounds with unprecedented imagination and creativity.

Figure 24.1
Duke Ellington. (Courtesy of Ray Avery.)

In 1930, Ellington composed *Mood Indigo,* a piece whose chromatic melodies, bitonal harmonies, and dreamy mood made it music to listen to as well as dance to. Ellington recorded many versions of *Mood Indigo,* some similar to and some entirely different from the performance heard in Listening Example 41.

Lyrics were added to *Mood Indigo* and other haunting melodies written by Ellington, producing popular songs of lasting appeal. He also wrote more serious concert music, including tone poems, ballet suites, and short concerto-like pieces such as *Concerto for Cootie* (Optional Listening Example), one of Ellington's most beautiful compositions, which he wrote to feature the trumpeter Charles "Cootie" Williams. Among his best-known

---

LISTENING EXAMPLE 41
Concert Jazz

Composer Duke Ellington

Title *Mood Indigo*

Instruments This is a big band arrangement, including five trumpets, three trombones, five saxophones (two tenor, two alto, one baritone), two clarinets, bass, drums, and Duke Ellington at the piano.

After a relaxed introduction played by muted sax accompanied by walking bass, the lovely theme is introduced by trumpets playing in a style appropriately warm and mellow rather than brilliant or virtuosic. The bass continues to provide steady support as the piano delicately embellishes the highly chromatic melody.

Even in this brief rendition of the romantic piece, the colors of the sounds change continuously, rendering the timbres endlessly interesting in their own right. Listening to other versions of *Mood Indigo* provides insight into Ellington's incredibly versatile and imaginative approach to orchestration.

Tempo Rather slow and bluesy. Although the performance is of a quality and style suitable for intense listening, it is also eminently danceable.

---

symphonic works is *Black, Brown, and Beige,* written in 1943 and played by the New York Philharmonic Orchestra in 1949 and by other orchestras in later years. He even wrote a **concerto grosso**—a multimovement Baroque form for orchestra and a small group of solo instruments, which in Ellington's piece *Harlem* (1950) is a jazz band. Another well-known piece, *Ko-Ko,* has a bluesy mood but modal effects and complex harmonies that place it in the realm of concert music.

Later, Ellington also wrote sacred choral compositions using jazz rhythms, timbres, and melodic effects and including brief improvisatory passages. When he died, he was writing a comic opera, *Queenie Pie,* which was finally staged on Broadway in 1986.

NEW
APPROACHES TO
SYMPHONIC JAZZ

In the forties, **Woody Herman** directed a band that included several French horns and a tuba, and performed multimovement orchestral works much in the style of European concert music. Stravinsky was so impressed with this symphonic approach to jazz that he wrote his *Ebony Concerto* for Herman's band in 1945.

Progressive Jazz

In 1949, pianist-arranger **Stan Kenton** (1912–1979) led a twenty-piece orchestra in a jazz concert at Carnegie Hall. His tightly organized and beautifully balanced ensemble played with elegance and precision. Kenton called the music **progressive jazz,** and that became the name of a new jazz movement.

LISTENING EXAMPLE 42
Progressive Jazz

Composer   Paul Desmond (saxophonist)

Title   "Take Five"

Performers   Dave Brubeck Quartet (piano, sax, bass, drums)

Meter Quintuple, or five beats per measure
   The piano marks the beginning of each measure with a low,
   accented pitch, while the sax and drum solos weave intricate patterns
   over the steady five-beat figure.

While Kenton and Herman were active in the East, **Dave Brubeck** was in the forefront of progressive jazz on the West Coast, where performances such as that in Listening Example 42 brought his quartet increasing fame and prestige.

Dave Brubeck is a pianist and composer who played with Dixieland and swing bands as a youngster. He majored in music in college and then studied composition with the French composer Darius Milhaud.

**Dave Brubeck
(b. 1920)**

Milhaud (1892–1974) was among several important European composers who escaped some of the horrors of World War II by living and teaching in America, thereby profoundly affecting the course of our music history. He was particularly interested in jazz, having written several symphonic pieces with jazzy rhythms and timbres. Milhaud encouraged Brubeck to apply jazz techniques to his compositions, but Brubeck also absorbed ideas from European art music.

For example, Brubeck was intrigued by the Baroque keyboard player's responsibility for improvising chords over a given bass line. In fact, some of Brubeck's polyphony is reminiscent of the seventeenth- and early-eighteenth-century style of music. His harmonies, however, are those of his own century, including atonal and polytonal effects.

Brubeck's rhythms are the complex rhythms, and sometimes polyrhythms, of modern jazz. He particularly likes unusual meters, using five or seven beats per measure instead of the usual two, three, or four.

Charles Mingus was also involved in progressive jazz. A double bass player, he made the bass line significantly more interesting and important than it had been in early or traditional jazz styles. During the 1960s, he became an extremely controversial figure because of his ideas concerning jazz composition.

**Charles Mingus
(1922–1979)**

Perhaps more than any other jazz musician, Mingus explored the relationships between jazz composition and improvisation. He established the

Charlie Mingus Jazz Workshop in New York for the purpose of experimenting with jazz composition techniques. Mingus prescribed a formal framework for each composition, but encouraged individual freedom and creativity within that framework. For that reason, he disapproved of a written score.

Mingus's "unwritten compositions" are rhythmically very complex. Instead of the requisite steady beat of earlier jazz styles, his rhythmic pulse is flexible, and he changed meters frequently. His bass line is sometimes modal, precluding the use of traditional chord changes and requiring musicians to improvise new kinds of melody lines instead of basing them upon given tunes. In short, Mingus's conception of jazz, as well as jazz composition, was revolutionary.

COOL JAZZ

At about the same time that progressive jazz was evolving, other jazz musicians were developing a style they called **cool.** In reaction to the complexity and exclusive nature of bebop, they organized larger bands and included the more sensuous sounds of symphonic instruments such as the French horn and oboe. More elegant and less hot than bebop, cool jazz reflected the influence of European concert music—especially the Impressionistic harmonies of Debussy and the sharp dissonances of Stravinsky.

Among the musicians involved in cool jazz was **Miles Davis** (fig. 24.2), who in 1949–1950 led the nine-piece orchestra that recorded the album later titled "Birth of the Cool."

MILES DAVIS (1926–1991)

Cool jazz was only one of Miles Davis's interests, for he made important contributions to several jazz styles over the years. He became particularly interested in expanding the melodic possibilities of jazz by basing melodies on modes rather than the major, minor, or blues scales. The music on Davis's album "Kind of Blue" was largely modal, and this album had important influence on many jazz musicians. Davis was a virtuoso trumpet player, an outstanding bandleader, a composer, and an innovator who continued throughout his life to experiment with new ideas in jazz.

JOHN COLTRANE (1926–1967)

John Coltrane (fig. 24.3) was a jazz saxophonist who, having worked with Miles Davis on "Kind of Blue," continued to use modal effects in some of his own compositions. Generally, Coltrane's music is dissonant and complex, with frequent harmonic changes and some polytonal passages; yet it is charged with intense emotional and even spiritual involvement. His name is sometimes associated with the free jazz style (see page 255) that emerged in the sixties.

Meanwhile, as Davis and Coltrane explored their various advanced ideas, other jazz musicians were experimenting with a manner of combining jazz and concert music in a way that allowed each to maintain the integrity of its own distinctive style—a new approach to jazz known as *third stream.*

Figure 24.2

Miles Davis. (© Shooting
Star.)

Figure 24.3

John Coltrane. (Historical
Pictures/Stock Montage.)

Third stream involves the interaction of jazz and classical music. However, unlike symphonic, cool, and progressive jazz, in which classical and jazz effects are variously *blended,* third stream allows each style to *retain* its characteristic qualities. The third-stream composer requires the listener to mix distinct sounds, much as an Impressionist painter expects the viewer to perceive orange when yellow and red are juxtaposed.

The composer who first attracted attention to this new idea, which had not yet been named, was **John Lewis.**

Lewis is a classically trained black pianist who has been particularly interested in the forms of European art music, especially of the Renaissance and Baroque periods. He founded the Modern Jazz Quartet (MJQ; fig. 24.4) in 1952 and wrote many compositions for that ensemble, often using forms—such as canon, fugue, or variations—of the earlier periods he admired.

Some of Lewis's compositions were to be performed by the MJQ together with a symphony orchestra or other classical music organization. In these pieces, the members of the quartet *improvised* some of their music, while the classical ensemble played what was *written.* Thus, each group remained true to its traditions, and their collaboration formed a new style of music.

Among the composers who also wrote music for the MJQ is the man who eventually coined the term "third stream"—**Gunther Schuller.**

THIRD STREAM

John Lewis
(b. 1920)

Figure 24.4

The Modern Jazz Quartet
(MJQ). (Courtesy of
Atlantic Records.)

Gunther Schuller (b. 1925)

Gunther Schuller is also a classically trained musician, whose interests are about equally divided between jazz and classical composition. He has played the French horn with major symphony orchestras and is a conductor, arranger, orchestrator, music critic, and composer of many kinds of music.

Like Charles Ives, Schuller recognizes no qualitative distinction between categories of music, admiring a good rag as much as a good symphony. He orchestrated Joplin's opera *Treemonisha* and led the Houston Opera Company in the successful premier performance. His transcriptions of several Joplin rags were used in the 1972 movie *The Sting*.

For a time at least, Schuller believed that jazz and classical music should be treated as separate but congenial entities. He found their interaction effective, but he distinguished between John Lewis's approach, in which each style retains its characteristic qualities, and symphonic, cool, or progressive jazz, in which they are variously blended. In 1957, Schuller referred to classical music as the "first stream" of music and to jazz as the "second stream," calling their combination in the manner Lewis prescribed "third stream."

Schuller, Lewis, Brubeck, and others have produced pieces for jazz band and orchestra, jazz quartet and string quartet, and other similar combinations, in which the jazz and classical styles are heard simultaneously but are not fused. However, third-stream music as these musicians conceive of it seems to have run its course and is seldom referred to today. Contemporary jazz players ("jazzers") sometimes loosely use the term third stream to refer to avant-garde jazz in general.

Anthony Davis frequently blends jazz and classical styles in his compositions. His avant-garde jazz ensemble Episteme has been involved in some third-stream performances with traditional, or classical, performers.

Davis is sometimes referred to as a **crossover** musician—one whose music is addressed to a certain audience yet has significant appeal to other audiences as well. (For example, a number of prominent opera singers have recently produced popular recordings of a wide variety of songs.) However, Davis steadfastly resists labels. He happens to be a jazz musician, a pianist, and a black person, but all kinds of music interest him. His first opera (*The Life and Times of Malcolm X*) was performed at the Metropolitan Opera House in 1986, and in 1988, he wrote a science fiction opera called *Under the Double Moon.*

Davis has a classical appreciation of formal structure, believing that "the ultimate freedom is to command form." His orchestral music is organized, in fact, according to clear formal designs, but it often includes improvisatory passages. Davis's *Violin Concerto* and *Notes from the Underground* are recent orchestral compositions with effective jazz undertones.

In 1960, **Ornette Coleman** (b. 1930) introduced free collective improvisation in an album titled "Free Jazz." The new style defied most people's perception of jazz. **Free jazz** was a difficult music, challenging to performers and listeners alike. There were no familiar chord changes, no references to popular songs or blues, and no steady beat. In free jazz, each musician improvised independently, aware of and responsive to the other players, but bound by no preset obligations. Even the initial phrases of a composition, played by the soloists together, were not necessarily in unison.

Thus, free jazz expressed in musical terms the freedom that blacks were demanding and finally experiencing in many areas of life. It was also related in concept to chance music and Abstract Expressionist art. Free jazz was free from the tyranny of bar lines, familiar melodies, established chord changes, and traditional instrumentation. No piano was required in free jazz ensembles, because there were no chord changes to play. Rhythm instruments assumed a new significance, assertive and independent rather than supportive as before, much in the manner that black individuals were assuming respected positions in life.

Free jazz also reflects an interest in some of the non-Western musics that have intrigued twentieth-century composers of classical music. For example, Coleman used microtones and certain rhythmic techniques derived from the music of India that heighten the emotional effect and the intellectual challenge of his performances.

The question arises as to whether these various concert styles are jazz at all. The answer, of course, is elusive, subjective—irrelevant, in fact, if the listener simply values each style and each piece according to its merits. In some situations, labels only get in the way.

SUMMARY

Since 1950, jazz musicians have formed alliances with the world of concert music. Jazz composers have produced symphonic works with jazzy flavors, jazz pieces in classical forms, and third-stream pieces in which jazz and classical music meet, yet retain their independent qualities. Many interests of composers working in the European art music tradition—modal melodies; Eastern scales, rhythms, and timbres; polytonality; twelve-tone and serial techniques—have also been reflected in jazz compositions intended for a listening rather than a dancing audience.

Certain individuals have been particularly influential in the field of concert jazz. Duke Ellington, whose natural musical language was that of jazz, wrote music for both the concert hall and the church and is considered one of America's greatest composers. Dave Brubeck extended the rhythmic concepts of jazz pieces by using unusual meters. Charles Mingus explored techniques of jazz composition, prescribing a formal framework but no written score for each piece.

The styles of concert jazz are many and diverse. Progressive jazz introduced a symphonic approach. Cool jazz added a sensuous element. Third stream combined classical music and jazz without mixing them. Free jazz declared independence from most of the preconceived notions about jazz. Through these and other concert styles, jazz has emerged as an important American art music of the twentieth century.

TERMS TO REVIEW

concerto grosso   A Baroque composition for orchestra and a small group of solo instruments. The form has been revived by some twentieth-century composers.

progressive jazz   A symphonic approach to jazz, introduced by Stan Kenton.

quintuple meter   Five beats per measure.

cool jazz   A style introduced about 1950 for large bands that included some symphonic instruments.

third stream   As coined by Gunther Schuller, the term refers to the combination, but not the blending, of jazz and classical music. The term is loosely used today to refer to avant-garde jazz styles.

crossover   Music that appeals to more than one kind of audience.

free jazz   A style of free improvisation introduced by Ornette Coleman in 1960.

KEY FIGURES

Duke Ellington

Woody Herman

Stan Kenton

Dave Brubeck

Darius Milhaud

Charles Mingus

Miles Davis

John Coltrane

John Lewis

Gunther Schuller

Anthony Davis

Ornette Coleman

OPTIONAL LISTENING EXAMPLE*

Duke Ellington: *Concerto for Cootie*

SUGGESTIONS FOR FURTHER LISTENING

Gunther Schuller: *Transformation* (for an eleven-piece ensemble)
Conversation (for the MJQ and the Beaux Arts String Quartet)
Seven Studies on Themes of Paul Klee (orchestral)

*Guides for Optional Listening Examples are in the Instructor's Manual and may be copied and distributed to students.

part 9

OTHER VERNACULAR MUSICS

COUNTRY MUSIC

Chapter 25

While various vernacular musics evolved in America's urban and rural environments throughout the nineteenth century, people living in certain remote areas of the eastern hills continued to sing and play their traditional music much as it had been performed in the countries of their ancestors. Relatively isolated from mainstream popular music and largely unaffected by modern trends, they passed the old tunes and performing customs from one generation to the next by oral tradition. In this way, many early folk ballads—especially those brought to America from the British Isles—were faithfully preserved.

However, after the Civil War, even isolated mountain areas were invaded by new influences that inevitably affected the music as well as every other aspect of life. Railroad lines were being laid, coal mines worked, and textile mills established in remote areas where tough union rules could be ignored. These and other enterprises attracted migrant workers, who brought new kinds of music and new musical instruments into the hills. Of particular significance was the five-string banjo, on which one string played a constant or repeated pitch called a **drone.** This instrument was ideal for accompanying hill or country music.

Conversely, mountain people began to take temporary jobs in the cities, from which they brought home new subjects for songs and new musical sounds. Soon new "folk" songs evolved, similar to the traditional ballads, but characteristically American in subject and style. Sometimes people lost track of the origin of a song, so that one included in the "folk" repertoire might actually have been composed rather than improvised, memorized, and passed down in the traditional way.

FROM COUNTRY TO CITY

In the early 1920s, commercial recording companies began to send talent scouts into the hill country searching for folk singers and instrumentalists with a distinctive sound. Thus, country musicians were enticed to come to the cities, where the market for recordings of "old time" music was growing. In 1925, four musicians from Virginia recording under the name Hill Billies gave rise to the term **hillbilly music,** which then was generally applied—often with scorn—to the music of country fiddlers, harmonica players, and singers of traditional country ballads.

The hill musicians traveled with tent shows, medicine shows, and vaudeville shows, appeared at county fairs, and participated in fiddlers' contests. Their songs, which concerned the elemental subjects of human experience—love, work, family life, and death—expressed the deepest emotions in a semi-detached, impersonal way that made them all the more moving. As city listeners perceived the wealth of beauty and entertainment in this unfamiliar style, country music's audience continued to expand.

Of course, this trend signalled the end of the old way of preserving original folk songs and performance practices. Professional country musicians soon adapted to the requirements of the commercial market, expanding their limited repertoire by writing new songs and learning to perform them in a manner acceptable to a city audience. Story-songs, or ballads, were particularly popular, and many were written on dramatic topics of the day: a coal mine disaster, a hanging, the sinking of a ship. By the mid-1920s, recordings of country music were widely available, bringing the country sound to a larger audience. Even the country people themselves began to lose track of which folksongs were traditional and which were modern.

In 1927, two different strains of hillbilly music were introduced to the public—one by a soloist from the Deep South and the other by a singing family from the mountains of Virginia.

Jimmie Rodgers came from Mississippi, but he wandered through several states in the course of his tragically brief career. He had little formal training but many creative ideas, and he was willing to try anything suggested by the record producers who promoted him. Although he was accompanied on his recordings by various and unusual combinations of instruments, Rodgers was probably most effective when he accompanied himself on the guitar, his simple self-accompaniments providing appropriate support for his clear, pleasant tenor voice that he sometimes used in the falsetto range. He also had a natural **yodel,** or rapid alternation between the full voice and falsetto, which was later imitated by many country singers. The thirteen songs called "blue yodels," for which Rodgers was particularly famous, had the form and harmonies of the twelve-bar blues, with his distinctive yodel added at the end of each verse.

Known as the "singing brakeman," Rodgers drew on his experiences as a former railroad man in some of his songs. He also sang of love gone wrong, of cowboys, and of country folk whom his listeners either recognized or idealized, as well as sentimental songs of the southern home he missed, such as "Daddy and Home" (Optional Listening Example).

Rodgers only performed professionally for about six years, dying of tuberculosis at the age of thirty-six. He had become extremely popular during his short career, having established the solo song as an important part of hillbilly music. He also became the first person elected to the Country Music Hall of Fame, which was established in Nashville, Tennessee, in 1961.

Jimmie Rodgers
(1897–1933)

Figure 25.1

The Carter Family. (Michael Ochs Archives, Ltd.)

The Carter Family

A. P. Carter (1891–1960), his wife Sara, and his sister-in-law Maybelle came from the mountains of Virginia and sang traditional songs, ballads, and hymns in the high-pitched, nasal voices characteristic of mountain people. Their accompanying instruments were the guitar and the **autoharp** (a simple folk instrument on which the strings are strummed or plucked with one hand while buttons are depressed to form chords with the other).

The **Carter Family** (fig. 25.1) represented a tradition quite different from that of Jimmie Rodgers. He typified the hard-living wanderer; they the close, conservative family. Rodgers made the solo country song popular, with a voice that was bluesy and relaxed, while the Carters performed as a group, their harmony close and their voices high-pitched and tense.

Several generations of Carters have continued to perform country music professionally. June Carter, who became the wife of singer Johnny Cash, is widely known, and their daughter Roseanne has been a major country music performer since the 1980s.

Radio Spreads the Message

By the late 1920s, most American homes had a radio, and from that time, radios brought hillbilly music and the religious country music called gospel into homes across the country. "The Grand Ole Opry" radio program in Nashville was the best-known, but not the only, popular radio program featuring hillbilly or old-time music.

The typical country radio program included sentimental parlor songs, gospel hymns, old English and American ballads, and work songs performed by country singers, usually accompanied by a fiddle or banjo and sometimes by a guitar. String bands, consisting of several fiddles, one or more banjos and guitars, and sometimes a string bass, provided rollicking dance tunes. The popular radio shows also included "dance songs," in which string bands alternated verses with a solo voice.

LISTENING EXAMPLE 43

Cajun Music

Title   Cajun Two-Step

Form   The two-step is a dance organized much like a rag or march in a series of four-measure strains. The taped excerpt includes **AABBAAC . . .** , and we sense, probably accurately, that the dance could continue almost indefinitely were it not for constraints of concert and/or recording time.

Meter   Duple, as the title implies.

Tempo   Fast. The insistently rapid tempo contributes to the exuberant nature of the piece.

Instruments   Accordion, or concertina, and triangle. The instrumentalists punctuate their performance with occasional joyous shouts.

Country musicians seem to have a special gift for absorbing influences and life experiences and for developing a characteristic music, country in flavor but distinctive in style. Thus, many kinds of country music have evolved across America, reflecting local experience and acculturation, and the rich collection called country music now includes many musics that sound quite different from each other.

Evicted from their homeland in Acadia (Nova Scotia) in the late eighteenth century, the **Cajuns** sought asylum in the bayous of southern Louisiana, finally settling in a remote area south of New Orleans. There they remained relatively isolated from the rest of American society, continuing to speak French and slowly evolving a *patois,* or mixed language, of their own. The Cajuns' music is similar in many ways to the folk musics of rural America, for it has absorbed some influence from the hillbillies and later country musicians, while they in turn—particularly in Louisiana and later in Texas— have been affected by Cajun sounds.

Cajun music is prevailingly lighthearted, with dance-related rhythms and delightfully syncopated melodies (Listening Example 43). The ensembles that accompany Cajun dancing or singing often include a small accordion known as a **concertina,** relatively unfamiliar to the rest of the country. Cajuns are particularly fond of waltzes and other dances, which they perform with rhythms and timbres as spicy as their highly seasoned food.

Zydeco

A recent black Cajun style called **zydeco** is attracting enthusiastic listeners around the country with its distinctive hot rhythms and unusual timbres.

STYLES OF
COUNTRY MUSIC

The Cajun Style

Figure 25.2

Bill Monroe playing the mandolin with his Blue Grass Boys at the Nightstage in Boston, Massachusetts. (© Cheryl Higgins 1989/Decisive Moment, Inc.)

Zydeco melodies and harmony are sounded with the rich timbres of accordion and harmonica, and the strongly syncopated rhythms are marked with a tambourine and sometimes with a modern version of the **washboard,** which the musicians strap on their chests for ready access. Contemporary zydeco bands combine the energy and amplification of the hottest rock groups with the exotic melodies and dialect of the Cajuns to produce an intoxicating new music.

Bluegrass

In the 1940s, a virtuosic instrumental style rooted in mountain music became widely popular and commercially important. This revival of a traditional music was eventually named after Bill Monroe's Blue Grass Boys (fig. 25.2), a string band that played the music on the radio and recorded extensively in the late forties.

The instruments of the **bluegrass** ensemble include a fiddle, guitar, string bass, and five-string banjo. Often there is also a **mandolin,** a popular Italian instrument that produces a delicate, yet vibrant sound when its strings are plucked. (Bill Monroe was a virtuoso on the mandolin.) Because only **acoustic instruments** (natural instruments) are used, the characteristic timbres of bluegrass music are light, but the fast tempos and virtuosic playing provide plenty of excitement.

Bluegrass is unique among country musics in being primarily instrumental. Although some performances include story songs, which are performed in the high pitch and with the close mountain harmony introduced by the Carters, the emphasis is still on important instrumental interludes or breaks. No less than other country musics, bluegrass has absorbed varied influences. For example, the verse-chorus form reflects the style of Tin Pan

> ## LISTENING EXAMPLE 44
> ## Bluegrass
>
> **Title**   "Earl's Breakdown"
>
> **Instruments**   Guitar (Lester Flatt), banjo (Earl Scruggs), mandolin, fiddle, bass
>
> Lester Flatt and Earl Scruggs left Bill Monroe's Blue Grass Boys to form their own group and develop a distinctive style of bluegrass.
>
> **Form**   Variations on a tune.
>
> 1. The banjo presents the tune, which has two parts, accompanied by the other instruments. In the second part, Scruggs uses a tuner to bend the pitches expressively.
> 2. The fiddle offers virtuosic variations on both parts of the tune.
> 3. Scruggs takes the tune back, with chromatic variations, again bending the strings in his distinctive style.
> 4. The fiddle ranges ever more widely in pitch, treating only the first half of the tune.
> 5. The banjo introduces a new picking style as the excerpt tapers off.
>
> Throughout the example, you are encouraged to listen to *all* of the instruments as they offer stimulating accompaniment to the exciting solo performances.

Alley, and the virtuosic instrumental playing owes homage to jazz. During the 1960s, the vibrant sound of the acoustic string instruments and the brilliant playing of the instrumentalists made bluegrass particularly popular on college campuses, in coffeehouses, and at folk festivals around the country. The virtuosic performance in Listening Example 44 indicates why bluegrass remains among the most appreciated styles of country music today.

The Nashville Sound

When rock and roll exploded on the popular music scene in the early 1950s, the country-western music industry faced disaster—even though, as we shall see, country was actually one of the main sources of rock and roll. While **rockabilly** responded to the threatening new music by combining country themes with the rhythms and instrumentation of rock and roll, the audience for traditional country music fell away, record sales decreased, and radio listeners disappeared. But Nashville, Tennessee, which had long been the center of the country-western business, met rock and roll on its own ground, introducing the **Nashville sound.**

The Nashville sound had country themes but pop instrumentation. That is, soloists sang of traditional country topics, but they were accompanied by electric and steel guitars, drums, electric bass, piano, and sometimes a string section. There was even a background chorus of voices singing not in the close mountain harmony of the Carters, but in a trained, professional style, much like the doo-wop singers of Motown rock and roll (see chapter 26). This was hardly true to the traditions of country music, but it helped attract an audience for country during the early days of rock and roll.

COUNTRY BECOMES COUNTRY-WESTERN

Even before bluegrass and the Nashville sound established popularity in the eastern United States, country music moved west, where it developed further distinctive styles. People displaced from their jobs by the economic turmoil of the Great Depression, or forced to abandon farms located in drought-stricken areas of the country, left their accustomed environments and roamed across the country, carrying with them their traditional music customs—and sometimes little else.

This kind of forced migration continued during World War II, as people left familiar rural areas to find jobs in the cities but brought along their country music tastes. Young people in the armed services had an unprecedented opportunity to associate with others from diverse backgrounds, and many who were from the city discovered that they liked the country music sound.

People living in western states welcomed and absorbed country music, adding distinctive flavors of their own. For example, Texans— residing in both the South and the West—reflected the mariachi sounds of Mexico, the Cajun music of Louisiana, the Hawaiian steel guitar, and the songs of lonesome cowboys in their own versions of country music, which may properly be called **country-western.**

Western Swing

Whereas country music in the eastern United States generally reflected the conservative mood and morality of the home, in the West, the country flavor was that of the dance hall. So in response to the dance craze of the thirties and forties, Texans developed a dance band style of their own: **western swing.** To the piano, sax, brasses, and jazz rhythm section of the eastern big band, Texans added fiddles and the steel guitar, while their singers added yodeling. The jazz influence on western swing was strong, rendering tempos fast, rhythms hot, and instrumental solos wonderfully virtuosic in this Texas big band style.

Honky-Tonk

While Texas dance halls rang with the sounds of western swing bands, another country-western style developed in the intimate Texas bars and clubs called honky-tonks. The patrons in these small, crowded rooms were more interested in listening than dancing to the **honky-tonk** songs, which dealt frankly with the hard subjects of life of relevance to the returning servicemen and uprooted or separated families: infidelity, divorce, alcohol, homesickness, separation, loneliness, prison. The harsh and realistic lyrics were delivered in an earthy, matter-of-fact style, typical of the country music manner.

Honky-tonk, like most country music, is primarily a vocal style, and sometimes an amplified piano was the sole accompanying instrument. Accompanying bands, if any, had a distinctive instrumentation, borrowed from the blues, jazz, or Hawaiian ensembles, and electrified in order to be heard above the noise of rough, drinking crowds.

Honky-tonk today retains that same honest, straightforward delivery style, but the lyrics avoid the gritty specifics of the songs of the forties. The past is often mourned, but it is never over-romanticized.

Cowboy Songs

From the time of the earliest talking pictures, Americans flocked to western films, and by the mid-1930s, the craze for westerns was full-blown. These films portrayed the West as Hollywood envisioned it: full of wide-open spaces, dramatic scenery, beautiful and virtuous women, and villains who were inevitably vanquished by brave and handsome cowboys—many of whom sang romantic cowboy songs.

Some of the Hollywood singing cowboys were actually from the West; **Gene Autry** and **Tex Ritter,** for example, came from Texas. But many of the songs Autry and Ritter sang were written by Tin Pan Alley professionals. Among the most famous were "Tumbling Tumbleweeds" (featured as a tremulous harmonica solo in the 1991 film *City Slickers*) and "Cool Water," both written by Bob Nolan, a founding member of the famous singing trio called the Sons of the Pioneers. Most of the songs sung by **Roy Rogers,** who, like Autry, starred in about one hundred western films, were also written by Nolan. Of course there were real cowboy songs as well, many of them lilting Irish tunes to which nineteenth-century immigrant Irish cowboys had set new words. These, together with the songs composed for western films, became part of the country-western repertoire.

By the late 1940s, cowboy songs had largely faded in popularity. Gene Autry had earlier recorded songs from the African-American blues tradition ("Black Bottom Blues," "Wild Cat Mama," and "Traveling Blues," for example), and he went on to sing songs in the popular rather than the western vein. (His best-known songs today are "Here Comes Santa Claus" and "Rudolph, the Red-Nosed Reindeer.") Tex Ritter's biggest hit, "High Noon," was high on the pop rather than the country-western charts.

COUNTRY POP

Patti Page's recording of "Tennessee Waltz" in 1950 proved how popular a country-style song could be if presented in pop format to a general audience, and soon **cover recordings** of country hits were made by Tony Bennett, Frankie Laine, and other popular singers. The smooth voices and polished styles of **Eddy Arnold** and **Jim Reeves,** often accompanied by a string orchestra, were also examples of country pop. **Chet Atkins** was a "country" singer who sang songs and played his guitar in a style close to that of Tin Pan Alley. The songs of **Hank Williams** (1923–1953) were firmly rooted in the genuine rural tradition of country music, but his performance style was widely accepted by the country pop audience. At the time of his early death, Williams was the best known and most financially successful country singer.

The Folk Revival

The folk songs of the urban folk movement that developed in the late fifties and remained popular through the succeeding turbulent decade also formed a part of the country pop repertoire. The most admired representative of the folk revival period was **Woodrow Wilson ("Woody") Guthrie** (1914–1967), who developed from a simple hillbilly singer into a sophisticated composer and performer of protest songs. Protest was not a traditional characteristic of country music, but social commentary was, so Guthrie's stirring poems and songs on a variety of social topics provided inspiration for the folk revivalists. In fact, some consider him America's greatest folk poet.

Other singers of protest songs in the urban folk style included **Joan Baez, Bob Dylan, Pete Seeger,** and groups such as the **Kingston Trio,** the **Limelighters,** and the **New Christy Minstrels.** These singers were city-bred musicians producing commercial music for a sophisticated urban audience, but they effectively stirred interest in the original folk styles. Joan Baez, for example, made serious studies of folk and country music, learning traditional songs and performance customs and bringing them to a modern and receptive audience.

MINORITY AND FEMALE REPRESENTATION

Minorities have not been well represented in country music. Certainly some black rural styles have interacted with country-western music: Zydeco is specifically a black style, and other country music shows the influence of rhythm and blues. But to date, **Charley Pride** remains the only black to have played a prominent role as a country star.

On the other hand, although few women were involved in the early country-western experience, more recently many have achieved wide acclaim. **Kitty Wells,** performing in the fifties, broke ground for later female stars. **Patsy Cline** was known as the "queen of country music" before her untimely death in 1963. Her recordings of "Walking after Midnight" and "I Fall to Pieces" were hits on the pop as well as the country charts. **Loretta Lynn** and **Dolly Parton** are not only outstanding singers in the genuine country style, but they have also written fine songs. (The 1980 film *Coal Miner's Daughter* is based on Loretta Lynn's life.) **Tammy Wynette** is another popular country star, though she performs in a style close to mainstream popular music. The **Mandrell Sisters** and Loretta Lynn's sister **Crystal Gayle** are among other familiar figures in country music, and more recently, **Patty Loveless** and **Reba McEntire** have become widely known.

COUNTRY IN THE NINETIES

More sophisticated in performance and broader in scope than ever, country music continues to hold a wide audience. Successful releases, including Dwight Yoakam's "Turn Me Loose," are now coming out of California as well as Nashville. The Kentucky Headhunters' recent hit "Rock 'n' Roll Angel" illustrates the new confidence that allows country musicians to refer comfortably and with humor to their formerly dreaded competition. Steve Wariner's "Domino Theory," accompanied by mandolin, steel guitar, and

Barbara Mandrell.
(© AP/Wide World
Photos.)

fiddles, bears recent evidence to the bluegrass influence. Restless Heart's
"Fast Moving Train" illustrates the modern "Hawaiian" sound—steel guitar
plus synthesizers.

And so the sounds have changed, but the essence of country music
remains the heartfelt, unpretentious, highly effective expression of basic
needs and human experience.

SUMMARY

Country-western music is rooted in rural and
mountain folk traditions. Hillbilly music
changed when it became commercial, but it has
never entered the mainstream of popular music.

Jimmie Rodgers made solo hillbilly songs
popular, and the Carters brought mountain
harmony to the city. First, recordings and later,
radio shows spread country music to an ever
wider audience.

In the 1930s, many rural people traveled to
new states, bringing their music with them.
World War II introduced country music to even
more city folk. Country musicians absorbed
varied influences, and soon new styles evolved.
Texans danced to western swing and listened to
honky-tonk. The cowboy songs of western films
joined the hillbilly repertoire to produce a new
genre, country-western.

Bluegrass is an instrumentally dominated
revival of mountain folk music. The "folk
revival" of the sixties, however, belonged to
country pop.

TERMS TO REVIEW

drone A single tone, sounded continuously or repeated.

hillbilly music A term applied to early country music.

yodel A singing technique that involves changing rapidly back and forth between the normal and falsetto voices.

autoharp A folk instrument played by strumming the strings with one hand and pressing chord buttons with the other.

Cajun Acadian. A French-speaking people who settled in Louisiana in the eighteenth century.

concertina A kind of accordion or portable reed instrument. Melody and chords are achieved by depressing buttons or keys, and the wind is supplied by a folding bellows.

zydeco A rock-flavored Cajun style of country music.

washboard Originally a laundry board scraped for its sound effects as a music "instrument." Modern imitations are strapped onto the player for easy access.

bluegrass A commercial instrumental style derived from mountain music.

mandolin A pear-shaped plucked string instrument.

acoustic instrument The natural, as opposed to electric, instrument.

rockabilly A close amalgamation of country music and rock and roll.

Nashville sound Country music's commercial response to rock and roll, with country themes, pop instrumentation, and a heavy beat.

country-western Western music with a country flavor, including western swing, honky-tonk, and cowboy songs.

western swing The Texas swing band style, influenced by Mexican and Hawaiian sounds and by jazz.

honky-tonk A Texas vocal style with harsh, honest lyrics.

cover, cover recording A re-recording of a popular record, sometimes intended to appeal to a broader audience than the original recording addressed.

KEY FIGURES

Early Country (Hillbilly) Musicians
Jimmie Rodgers
The Carter Family

Cowboy Singers
Gene Autry
Tex Ritter
Roy Rogers

Country Pop Singers
Eddy Arnold
Jim Reeves
Chet Atkins
Hank Williams

Urban Folk Singers
Joan Baez
Bob Dylan
Pete Seeger
Kingston Trio
The Limelighters
New Christy Minstrels

Composer, Poet
Woody Guthrie

Female Country Stars
Kitty Wells
Patsy Cline
Loretta Lynn
Dolly Parton
Tammy Wynette
The Mandrell Sisters
Crystal Gayle
Patty Loveless
Reba McEntire

Black Country Star
Charley Pride

SUGGESTIONS FOR FURTHER LISTENING

The Carter Family: "Keep on the Sunny Side" (their theme song) or any recordings available to you

Cajun music: "Fais Pas Ça" ("Don't Do That")

The Smithsonian Collection of Classic Country Music

ROCK AND ROLL

Chapter 26

The baby boom of World War II produced a fifties "teen boom" of unprecedented numbers, wealth, and influence. These young people had little interest in the sentimental popular music of the depression and war years, for their frustrations were of a different order from those of the preceding generation. For them, songs about loneliness, separation, and hope for the future were meaningless. They craved excitement; they wanted to dance; and for the first time they had enough money to affect the popular music industry.

Several postwar conditions fostered a sense of independence, and even rebellion, among American youth. For example, they found it difficult in such a prosperous time to accept the frugal ways of their parents who had survived the Great Depression and years of wartime austerity. Those in military families experienced frequent relocation, which is particularly unsettling to children and teens. These and other social and economic conditions caused an unprecedented gap in communication and understanding between adolescents and their parents.

THE GENERATION GAP

The spirit of rebellion was particularly strong among young blacks, some of whom returned from war to find the equality they had experienced on the battlefield denied them in the work force. As the injustice of social discrimination became ever more apparent, the civil rights movement steadily gained momentum, and black power became a force to be reckoned with. The white, middle-aged middle class—conservative, content, moralistic—was about to clash with the passionate youth. Out of that conflict came a provocative, energetic new music.

During the years immediately after World War II, popular music became increasingly diversified. Generally, there was a move away from instrumental music and a return to song. Swing bands were considered too polished, the dress too formal, the performances too structured; and jazz was too complex to appeal to the restless young audience.

THE ROOTS OF ROCK AND ROLL

Mainstream pop featured sentimental ballads suitable for the slow dances popular at the time. The protest songs of the urban folk movement also had wide appeal. But it was two popular musics that lay *outside* the mainstream—country-western and rhythm and blues—that formed the roots of rock and roll.

Rhythm and Blues

For many years, the unfortunate term "race records" continued to be used by the popular music recording industry for the music they produced for black listeners. This included a wide range of styles, from country and urban blues to gospel, jazz, and some white-style ballads. However, much black music was based upon the form and harmonic pattern of the blues. Most of it was in quadruple meter, with strong **backbeats** on the normally weak second and fourth beats of the measure. And most of it was danceable. In 1949, the industry trade journal *Billboard* grouped all of the music intended for a black audience under the term **rhythm and blues (R & B),** and for several years that phrase was generally used for black popular music.

Rhythm and blues ensembles included swing-style bands and small combos, but even the small combos were loud. They usually had an electric guitar and sometimes other electrified instruments as well. They normally included at least one singer, and all-male vocal groups were popular. The lyrics of most R & B songs were good-natured, though frankly, unself-consciously, and even blatantly sexual. The singers had to shout or scream to be heard above the instrumentalists, and this contributed to the emotional intensity of rhythm and blues.

White listeners had previously accepted the music of black performers—but not necessarily black music. That is, male ensembles such as the **Mills Brothers** and the **Ink Spots,** featuring high falsetto voices, smooth harmonies, and subtle rhythmic backgrounds, were very popular, and the black soloists **Lena Horne, Nat "King" Cole,** and **Ella Fitzgerald** also had hits on the pop charts. But most of their repertoire was from Tin Pan Alley, and their performances were relatively close to white in style. Black listeners tended to prefer rhythm and blues, and by 1950, increasing numbers of young whites did too.

Country Music Meets R & B

Black rhythm and blues and white country-western had a number of characteristics in common. Both lay outside the popular mainstream. Both were rooted in the South. Both were danceable. Both consistently involved the guitar—acoustic, electric, or amplified. Both had frank lyrics and earthy delivery styles. And both were sung with dialects different from that of the white urban population.

In the early fifties, the two dissident styles met and fused, producing the most widely and wildly hailed popular music the world has known: **rock and roll.**

THE BIRTH OF ROCK AND ROLL

Rhythm and blues hits were not widely programmed on radio, for producers and executives were convinced that their white listeners would turn away. But a disc jockey in Cleveland, Ohio, named **Alan Freed** understood that many white teens preferred R & B hits to mainstream popular music.

Beginning in 1951, he played increasing numbers of rhythm and blues records on his radio programs, which reached a broad general audience. Freed also promoted live stage performances of music in R & B style, with both blacks and whites present on the stage and in the audience.

Next, white performers began to make cover recordings of black hits. The early covers were tame, toned-down versions of R & B songs; the sexual references were less blatant and the rhythms less hot. Radio stations that had never programmed R & B willingly played the cover recordings, which they considered more suitable for the general audience. On television, the popular "American Bandstand" program hosted by **Dick Clark** featured white teen idols, such as **Paul Anka, Bobby Darin, Fabian,** and **Frankie Avalon,** singing respectable, urban versions of rock and roll songs.

Then two young white country singers with black delivery styles entered the picture. The terms "rock" and "roll" had long been familiar and suggestive in black popular music, but Alan Freed is credited with coining the term "rock and roll" for the new style with which Bill Haley and Elvis Presley revolutionized the popular music world.

When **Bill Haley and his Comets,** which began as a country-western group, recorded "Shake, Rattle and Roll" (1954)—already an R & B hit as recorded by the black singer **Joe Turner**—their cover recording was widely played by radio stations that would not have touched the R & B version, and it quickly soared to the top of the popular music charts. The next year, the Comets' recording of "Rock around the Clock" was used as the theme for the movie *Blackboard Jungle* and became the first international rock and roll hit.

Bill Haley (1925–1981)

Much the same course from country to rock and roll was followed by **Elvis Presley** (fig. 26.1), but the popularity he achieved was unprecedented and, for a solo singer, remains unsurpassed. Presley was another country boy who grew up in poverty in Mississippi. Through a combination of talent, persistence, and luck, he achieved a recording contract and soared to the top of his profession with dizzying speed.

Elvis Presley (1935–1977)

Presley's early rockabilly or country rock records were actually more popular with blacks than whites, but his appeal soon became interracial and international. His 1956 cover recording of "Hound Dog" by **Willie Mae "Big Mama" Thornton** reached the top of first the black and then the white pop charts. Another early recording, "Heartbreak Hotel," revealed the range of his expressive gifts, from wild and raucous to wrenchingly tender.

Elvis was self-taught, but he had a beautiful and amazingly versatile voice to which he added warmth and intensity by the use of **vibrato**—a slight wavering between pitches that singers use to color the sound of their voices. The vocal slides and catches typical of black singing styles came to him naturally, and he used them with poignant effect. He could shout or croon, sing gospel, folk, or rock and roll, and in every case mesmerize an audience with his voice and his electrifying stage presence. Known as Elvis

the Pelvis for his sexy gyrations on stage, he epitomized all that youth loved and middle-class adults feared about rock and roll.

EARLY CHARACTERISTICS OF ROCK AND ROLL

Most early rock and roll songs were close in form and harmony to the twelve-bar blues. Accompanying instruments included one or more amplified guitars, a saxophone, and sometimes a trumpet, over which a singer screamed or shouted. The meter was quadruple, with strong backbeats, and the tempo was danceable.

Black musicians soon began to develop their own distinctive styles of rock and roll.

Black Rock and Roll

Whereas Presley's style was rooted in country-western music, a number of impressive black rock and rollers stayed closer to rhythm and blues. **Bo Diddley** played his electric guitar with terrific rhythmic vitality, achieving an amazing range of sounds in an age before technology made such effects commonplace. **Little Richard** thumped his piano and screamed his lyrics—whether sacred or profane—with equal fervor. Little Richard left rock and roll temporarily for religious reasons, but returned after several years to resume his highly successful career.

Chuck Berry (b. 1926)

Chuck Berry (fig. 26.2) was among the most talented early black stars of rock and roll. He was a great guitarist, a talented songwriter, and an effective singer who shouted protest and rebellion over his highly amplified

Figure 26.2

Chuck Berry. (© UPI/ Bettmann Newsphotos.)

guitar. Berry had a gift for melodic improvisation and was a more sophisticated performer than either Bill Haley or Elvis Presley. He had important influence upon the Beatles and the Rolling Stones, who later sang his songs and imitated his distinctive style.

In 1959, Berry returned to America from abroad and produced one of his biggest hits, "Back in the USA." That same year, his serious, sentimental, well-written song "Memphis" also hit the charts.

The End of the First Era

But the end of the fifties was a dark time generally for rock and roll. Elvis was in the army; Little Richard walked away from rock and roll; and Buddy Holly was killed in a plane crash. Scandal plagued some of the stars (notably Jerry Lee Lewis, who had married his very young third cousin, and Chuck Berry, who was arrested for taking a minor across state lines). And the **payola** investigation, which revealed that disc jockeys had routinely been accepting money and gifts for playing (plugging) certain records, tarnished even Dick Clark. Rock and roll lost its hard edge and energy, and pop became more bland than ever.

Even the turbulent sixties got off to a slow start.

SURFING MUSIC

The early 1960s experienced unprecedented social unrest and violence. True, the civil rights movement made dramatic breakthroughs, but often at tragic cost. President Kennedy spoke of a new frontier and challenged young people to make sacrifices in order to realize high ideals. But in sunny Southern

California, Kennedy's challenge seemed remote and unreal. There, warm, relaxed, materialistic youth considered that the ideal existence consisted of sun and fun, girls and cars, and the beach. **Surfing songs** about the easy California life provided vicarious pleasure to young whites in other parts of the country as well.

The Beach Boys

The **Beach Boys** were formed by Brian Wilson in the early sixties and included two of his brothers, a cousin, and a friend. Wilson, who led the group and wrote some of the songs, had a pleasant falsetto voice, and the Beach Boys sang their simple songs with smooth and soothing harmony.

As the decade evolved, so did the Beach Boys, who changed both their leader and their image after 1966. They grew long hair and beards, added sophisticated electronic effects, and included protest songs in their repertoire. But the lasting fame and influence of the Beach Boys rest upon their days of singing about sun, sand, and surf.

REBELLION

Surfing music had little significance for young blacks, whose challenges were of a different kind. They were angered to see white performers making huge sums of money from covers of black hits and from bland surfing songs. In 1959, a young black songwriter named **Berry Gordy, Jr.,** formed a company called Motown for the purpose of marketing black rock and roll as aggressively and lucratively as the products of white musicians.

Motown

Motown was established in the "motor town," Detroit, which became to rock and roll what Nashville was to country. The records produced by Motown were technically perfect, efficiently marketed, and of broad crossover appeal.

Gordy custom-designed his singers. He had them take classes in diction, grooming, stage presence, and choreography, and he carefully supervised their repertoire. Under his guidance, they turned out hit records as efficiently as assembly lines turned out cars.

The Motown sound was lighter, smoother, and less sexy than other rock and roll. There was usually a lead singer and a background vocal **doo-wop** group, who enriched the sonority by singing nonsense syllables. Early Motown records used very simple instrumentation, but strings and other orchestral instruments accompanied later performances. "Only You" and "My Prayer," the doo-wop recorded by **The Platters,** are well-known examples of the early style. The outstanding Motown group was **The Supremes** (fig. 26.3) with their lead singer **Diana Ross. Stevie Wonder** also recorded for Motown, though he became the first member of that group to achieve artistic independence and gain control over his own recordings.

Although Motown made a lot of money for black singers, the music they produced was actually more popular with white than with black listeners. By the mid-sixties, black musicians were effectively asserting themselves with their own new music, "soul." But first, an invasion from abroad revitalized the fading American rock and roll.

Figure 26.3

The Supremes. (The Bettmann Archive, Inc.)

The baby boom that followed the war years produced a generation of underemployed, undereducated, and often underfed English teenagers, some of whom vented their frustrations in various antisocial ways. Many joined one of two rival gangs, the Rockers or the Mods, which provided a sense of identity and belonging but also fostered rough, delinquent behavior.

Many young gang members were avid fans of rhythm and blues and rock and roll, because popular American recordings were well known in England by the late 1950s, and several successful concert tours had taken place there. But the young English fans were disturbed at the commercialization that was diluting their favorite music and threatening to render rock and roll obsolete. In fact, it was the unlikely combination of four English Rockers who effectively revitalized the fading American style.

The remarkable group that became known as the **Beatles** (fig. 26.4) began as a Liverpool gang more interested in getting into trouble than changing the course of rock and roll. **John Lennon** formed the group, which included **Paul McCartney** and soon **George Harrison.** It is not surprising that music was among the more innocent activities of three such talented, though largely untrained, musicians. However, it is astonishing that—having replaced their early drummer with the already popular **Ringo Starr** in 1962—

THE BRITISH INVASION

The Beatles

Figure 26.4

The Beatles in 1963. Pictured left to right: bass guitarist Paul McCartney, guitarist George Harrison, guitarist John Lennon, and drummer Ringo Starr. (AP/Wide World Photos.)

they attracted a producer, quickly became famous in England, and very soon were rocking the world with their own brand of rock and roll.

The Beatles' early songs were pleasantly simple and naive, and their performance style was rather primitive. Lennon was more inclined to shout than sing. McCartney had a beautiful voice, and Harrison played the guitar extremely well, but Ringo Starr was the only one of the group who was well known. Then, in 1962, the Beatles shared a London performance with Little Richard (who had recently returned to rock and roll) and became an overnight sensation. By 1963, their records were hugely popular in America as well.

Impressed with their growing fame, television host Ed Sullivan invited the Beatles to perform on his popular television show in 1964, little anticipating the riot of enthusiasm their arrival in America would cause. Their lighthearted, good-natured songs with catchy melodies and fairly innocent lyrics ("I Want to Hold Your Hand") lifted the spirits of American youth and inaugurated Beatlemania. Their clothes, hair styles, and foreign accents made a terrific impression on American teens, who screamed and swooned with adulation.

The Beatles' first film, *A Hard Day's Night,* was also made during 1964. It included several hit songs, but the album compiled from the film is loosely structured with no unifying theme. Later Beatles albums (especially "Sgt. Pepper's Lonely Hearts Club Band" and "Abbey Road") were sophisticated productions conceived not just as a series of hit singles but as tightly integrated productions.

Highly successful and well-to-do by 1966, the Beatles stopped touring, preferring to record in studios using the new technological facilities they could by then well afford. They also made several more films. Lennon, McCartney, and Harrison all composed for the group, but Lennon's poetry was especially effective. His later verses, symbolic and complex, address subjects of universal interest and are often laden with idealistic messages.

The band's instrumental music had more significance in later days as well. Their playing had improved, and their albums began to include more instrumental passages. Eclectic in their interests, they proved to be incredibly versatile musicians. Toward the end of the sixties, the Beatles' compositions and performances reflected the influences of Harrison's travels in India. The group also learned to take advantage of the most sophisticated studio facilities and to use advanced electronic techniques.

At the end of just a decade, the Beatles separated, each wishing to satisfy his own creative needs. John Lennon remained largely secluded from that time, working with his wife Yoko Ono on various artistic projects until his tragic death in 1980. Today the three surviving Beatles continue to generate innovative musical ideas and occasionally collaborate on new projects. Paul McCartney formed a successful group of his own, Wings, which has periodically disbanded and re-formed. He now lives quietly at his home in England, where he has recently completed a new record album in his private studio. The other two Beatles have remained less active musically. However, George Harrison has made several record albums and worked on films with members of the British comedy team Monty Python, while Ringo Starr continues to perform as a singer, actor, and drummer. He toured the United States during the summer of 1992, having just released "Time Takes Time," his first studio recording since 1983.

POST-BEATLES ENGLISH ROCK

Elton John (born Reginald Kenneth Dwight) became a popular rock pianist and singer in both England and America in the early 1960s. His music is distinctive in that it reflects country-western styles. Elton John attracted as much attention with his appearance as with his songs, wearing outlandish clothes and spectacular spectacles—but these techniques could not detract from his talent, which was genuine. (In 1988, no longer needing such gimmicks, he sold some of his adornments very profitably at auction.)

The Who evolved later in the sixties, an unlikely combination of talented but disparate individuals, each of whom performed in a style unlike the others. Yet somehow their brand of chaos worked, and they became quite popular in the United States. Their rock opera *Tommy,* written in 1969, was made into a successful film in 1975.

The Rolling Stones were another hugely influential English group. However, although they began to perform in the early sixties, their style and influence belong to the next decade, and we will discuss them in chapter 27.

While English groups and soloists were having an impact upon rock around the world, American blacks were seeking to regain the initiative they had temporarily lost.

BACK TO
BLACK ROCK

Relationships between black and white rock and roll have been curious and complex. With roots in both cultures, rock was primarily a black concept; yet white country singers who *sounded* black made the style popular, and the Beatles gave it the shot of energy that rescued it from early death.

By the mid-sixties, "black power" and "black is beautiful" were potent slogans in the United States. Blacks were generally less interested in integrating with whites than in establishing their own cultural identity, and they resented the basically white flavor of the Motown sound. Some black musicians began to perform a kind of updated rhythm and blues, which they named *soul,* after the fifties term for black pride.

Soul

At first, **soul** was a new blues, sung by small vocal groups with harsh voices and a rough delivery style. The small accompanying combos usually included a saxophone. The new black music had an added intensity of conviction, passion, and sincerity that remained inherent even when the term soul was applied to a broader stream of music.

Aretha Franklin (fig. 26.5), known as "Lady Soul," began her music experience in church. The sound of soul is rooted, in fact, in gospel as well as blues. Like many soul singers, Franklin transferred the emotional gospel style to popular and rhythm and blues songs.

The African roots of soul are apparent in the harsh, intensely emotional singing of another great soul singer, **James Brown** ("Mr. Dynamite"). But the acknowledged genius or "father" of soul is **Ray Charles.**

Ray Charles
(b. 1930)

Blind from the age of seven, Ray Charles received excellent music training in his teens. He became a fine pianist and singer and also learned to play the saxophone. Charles was among the first blacks to become technically expert with studio recording technology, thereby enhancing the quality of recordings by himself and other blacks. He also has a great gift for involving an audience in his performances, effectively using call-and-response to capture their attention and participation.

Charles is, in fact, a knowledgeable and complex musician. He blends the improvisation of jazz, the beat of rhythm and blues, and the emotional fervor of gospel, delivering all in his infectious, inimitable style.

FROM "ROCK
AND ROLL" TO
"ROCK"

Ominous social events of the mid- to late sixties again changed the mood and the music of youth. There were riots in the ghettos of Harlem and Watts in 1965, further race riots in 1967, and the murder of Martin Luther King in 1968. Students held sit-ins at colleges across the land, protesting discrimination, authoritarianism, and eventually the war in Viet Nam.

Of course, popular music reflected the new mood. The carefree days of early rock and roll were gone, and the vivid new music was collectively called **rock.** Some urban folk singers reflected this new mood by blending light rock effects with their tuneful melodies and protest lyrics to produce **folk rock.**

Figure 26.5
Aretha Franklin. (© UPI/
Bettmann Newsphotos.)

The urban folk singers who included protest songs in their college and night club performances were addressing rock audiences as well by 1965. The mood of protest had strengthened, and rock crowds wanted more than entertainment. Groups like Peter, Paul and Mary, unable or unwilling to update their lyrics and their style, became less relevant and, of course, less popular.

Folk Rock

Joan Baez (fig. 26.6; see page 266) was among the singers who intensified the emotional content of their songs and addressed topics of current controversy and concern. Drawing upon the examples of Woody Guthrie and Pete Seeger, other folk musicians also began adding elements of rock to their performances, thereby reaching a wider audience.

Bob Dylan switched to folk rock in 1965, using an electric guitar and a rock rhythm section in place of the acoustic instruments of his early days. (He remains a fine poet, and his powerful messages of protest and reform are very moving. Some think, in fact, that Dylan's poems are destined to survive his music.) Soon, however, Dylan began to sing of personal rather than social or universal problems. His switch to folk rock had already confused some fans, and his new approach antagonized others.

Several groups joined the folk rock movement. **The Mamas and the Papas** simply added a light rock flavor to their familiar style of folk music. **Crosby, Stills, Nash and Young** also updated their sound by adding light rock effects. **Simon and Garfunkel** and **The Fifth Dimension** performed in folk rock style as well.

Figure 26.6

Joan Baez performing at Big Sur. (Bettmann Newsphotos.)

The Byrds were even more strongly affected by Bob Dylan's new approach, and they became the group most closely allied to the folk rock style. Their recorded versions of Dylan's "Mr. Tambourine Man" and Pete Seeger's "Turn! Turn! Turn!" made a very strong impact. Among their distinctive techniques were the amplification and distortion of instrument sounds for expressive effect.

Acid Rock

Figure 26.7

Janis Joplin. Acid rock was a means of expressing frustration with the values of an older generation. (Wide World Photos.)

"Psychedelic" or **acid rock** began in San Francisco about 1965 as an attempt to reproduce the sensations experienced by someone under the influence of LSD (called "acid" in street slang). The music was to be *felt,* rather than just heard, so the sound was amplified to unprecedented levels. Music pieces were often extremely long, for time is meaningless to someone in a psychedelic haze.

During performances, dramatic light shows, smoke and fog machines, and other special effects produced a kind of psychedelic experience in themselves. In fact, a rock concert had become a theater experience in which music was only one of the entertainment elements, and the audience was expected to be totally involved. **Jimi Hendrix** set fire to his guitars on stage. **Janis Joplin** (fig. 26.7) sang passionately of her sad and hopeless life, and the audience felt her pain.

References to drugs were sometimes expressed in code to avoid censorship, but they became more and more overt in time. "White Rabbit," performed by **Jefferson Airplane,** never pretended to be about anything else. Some acid rock groups, such as **The Doors,** sang of sex and death and self-destruction. **The Grateful Dead,** although associated with the same movement, were milder—or at least less violent—in style. The members of that group lived for a time in the Haight-Ashbury district of San Francisco, actively sharing the hippie experience that they related in their music.

Toward the end of its second decade, rock was celebrated at major rock festivals across the country. The most notable took place at Woodstock, New York, in August of 1969, and was attended by more than 400,000 people. Some of the festivals spawned violence and tragedy: Four people died at Altamount Speedway near San Francisco, and three were killed at the "Celebration of Life" on the banks of Louisiana's Atchafalaya River. Although rock music had grown strong and varied, its future was insecure as the 1970s approached.

SUMMARY

In the 1950s, the popular music industry responded to the desires and the dollars of American teens, as elements of black rhythm and blues and white country-western music combined to produce rock and roll. Bill Haley and Elvis Presley, white singers with a black delivery style, made the new music widely popular, and soon cover records of rhythm and blues hits were making significant money. In rebellion against this trend, Motown produced records that were popular with whites but earned money for black performers, and soul brought music of a new intensity and sincerity to rock and roll.

In the sixties, the Beatles reacted against the overcommercialization of rock and roll, revitalizing the music with their energy and style. Urban folk singers used light rock effects in protest songs on topics of current social interest. Acid rock sought to evoke as well as describe a psychedelic experience.

TERMS TO REVIEW

backbeat A heavy accent on the normally weak second and fourth beats of a measure.

rhythm and blues (R & B) Broadly, black popular music of the 1950s. More specifically, a black popular style in quadruple meter, with strong backbeats and a danceable tempo.

rock and roll A popular music of the mid-fifties to mid-sixties that combined characteristics of rhythm and blues and country-western music.

vibrato A slight variation in pitch that adds warmth and intensity to vocal or instrumental sounds.

payola The acceptance by disc jockeys of money and gifts in return for plugging recordings.

surfing songs Songs by the Beach Boys and other groups reflecting the easy California life-style.

Motown A highly successful black company that recorded, published, and sponsored black popular music.

doo-wop The name given background vocal ensembles that accompanied Motown singers, often by singing neutral or nonsense syllables.

soul A fervent, emotional black style, rooted in gospel and the blues.

rock A collective term encompassing many styles of popular music that evolved from and succeeded rock and roll.

folk rock The addition of light rock effects to urban folk music.

acid rock Sometimes called "psychedelic rock." Music that attempts to evoke the sensations experienced by a person under the influence of LSD.

KEY FIGURES

Black Singers with a White Style
Mills Brothers
Ink Spots
Lena Horne
Nat "King" Cole
Ella Fitzgerald

Disc Jockey
Alan Freed

**Host of American Bandstand
Television Program**
Dick Clark

Teen Idols
Paul Anka
Bobby Darin
Fabian
Frankie Avalon

Rhythm and Blues Singers
Joe Turner
Willie Mae "Big Mama" Thornton

Early Rock and Roll Stars
Bill Haley and the Comets
Elvis Presley

Black Rock and Roll Stars
Bo Diddley
Little Richard
Chuck Berry

Surfing Music Group
Beach Boys

Motown
Berry Gordy, Jr.
The Platters
The Supremes
Diana Ross
Stevie Wonder

Early British Rock Stars
The Beatles
John Lennon
Paul McCartney
George Harrison
Ringo Starr
Elton John
The Who

Soul
Aretha Franklin
James Brown
Ray Charles

Folk Rock
Joan Baez
Bob Dylan
The Mamas and the Papas
Crosby, Stills, Nash and Young
Simon and Garfunkel
The Fifth Dimension
The Byrds

Acid Rock
Jimi Hendrix
Janis Joplin
Jefferson Airplane
The Doors
The Grateful Dead

SUGGESTIONS FOR FURTHER LISTENING

Atlantic Rhythm and Blues, vols. 1–7

Bill Haley: *Golden Hits*
    Greatest Hits

Elvis Presley: *Golden*, vols. 1–4

Chuck Berry: *Greatest Hits*

Beach Boys: *Best—Beach Boys*

Beatles: *Abbey Road*
    Early Beatles
    Yellow Submarine

Elton John: *Live*–Collection

The Who: *Magic Bus/My Generation*
    Tommy

Bob Dylan: *Times They Are a-Changin'*

Ray Charles: *Rock Begins*, vol. 1

THE MANY MOODS
OF ROCK

Chapter 27

The year 1970 had devastating social and political significance in the United States. At Kent State University, students protesting America's war policy were shot at by National Guard troops, who killed four and wounded ten others, whereupon student riots broke out on campuses throughout the country. Militant protesters marched and were arrested—yet finally, they succumbed to a sense of demoralization and helplessness.

Rockers were deeply affected by the mood of the time, which darkened further with the deaths of several prominent rock figures. In 1970, Jim Morrison of The Doors died of a heart attack, Jimi Hendrix from an overdose of sleeping pills, and Janis Joplin from an overdose of heroin.

Musical innovation temporarily lessened as rockers absorbed these shocks and looked ahead. By that time, almost any kind of popular music was loosely called "rock." Solo singers, many of whom wrote their own songs, acquired new significance, and as the sound engineer became an essential partner in performance, some groups abandoned live performances entirely. Synthesizers and other electronic instruments increasingly varied the sonorities of live and recorded performances, and concerts and recordings achieved new levels of sophistication.

The music of a British group, contemporary with but entirely different from the Beatles, helped bridge the gap from the past to the future of rock.

THE ROLLING STONES

We have seen that the Beatles belonged, in actual time and in style, to the sixties. A rival British group, the **Rolling Stones** (fig. 27.1), also began performing in the early sixties, but their style was always closer to the acid rock and punk of the seventies; and unlike the Beatles, the Rolling Stones have remained active to the present day.

From the beginning, the Stones differed from the Beatles in nearly every respect. They were led by **Mick Jagger,** who came from a comfortable middle-class home. Although all of the Stones were white and relatively well off, they identified with the music of poor black Americans and sang in black style. However, their values were highly materialistic, and they soon developed an insatiable lust for wealth.

Figure 27.1

The Rolling Stones in 1964. (Michael Ochs Archives, Ltd.)

Again unlike the Beatles, whose messages were generally hopeful and sometimes pleasantly naive, the Stones sang aggressive songs of revolt and destruction. Their style has evolved over the decades, though always strongly influenced by black music, and they have survived, with occasional changes in personnel, to maintain long-lived, if limited, popularity.

COLLABORATION AND ACCULTURATION

Beginning in the 1970s, rockers began to collaborate in imaginative ways with musicians in other areas of performance and from other cultures, thereby producing several interesting new styles of rock music.

Jazz Rock

Because both jazz and rock are closely related to the blues, it is not surprising that several groups have achieved an imaginative meld of jazz and rock. **Jazz rock,** sometimes called **fusion,** marries the instrumentation of rock with the improvisation, lighter beat, and flexible rhythms of jazz. (Some people distinguish between jazz rock and fusion, claiming that fusion is more jazz-oriented than jazz rock and excludes the use of vocals.)

Beginning in 1969, Miles Davis experimented with jazz-rock combinations. **Blood, Sweat and Tears** is a rock quartet with a brass section, and later a saxophone, that produces a sound closer to jazz than rock, while the even more popular group **Chicago** is composed of rock musicians who include some elements of jazz.

Art Rock

Although rock and classical music are a less likely combination than the vernacular musics rock and jazz, various effects have been tried, some more successful than others. The superficial quoting of themes from familiar classics, as in Ekseption's "The Fifth," based on themes of Beethoven, is musically insignificant, and most arrangements of classical pieces that use rock instrumentation and rhythms are not of much interest.

However, some ensembles—several if not most of them British—have achieved an effective blend of serious concert music and rock, called **art rock. Emerson, Lake and Palmer** related rock to classical music in several pieces. The **Moody Blues** produced an art rock album with the London Festival Orchestra in 1967. **Genesis, King Crimson, Pink Floyd,** and **Yes** are among other English groups who have explored the concept of art rock.

A Dutch group, Focus, and a New York ensemble, Ars Nova, have also experimented with art rock. Leonard Bernstein's *Mass,* written for the opening of the Kennedy Center for the Performing Arts in Washington, D.C. (1971), represents another approach to the combination of art and rock styles. Some individuals in today's rock audience also show interest in the non-Western and experimental techniques that intrigue certain composers of art music, and these will be discussed in the Postlude that follows this chapter.

It should be pointed out that the term art rock is not intended to imply that other rock styles are not artistic. It is simply a convenient way to describe the combination of rock with concepts of "classical," "concert," or "art" music. Each of those terms is flawed as well, and the conscientious musician uses them with qualification.

Reggae

The style of music known as **reggae** fused elements of North American and African-Jamaican music to form a kind of "acculturated rock" that became popular in England in the 1960s and in the United States a decade later. **Bob Marley** (1945–1981) (fig. 27.2) was a Jamaican reggae performer who became very well known in the United States.

There are several styles of reggae, but all are roughly related to rhythm and blues. However, the rhythms of reggae include African polyrhythms far more complex than those of rhythm and blues. Also bass lines are stronger and tempos slower. Reggae combos consist of electric guitars, electric organ, electric bass guitar, and drums. Electronic studio techniques are sometimes of great significance as well.

This exciting music is an excellent example of acculturation, since a vernacular music (rock) has been borrowed and transformed by a culture other than the one that introduced it to form a new style. Reggae is also an example of a popular music that has strong religious connotations, because it is associated with a black religious movement called Rastafarianism. In addition, many of the songs have urgent political content, promoting the "back to Africa" movement that emerged in the sixties.

Jamaican disc jockeys developed a technique of rapid patter-talking over the sound of the records they played. Called "toasting" or "dubbing," this practice had far-reaching effects, contributing to the development of *rap* music in the seventies and eighties.

HEAVY METAL

The music style called **heavy metal** emerged from the explosive sound of such guitar heroes as Jimi Hendrix and from the wild, frenzied performances of several British groups. The sound was extremely loud and often

Figure 27.2

Bob Marley. (Michael Ochs Archives, Ltd.)

electronically distorted. The British group **Led Zeppelin,** the premier heavy metal band, developed a huge and nearly fanatical following in the United States. **AC/DC, Black Sabbath,** and **Deep Purple** were other British groups who were also extremely influential in America in the 1970s.

FUNK AND RAP

Funk began as a new expression of black consciousness, rooted in soul, but often having lyrics that referred specifically to interracial issues. Interestingly, the style was soon copied by white musicians, and in a sense, funk formed a bridge between sympathetic whites and blacks.

Although related to the blues, funk follows no prescribed harmonic pattern; in fact, it typically involves little harmonic change. There is a strong bass-guitar line, with simple, repetitive harmonies filled in by guitars and/or keyboards. Rhythms—often complex polyrhythms—are punctuated by a variety of drums. The meter is quadruple, frequently with all four beats accented evenly—a striking difference from the strong backbeats characteristic of much rock music.

The 1970 recording of "Thank You (Falettinme Be Mice Elf Agin)" by **Sly Stone** introduced the bizarre spellings that were imitated by some later funk musicians. **George Clinton,** leader of the group called **Funkadelic,** is considered a rigorously pure funk musician, but many other groups participate in funk with less consistency and dedication. **Earth, Wind and Fire,** for example, is considered a jazz-funk group. The funk music of **Kool and the Gang** includes their 1970 recording "Funky Stuff" and, from later in the seventies, "Celebration." The **Commodores** are a smooth funk band who have crossover appeal to the disco audience.

Rap began to be popular in New York in the mid-seventies, developing even wider appeal throughout the next decade. The rapid spoken patter accompanied by funk-style rhythms evolved partly from the complex rhythms and the message songs of James Brown in the sixties. But as we have already seen, an even stronger influence was the Jamaican-based reggae.

Disco was a commercial dance music of the 1970s—optimistic, good-time, escape music that served its purpose during that troubled decade. People danced to recorded disco in huge, colorful dance halls, where the entertainment was provided by swirling lights and by the dancers themselves. John Travolta in the 1977 movie *Saturday Night Fever* did much to popularize the style and encourage the dance craze that swept the country. Disco was not a compelling or innovative music of lasting influence, but **Donna Summer, Diana Ross, Chuck Mangione,** and the **Bee Gees** are among the artists who contributed to the celebrated, though short-lived, disco movement.

By the late 1970s, most rock musicians were performing more for the sake of money than for art, blatantly adjusting their styles to meet popular demand. Again it was in Britain that an idealistic reaction arose against the betrayal of the essence of rock, and again the British rescued rock from succumbing under the weight of its own success. In short, they invented **punk.**

Much as conditions in the early sixties had spawned the Beatles, the mid-seventies produced a number of young Britishers who were poor, unemployed, and resentful of social inequities and political hypocrisy. They also resented rich rock stars! It was their contention that society must be overturned in order to make the world a better place, and this was the message of their songs.

The first successful—or, more accurately, notorious—punk group was the **Sex Pistols** (fig. 27.3). Other groups soon sprang up, revolutionizing rock as they wished to revolutionize society itself. The striking visual effects of punk dress, hair, and makeup strongly influenced art and fashion around the world.

In America, punk turned negative, promoting nihilism rather than constructive change. Paradoxically, however, American society effectively put down punk—not with censorship, as might have been expected, but with imitation! As fashion models spiked their hair and fastened gaping holes in their clothes with safety pins, the movement lost its anger and became simply another style of rock among many.

New wave groups, neither angry nor political, further defused punk by emulating its manner but not its substance. The term "new wave" was loosely applied to several sounds of the mid-eighties, some of which reflected certain characteristics of earlier styles. But the term always referred to new or progressive music, conceived with the aid of modern studio and electronic techniques.

Figure 27.3

The Sex Pistols. (Michael Ochs Archives, Ltd.)

Although new wave music contained some of the elements of punk, it was broader in concept, and in fact referred to a way of life as well as a musical style. One outstanding American new wave group is the Talking Heads, much of whose music is based upon the simple harmonies and complex rhythms of Africa. Other well-known new wave bands include the **B-52s,** the **Cars,** and especially, the **Police.**

A MULTIPLICITY OF STYLES

By the mid-1980s, popularity had shifted away from new wave, as many bands and several individuals with distinctive styles became rich and famous. They were variously identified by a string of labels (*new romantics, blitz, punk-jazz, blue wave, techno-pop,* and *techno-funk,* among others). Prince, Michael Jackson, Lionel Richie, Madonna, Cyndi Lauper, and Sting (formerly of the Police) are among the best-known names of recent rock.

"The Boss" **Bruce Springsteen,** probably the most successful rock star of the late seventies, revitalized the rock music of the mid-eighties with his stirring songs on socially relevant topics. He seems, in fact, to have pointed rock in a new direction in his 1982 album *Born in the U.S.A.* The social concerns eloquently expressed there were further implemented by Springsteen and other like-minded rock stars in the rock-sponsored benefits for starving masses in Ethiopa, "We Are the World" and "Live Aid."

A PROMISING FUTURE

As we approach the mid-1990s, many rock musicians have returned to their roots, and rhythm and blues, rockabilly, soul, and psychedelic music can all be heard today. Social consciousness continues to stir rockers' emotions and stimulate their talents. The newest technology produces an array of sophisticated effects, and acculturation becomes ever more significant as improved communication and expanded travel bring fascinating new sounds to the Western vernacular music experience.

SUMMARY

The Rolling Stones, who came from comfortable English backgrounds, sang of the experience of poor black Americans, but their own values were highly materialistic. Later in the 1970s, other British rockers introduced punk in reaction against rich rock stars, though in America, punk turned fashionable.

Rock joined with jazz and art music to produce several new styles, and with Jamaican influences to produce reggae. Although nearly all popular music was called "rock" in the seventies and eighties, there were actually significant differences between the many kinds of rock that evolved. Heavy metal was wild and frenzied; funk's lyrics typically dealt with racial relations; rap reflected the reggae influence; disco was a commercial dance music; and new wave was a broad concept embracing varied sounds. Today's rock acknowledges its roots but is enriched by social consciousness and increased acculturation.

TERMS TO REVIEW

jazz rock or **fusion**   Rock instrumentation blended with the improvisation and flexible rhythms of jazz.

art rock   A blend of rock and symphonic or concert styles.

reggae   A blend of rock and African-Jamaican styles.

heavy metal   Loud, heavily electronic music, often with distorted sound.

funk   Rooted in soul, but with lyrics that express interracial concerns.

rap   Rapid spoken patter accompanied by funk-style rhythms; derived from reggae performance practices.

disco   Commercial dance music popular in the 1970s.

punk   A British reaction to flagrantly commercial rock and roll.

new wave   A term encompassing several styles, all conceived within the context of modern studio and electronic techniques.

KEY FIGURES

Rebellious British Stars
Rolling Stones
Mick Jagger

Jazz Rock
Blood, Sweat and Tears
Chicago

Art Rock
Emerson, Lake and Palmer
Moody Blues
Genesis
King Crimson
Pink Floyd
Yes

Reggae Star
Bob Marley

Heavy Metal
Led Zeppelin
AC/DC
Black Sabbath
Deep Purple

Funk Stars
Sly Stone
George Clinton
Funkadelic
Earth, Wind and Fire
Kool and the Gang
Commodores

Disco
Donna Summer
Diana Ross
Chuck Mangione
Bee Gees

Punk Stars
Sex Pistols

New Wave Stars
B-52s
Cars
Police

Idealistic Rock Star
Bruce Springsteen

SOME NEW SOUNDS
OF MUSIC

Postlude

The meaning of music and the concept of musical sound have changed rapidly and dramatically since 1960. Among the sources of the new sounds is the music of other cultures, including some quite distant from twentieth-century America in terms of time and/or place. These influences have stimulated American composers to explore musical sounds as never before. Composers of concert music have also borrowed ideas and techniques from jazz and other recent vernacular musics. And modern technology, including sophisticated electronic equipment, has provided further important new musical resources.

Thus, today's music comes in all sizes, forms, and styles. Provocative ideas continue to emerge, and new concepts range from the stark simplicity of minimalism to the dizzying complexity of some electronic music. As Milton Babbitt has said, the range of musical experience is limited now only by the limitations of human perception.

RECENT
DEVELOPMENTS
IN AMERICAN
ARTS

The incredible capabilities of modern technology in the nineties have inevitably changed our perceptions of the meaning and the goals of life. Now we literally have the capacity to destroy our own earth. So-called "fixed" laws of science and nature have been replaced by laws of relativity, weakening our sense of stability and expanding the range of our imagination. We have come to expect the unpredictable, for we know that in life things are not always as they seem. Inevitably, then, American music of recent years reflects the trauma, and the wonder, of our changing sensibility.

Of course, new technology has immeasurably enhanced the development of new methods of expression in *all* of the arts. Recently, an unprecedented degree of collaboration between painters, dancers, poets, playwrights, and musicians has produced a wealth of interdisciplinary performances, awakening a healthy appreciation for the arts among audiences whose previous interest and exposure was quite limited.

NEW RELATIONS
BETWEEN
THE ARTS

We have already considered some of the relationships between Abstract Expressionist painters, composers of chance music, and free jazz musicians, and these ideas may be expanded upon here. For example, Abstract Expressionists play with colors as Milton Babbitt plays with sounds, and in their "action paintings," Abstract Expressionists explore the mind and express raw emotions much as **Expressionist** composers do in their music.

Pop artists reacted against the romantic individualism and perceived lack of discipline of the Abstract Expressionists by painting clearly recognizable subjects drawn from modern city life. In the machines, advertisements, and various familiar objects painted by **Andy Warhol** and **Jim Dine,** we see the simplicity and repetition characteristic of musical *minimalism* (see pages 295–96) and other music of the seventies and eighties. **Op art,** like chance music, involves active rather than passive participation, for lines and colors are combined to create optical illusions that "activate" the eye instead of "acting upon it" as traditional art does.

Some painters add a third dimension to their work by affixing pieces of fabric or other foreign objects to their surfaces. Others build up their surfaces by applying thick layers of paint. Sculptors, too, avail themselves of nontraditional materials—wood or plastic, for example, instead of marble or bronze. Similarly, composers vary the texture of their works by superimposing unrelated timbres or chords, or by combining complex layers of sound. Much as pointillist painters treated spots of pure color as entities, composers sometimes treat pitches or timbres as isolated phenomena with independent, as opposed to interdependent, values.

The new collaborative spirit has led some painters and sculptors to combine shapes, colors, and even sounds in large "environmental" works. Composers, too, have conceived multimedia compositions in which two or more of the senses are simultaneously addressed and spectators may participate in an active manner.

Dance

Dance has now been liberated from the expectation that it will tell a story. Movements and gestures, previously stylized, are limited only by the imagination and creativity of a choreographer. Jazz rhythms and electronically produced sounds also dramatically widen the range of dance experience. Some choreographers have designed dances that are entirely independent of music or sound, but most still consider music an inherent and vital dimension of dance.

Literature

Throughout the twentieth century, some writers have chosen words for their sounds rather than their meanings. Neither Gertrude Stein's libretto for Virgil Thomson's *Four Saints in Three Acts* (see page 187) nor the stream-of-consciousness prose of William Faulkner makes any attempt to follow the rules of grammar or syntax. Poetry may have visual as well as intellectual values, and **shaped poems** are placed on the page for visual effect that may enhance the literary meaning. Each of these literary concepts is related to a painter's subjective choice of colors and a composer's choice of pitches for their timbre rather than for their functional value. Chance, too, is represented in literature, for novels may be written today in *hypertext,* a computer technique that allows readers to follow subplots at will, as through a maze, rendering a book's form and conclusion indeterminate.

Contemporary American modern dance. (The Bettmann Archive.)

Thus, artists in every medium share an expanded perception of their own discipline and an interest in the interrelationships and interaction between the arts.

THE QUALITIES OF TODAY'S MUSICAL SOUNDS

Timbre has replaced *melody* as the element of primary interest for many contemporary composers, as it did for experimentalists half a century ago. Therefore, sounds that were previously considered noise are often accepted today as appropriate material for the composition of music. Besides, of course, unlimited *new* sounds can now be created through electronic techniques.

Many composers use musical instruments, including the voice, to produce sounds that do not conform to the traditional concept of "beauty." For example, in *Voice of the Whale* (scored for three masked musicians playing flute, violoncello, and piano), **George Crumb** (b. 1929) requires the flute player to hum while playing the instrument, achieving a sound eerily like that of the humpback whale. Players may be directed to produce breathy, squeaky, or raucous sounds, sometimes—but not always—for programmatic effect. Microphones are placed inside music instruments to amplify the sound, to alter or distort the timbre, or to produce echo effects. Several composers have found that the resonant timbres of mallet instruments, such as the **marimba, xylophone,** or **glockenspiel,** offer attractive alternatives to traditional orchestral or other Western sounds. The precise rhythmic effects expert players can achieve on mallet instruments further enhance their appeal for many composers today.

Philip Glass. (© UPI/ Bettmann Newsphotos.)

Pauline Oliveros began composing music in a traditional manner, but soon became fascinated with the qualities of *all* sounds, including those of nature and machinery. Her heightened sensitivity to timbre has led her to explore and experiment extensively with vocal and instrumental colors, often with stunning effect.

    Oliveros's *Sound Patterns* is a choral work that has no text. The voices produce abstract sounds, unrelated to traditional concepts of melody and harmony—much as abstract paintings are unrelated to the shapes and colors of representational art. Oliveros also uses tape and other electronic techniques to create distinctive pieces of sound imagery.

Pauline Oliveros (b. 1932)

Philip Glass, whose opera *Satyagraha* was referred to on page 191, is among those composers who are more interested in the *sound* than the *form* of a piece. Because performers of his music are often required to have creative as well as interpretive skills, he formed his own Philip Glass Ensemble, consisting of players who are able and willing to perform in this new and challenging way. Some of his music is specifically conceived for their interpretation.

    The Ensemble, which Glass himself directs, consists of two electric organs, four woodwind players who double on several amplified wind instruments, and a female singer who uses her voice as another, wordless "instrument." Glass often leaves the choice of instrumentation of a piece to the Ensemble members, so that the sound of a particular composition is actually determined at the time of each performance and may differ considerably from one concert to the next.

The Philip Glass Ensemble

EXPANDED RHYTHM CONCEPTS

Rhythm systems and practices derived from other cultures have greatly affected the recent music of Western composers. For example, Pauline Oliveros avoids the meter and pulse characteristic of Western music in favor of rhythms that shift, expand, and contract more or less systematically.

Having studied traditional composition techniques with Nadia Boulanger and Darius Milhaud, Philip Glass was subsequently impressed by the incredibly sophisticated rhythms of Africa and India. He studied with **Ravi Shankar,** a famous Indian musician who plays the string instrument called a **sitar,** and who interpreted various complex and subtle Indian rhythmic techniques for Glass.

From Indian practice, Glass derived a rhythmic system that he has applied to some of his own music, called *minimalist* in style. Unlike the Western metric system, which *divides* measured units (see table P1.1), Glass's system is an *additive* procedure. He starts with a simple rhythmic pattern, repeats it for some time, and then alters it very gradually by systematically adding or removing units. Minimalism (a term that, like many others in music, is borrowed from painting) will be considered in more detail on page 295.

Steve Reich (b. 1936)

Steve Reich (pronounced "Rike") has also been associated with minimalist music, but although his music often moves very slowly, it usually has a discernible pulse or beat.

Reich studied African drumming techniques, and he has achieved exotic rhythmic effects in his compositions, including some for mallet instruments (*Six Marimbas,* for example). He has also been strongly influenced by the gamelan and other non-Western percussion instruments, such as the Latin American **claves.** Both Glass and Reich are interested in the rhythms and procedures of progressive jazz as well.

Another new approach to rhythm, called **metric modulation,** was devised by **Elliott Carter** (b. 1908).

Metric Modulation

Just as a musical piece may modulate from one key to another (see page 152), Carter "modulates" to new metric patterns by slowly and methodically altering the value of a basic note. For example, by changing the value of the quarter note from 60 to 80 beats per minute, Carter of course increases the tempo of his music; but he may also use the new quarter note as the base value of a new meter. The concept of metric modulation is intellectual and the realization complex, but Carter's music is clear and quite accessible to the interested and prepared listener.

Carter's *String Quartet No. 2* illustrates his rhythmic techniques. The work has the traditional four movements, which are linked by solo cadenzas—one for the cello, one for the viola, and one for the first violin. There is also an Introduction and Conclusion to the piece. Each instrument is treated in a far more individualistic manner than in traditional string quartets, and Carter has suggested that they be placed at some distance from each other on the stage to enhance their independence. Metric modulation and other complex rhythmic techniques render the piece challenging to the performers, but the work, which won the 1960 Pulitzer prize in music, is not forbidding from the listener's point of view. (Elliott Carter's Double Concerto for Harpsichord and Piano with Two Chamber Ensembles is an Optional Listening Example.)

It is not often true that a contemporary piece has "no melody"—no meaningful succession of tones that form a musical line. However, modern melodies are often more angular in contour than were the songlike melodies of the nineteenth century. A few composers continue to base their melodies upon twelve-tone and serial techniques. Some composers write melodic contours, or "gestures," within a given range but without precise pitch notation. Others who specify pitches choose them from a continuum ranging between extremely high and low tones.

    On the other hand, familiar tunes are sometimes quoted in a new piece, often for programmatic purposes, and some composers retain a preference for a lyrical style. (The exciting thing about American music today is its diversity, and the danger to avoid in discussing it is overgeneralization.)

NEW KINDS OF MELODY

Some contemporary composers have adapted the symphony, concerto, and other traditional forms to suit their modern needs. For example, Elliott Carter has written string quartets, a piano sonata, and several ballets and choral works with a distinctive twentieth-century sound.

    However, many composers view traditional forms, such as ABA or sonata allegro, as formulas too tied to earlier concepts of symmetry and tonal relationships to be stimulating today. Some actually invent a form for each new composition, believing that the form should be determined by characteristics of the piece itself.

    Modern concepts of form are generally based upon principles of repetition with variation, rather than the complex development of motivic ideas characteristic of music in the classic style. The minimalist works of Steve Reich, Philip Glass, and other composers have attracted attention to a new concept of musical form.

FORM

The new interest in sonority led Glass, Reich, John Adams, and other composers to linger for such long periods on interesting sounds that all sense of pulse became obscured. Thus, **minimalism** began as a kind of "dream music," with simple sonorities that changed very slowly over a drone. Changes in melody, harmony, and rhythm were also minimal, and the structure simply evolved as the music continued.

    Some listeners find minimalist music monotonous; yet it has attracted many enthusiasts, who find the music soothing, easy to follow, and stimulating in a new way. It addresses an increased interest in various non-Western concepts and techniques, including meditation and an unhurried, more relaxed, less organized approach to life. It is a controlled, but not an

Minimalism

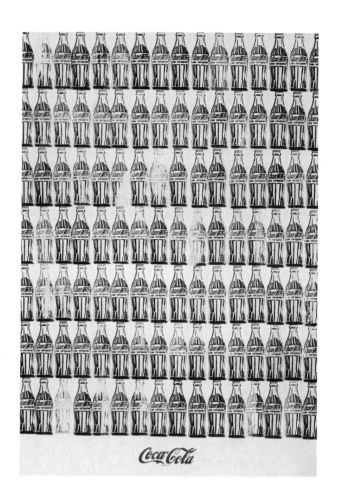

Andy Warhol, *Green Coca-Cola Bottles,* 1962. The repetitiveness of Warhol's painting is related to the concept of minimalist music. Oil on canvas, 82½ × 57 in. (209.6 × 144.8 cm). (Collection of Whitney Museum of American Art. Purchase, with funds from the Friends of the Whitney Museum of American Art, 68.25.)

intellectual, music style, and its simple and naive effect has been compared with that of popular music.

Glass, who says he was inspired by the work of certain sculptors who stripped their works of all superfluous lines to produce figures of extreme simplicity, varies the sound in his minimalist works by occasional abrupt shifts of timbre or harmony. Reich prefers a gradual and systematic change, which allows him, as he says, to "hear the process happening." Reich considers music, in fact, a continuing "process," whose evolution is of interest in itself.

Process Music

Reich has worked with loops of tape, playing them over and over so that their sounds formed repeated cycles. By playing two or more tape loops simultaneously at slightly different speeds, he created a form based upon the gradual unfolding of a simple idea that he refers to as **process music.**

Reich has also created process music for live performance. As instrumentalists repeat simple ostinatos, some move gradually ahead of others, producing the same "out of sync" effect that may be achieved with tape loops.

Chance, aleatory, or indeterminacy (three ways of saying the same thing) continue to be significant in new music. Many composers who desire a degree of indeterminacy in their music have recently devised ingenious techniques for indicating the parameters within which performers are to interpret their compositions.

Indeterminacy

Lukas Foss (b. 1922), who began composing lyrical melodies in neoclassical forms, became interested in chance music and has developed a kind of compromise between old and new sounds. His Improvisation Chamber Ensemble, established at the University of California in Los Angeles in 1957, improvised freely within limits he defined in his own unconventional notation. Foss finally disbanded the group, feeling that their improvisations had become too predictable. In spite of his aleatoric inclinations, however, Foss controls the form of his works, and his German Romantic heritage is apparent in the lyricism of his melodic lines.

Baroque Variations by Foss (1967) reveals his mixed appreciation for old and new, order and chance. It is a kind of surrealistic montage of references to music by composers from the Baroque era (Domenico Scarlatti, Handel, and Bach). Yet the performers are required to improvise, and the music has a very contemporary sound.

Because music for tape requires visual or dramatic interest for effective performance, some recent compositions involve a combination of live and taped music. **Theater scores** are even more elaborate conceptions, requiring musicians to act as well as play instruments and sing. John Cage's indeterminate *Theatre Piece* of 1960 is an example of a composition that includes visual and environmental, as well as musical, elements. The performers in George Crumb's *Voice of the Whale* (see page 292) wear masks to obscure their identity, and the stage is bathed in the deep blue light of the sea. Some performances today are "happenings" that combine live and/or taped music with film, slides, speech, lighting, and dance, gestures, or movement of some kind. In some cases the audience is invited to participate.

THEATER
SCORES

Theater scores are among the many kinds of contemporary music that often require new methods of notation. Composers have also invented symbols in order to indicate new techniques of playing on traditional instruments. Composers may indicate only the start and finish of very rapid passages in which the sounds occur too fast to be distinguished clearly. When pitch is of minimal importance, composers may indicate clusters of a particular *number* of tones, but leave the selection of actual *pitches* to the players.

NOTATION

Nontraditional notation by
John Cage.

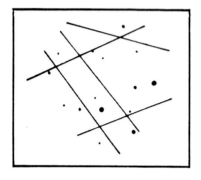

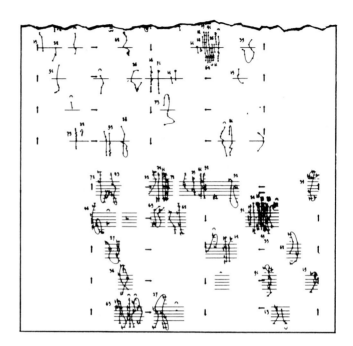

Sometimes graphs serve modern needs better than does traditional notation. For example, the parameters within which pitches, rhythms, durations, and metric patterns are to be determined may be effectively indicated in graphic style. Extremely complex divisions of beats are also sometimes indicated in graphic notation. Very long durations are better expressed in seconds of time than in quarter, half, and whole notes. Sometimes, in fact, composers simply indicate durations in terms of their proportional relationships—for example, one sound is to be twice as long as another.

THE NEW VIRTUOSITY

We have seen that new music places extensive and complex demands on the performer, often requiring extreme flexibility and virtuosic technique. Frequently performers have to study extensive explanatory notes at the beginning of a composition in order to realize the composer's intentions. Singers may be asked to shout, whisper, or sigh; to produce a pure, straight sound or one with slight or extreme vibrato; to sing quarter tones; to read new kinds of notation; to sing in extremely high or low ranges; to "pull pitches out of the air"; and to control a very wide range of dynamic levels. Extreme pitch and dynamic ranges of other instruments are exploited as well, and players may be required to strike or slap their instruments, blow into them, speak or whisper while playing, or make performance decisions within the parameters outlined by the composer. Players of brass instruments are sometimes required to master new mouthpiece techniques.

Although the number of performers able to meet these demands is increasing rapidly, it remains difficult to achieve a good performance of avant-garde compositions. For this reason, as we have seen, some composers have formed their own ensembles, and others have relied upon tape techniques to reproduce their intentions accurately. Listeners must be wary of judging the quality of a composition without considering the quality of its performance.

THE CHARGE

In order to understand and enjoy the art of our time, we must abandon preconceived notions and approach the new with a spirit of curiosity and happy expectation. Of course it is *safe* to listen to a work that has long been acknowledged as a masterpiece, but it is *exhilarating* to hear the first performance of a potential masterpiece of our own day.

To condemn a piece for having "no melody" may be comparable to condemning a doughnut for having no center, a piece by Mozart for having no electronic synthesizer, or an African dance for not being orchestrated. Inappropriate expectations lead to disappointment, of course, but the adventurous, prepared, receptive, creative listener of today has an unprecedented wealth of listening experiences in store. Enjoy!

SUMMARY

The meaning and concepts of music and art have changed more significantly in the last thirty-five years than during the previous three centuries. The visual arts, dance, literature, and music have shared in this dramatic change and have collaborated to produce many kinds of multimedia performances.

The music of foreign cultures and the availability of electronic techniques have broadened the concept of musical sound. Composers use voices and instruments in unusual ways, and have devised new methods of notation to express their requirements. Rhythm has been affected by non-Western techniques. Melody is apt to be angular in contour and is often less noticeable than the timbres and rhythms of a piece. Forms are sometimes invented for specific works.

Not all performers are able to interpret complex new styles effectively, and listeners must be aware of the quality of the performance before judging the quality of a new work.

TERMS TO REVIEW

Expressionism   A style of art that explores the mind and expresses raw emotion.

pop art   A style of painting that uses familiar, often commercial, subjects from everyday urban life.

op art   Combines lines and colors to create optical illusions.

shaped poem   A poem whose pattern formed on the page ties in with the theme of the poem.

marimba   A series of wooden bars suspended over resonators and played with rubber or felt-headed mallets.

xylophone   A series of wooden bars struck with a wooden mallet.

glockenspiel   A series of steel bars struck with a mallet.

sitar   A string instrument from India.

claves   A pair of wooden cylinders, one of which is struck against the other.

metric modulation   Elliott Carter's term for the evolution of one metrical pattern to another through the systematic lengthening or shortening of basic units.

minimalism A style of music based upon many repetitions of simple melodic and rhythmic patterns.

process music Steve Reich's term for music whose form can be heard to evolve from the repetition of patterns slightly out of synchronization with each other.

theater scores Concert pieces that include visual and dramatic elements as well as music.

KEY FIGURES

Pop Artists
Andy Warhol
Jim Dine

Contemporary American Composers
George Crumb
Pauline Oliveros
Philip Glass
Steve Reich
Elliott Carter
Lukas Foss

Musician from India
Ravi Shankar

OPTIONAL LISTENING EXAMPLES*

Elliott Carter: Double Concerto for Harpsichord and Piano with Two Chamber Ensembles

George Crumb: "El niño busca su vos" ("The little boy was looking for his voice") from *Ancient Voices of Children*

Steve Reich: *Drumming*

SUGGESTIONS FOR FURTHER LISTENING

Philip Glass: *Music in Fifths*
Music with Changing Parts

Pauline Oliveros: *Sound Patterns*

George Crumb: *Voice of the Whale*
Ancient Voices of Children

Elliott Carter: String Quartet no. 2
Holiday Overture

Lukas Foss: *Baroque Variations*
Time Cycle

*Guides for Optional Listening Examples are in the Instructor's Manual and may be copied and distributed to students.

CODETTA

You are now well prepared to enjoy a concert of American music. You know about the music of the Yankee pioneers, intended for utilitarian purposes but still delighting listeners today. You have seen how the songs of the singing school masters provided melodic material for some modern concert pieces. You have learned about our vernacular musics—from Stephen Foster's songs and Sousa's marches through ragtime, jazz, rock, and musical comedies. You have followed the development of American concert music and have seen how we became leaders in the field of experimentalism.

American music, like the American experience itself, is rooted in the cultures of Europe, Africa, the Orient, and Latin America. Now it stands, brave and free, a monument to *our* culture, and a source of infinite pleasure and stimulation.

GLOSSARY

A

Abstract Expressionism A mid-twentieth-century art style in which painters allowed chance to determine aspects of their work.

a cappella Unaccompanied. Term used for choral music performed without instrumental accompaniment.

accent A strong sound.

acculturation The process by which one culture absorbs characteristics of another.

acid rock Sometimes called "psychedelic rock." Music that attempts to evoke the sensations experienced by a person under the influence of LSD.

acoustic instrument A natural, as opposed to electric, musical instrument.

Ainsworth The Pilgrims' psalter, published in Holland in 1612.

Alberti bass A broken-chord pattern used as an accompaniment in keyboard music.

aleatoric music Sometimes referred to as **chance** or **indeterminate** music. Music in which the composer has left significant decisions to the performer or to chance. An extreme example is called **random** music.

alto or **contralto** The low female singing voice.

answer In a fugue, the second presentation of the subject, at the dominant.

anthem A through-composed religious song, usually with a biblical text, to be performed by a choir rather than the congregation.

aria A songlike piece in opera, oratorio, or other dramatic vocal work.

armonica or **glass harmonica** A musical instrument invented by Benjamin Franklin.

arpeggio The notes of a chord played successively in ascending order.

arrangement In jazz, a written musical score that includes most or all of the notes to be played.

art rock A blend of rock and serious concert music styles.

art song The setting of a secular poem by a recognized poet to music by a known composer. Intended for concert or recital performance.

atonality Music that has no tonic note or tonal relationships.

augmentation A rhythmic variation in which note values are doubled, making a theme twice as slow as it was originally.

autoharp A folk instrument played by strumming the strings with one hand and pressing chord buttons with the other.

B

backbeat A heavy accent on the normally weak second and fourth beats of a measure in quadruple meter.

ballad A folk song, strophic in form, that tells a story.

ballade A character piece in dramatic or heroic style.

ballad opera An English dramatic form in which comedy and satire were set to popular tunes.

ballet A formal, stylized dance form that evolved in seventeenth-century France.

bamboula A dance in duple meter, with strongly marked accents, particularly popular in nineteenth-century New Orleans.

banjo A string instrument, usually with six strings, derived from a folk instrument brought by slaves from Africa.

Baroque The dramatic, emotional artistic style prevalent from about 1600 to 1750.

bass The low male singing voice.

bass clef (𝄢) Usually used to notate lower pitches.

Bay Psalm Book A psalter; the first book printed in America.

beat Another word for pulse in music.

bebop A complex, highly improvised jazz style, largely developed by Charlie Parker and Dizzy Gillespie.

berceuse Lullaby; a character piece with the mood of a lullaby.

big bands Popular dance ensembles of the 1930s and 1940s, consisting of twelve to eighteen players in brass, reed, and rhythm sections.

binary form A two-section form, the first section beginning in the tonic and modulating to the relative major or another key, and the second beginning in the new key and returning to tonic.

bitonality Two keys at the same time.

bluegrass A commercial instrumental style derived from mountain music.

blue notes Flexible notes, usually slightly under normal pitch.

blues A black vocal folk music.

blues scale A seven-note scale in which the third and seventh, and sometimes the fifth and sixth, notes are expressively lowered.

bones A folk percussion instrument consisting of a pair of castanets tied together and held in one hand.

boogie-woogie or **piano blues** A popular piano style with the form and harmony of the blues, but a faster tempo and a dance beat.

Boston Classicists Nickname for members of the Second New England School of composers.

break A dramatic, unstable, strongly rhythmic section, as in a march.

broken chord The notes of a chord played in succession, one at a time.

broken triad The notes of a triad played in succession.

burlesque A variety show featuring satirical humor; later associated with striptease acts.

C

cadence A melodic or harmonic closing pattern.

cadenza A passage for solo instrument within an ensemble work. In keyboard music, a virtuosic passage for one finger at a time.

Cajun Acadian. A French-speaking people who settled in Louisiana in the eighteenth century.

cakewalk A plantation dance with syncopated melodies, including the short-LONG-short figure characteristic of ragtime.

call-and-response A method of performing music, based upon African customs, in which a leader sings a line or verse and the participating group responds with a repeated phrase or refrain.

canon A polyphonic composition in which all of the voices perform the same melody, beginning at different times.

cantata A relatively short choral work on a religious or secular subject, accompanied by organ or orchestra.

Carnegie Hall A recital and concert hall in New York City.

chamber music Music for a small number of instruments, with one instrument per line of music.

chamber opera An opera for a small number of performers.

chamber orchestra A small orchestra with a few instruments per line of music.

changing meters A different number of beats to the measure within a piece or section.

chantey A song about the sea.

character piece A relatively short piano piece, often in ternary form, of a characteristic style or mood.

chorale A religious song with simple tune and vernacular language.

chord A meaningful combination of three or more tones.

choreography The steps and movements of dancers.

chorus A large choral ensemble, or choir. In a Tin Pan Alley song, the refrain or tuneful section repeated after each verse.

chromatic tones Tones that do not belong in a particular major or minor scale.

Classical period The period from about 1750 to 1820, also known as the Age of Reason.

classical style A restrained, objective style of art. Spelled with a capital letter, refers to music of the Classical period.

claves A pair of wooden cylinders, one of which is struck against the other.

clef A sign placed on the staff that fixes the pitch of each line and space.

coda A closing section. (Coda means "tail" in Italian.)

coloratura Brilliant vocal display, usually consisting of extremely high pitches sung with neutral syllables.

combo. A small jazz ensemble.

compound meter Each beat in a measure is divided by three.

concert band An instrumental ensemble that includes brass, woodwind, and percussion instruments, and sometimes cellos or string basses as well. Also called a **symphonic band.**

concertina A kind of accordion or portable reed instrument. Melody and chords are achieved by depressing buttons or keys, and the wind is supplied by a folding bellows.

concerto A multimovement (usually three-movement) composition for orchestra plus a solo instrument.

concerto grosso A Baroque composition for orchestra and a small group of solo instruments. The form has been revived by some twentieth-century composers.

concert overture A one-movement programmatic orchestral composition, often inspired by literature and dramatic in style. The organization is generally intellectual as well as programmatic.

concrete music or **musique concrète** Music that has been created by manipulating taped sounds.

conservatory A professional music school.

consonance Musical sounds that seem to be passive or at rest.

container rattles Sound instruments consisting of a container made of gourd, hide, or other material, with a rattle element inside. They are shaken to make a sound.

continuum of pitches The continuous series of pitches of a voice or instrument, including those that lie between half steps.

contour The shape or outline of a melody formed by its notes.

contrapuntal Another term for **polyphonic.**

cool jazz A restrained style introduced about 1950 for large bands that included some symphonic instruments.

Copland-Sessions concerts A series of concerts sponsored by Aaron Copland and Roger Sessions from 1928 to 1931 for the purpose of promoting music by American composers.

cornet A brass instrument similar in shape to the trumpet, but smaller in size and more mellow (less brilliant) in timbre.

countermelody A melody performed together with another melody.

country-western Western music with a country flavor, including western swing, honky-tonk, and cowboy songs.

cover recording A re-recording of a popular record, usually to make it appeal to a broader audience.

Creole In nineteenth-century New Orleans, a person born in America of a family native to another country. Later the term was used for people of mixed racial heritage.

crossover Music that appeals to more than one kind of audience.

D

da capo "From the beginning." A three-part design (**ABA**), the last part a repeat (with or without embellishments) of the first.

dance piece A recital or concert piece reflecting the mood, style, meter, and tempo characteristic of a particular dance.

development In sonata-allegro form, the section that moves through many keys.

diatonic scales The major and minor scales.

diminution A rhythmic variation in which note values are halved, making a theme twice as fast as it was originally.

disco Commercial dance music popular in the 1970s.

dissonance Musical sounds that imply tension, drive, or activity. More generally, sounds that are not consonant.

Dixieland A white imitation of New Orleans-style jazz.

dominant triad The triad built upon the fifth note of the major or minor scale, and the chord most closely related to tonic.

doo-wop The name given backup vocal ensembles that accompanied Motown singers, often by singing neutral or nonsense syllables.

do, re, mi, fa, sol, la, ti The syllables of the major or minor scale.

double bass (See **string bass.**)

drone A single tone, sounded continuously or repeated.

duet An aria for two singers who sing different lines of music.

dynamic level The level of volume (loudness or softness) of a musical sound.

E

eight-to-the-bar The ostinato that accompanies a boogie. Each of the four counts in a measure is divided into a long and a short beat.

electronic synthesizer An electronic sound generator capable of producing, imitating, and altering sounds.

elements of music The basic materials of which music is composed: rhythm, meter, melody, harmony, and timbre.

en pointe The female ballet dancer's technique of dancing on the tips of her toes.

ensemble A performing group. In music theater, a group of solo singers, each performing different words and music at the same time.

ensemble finale An ensemble scene at the end of an act or at the end of the show.

ethnomusicologist A scholar who studies the music of other cultures.

étude A study of a virtuosic technique. An étude may be an exercise to build technique, or it may be suitable for concert or recital performance.

experimentalist A composer who challenges traditional concepts of musical sound.

exposition The first section of a fugue or a sonata-allegro.

Expressionism A style of art that explores the mind and expresses raw emotion.

F

falsetto The singing voice above the normal (full or chest voice) range.

fanfare A brief, dramatic piece for brass instruments, with the character of an announcement or celebration.

federal period The period in American history that succeeded the American Revolution.

fiddle A precursor of the violin, smaller and lighter than the modern instrument. (The term is sometimes used today as a colloquialism for the violin.)

field holler An emotional vocal phrase, sung as a long, loud shout, developed by blacks as a kind of communication with fellow workers.

fife A small flute.

figured bass A system of musical shorthand by which composers indicated intervals above the bass line with numbers instead of notated pitches.

finale In music theater, the final scene of an act or of the show.

fingerboard A board on the synthesizer that is uninterrupted by keys or frets, allowing a player to slide through the continuum of pitches.

First New England School America's first composers. Also known as Yankee pioneers and singing school masters, they lived in New England in the late eighteenth century and wrote music to use as teaching materials.

flat (♭) Lowers a tone one-half step.

flute A wind instrument capable of producing a series of pitches. The flute is the only true melodic instrument found in American Indian cultures today.

folk music Usually music of unknown origin, handed down by oral tradition and enjoyed by the general population. Also, pieces deliberately composed in that style.

folk rock The addition of light rock effects to urban folk music.

forte Loud (**f**).

fortepiano The early piano, smaller and less sonorous than the modern instrument.

fortissimo Very loud (**ff**).

fortississimo Extremely loud (**fff** or **ffff**).

fox-trot (See two-step.)

frame drum A narrow frame covered by a membrane and struck with a drumstick or beater. The drum may or may not have a handle.

free jazz A style of free improvisation introduced by Ornette Coleman in 1960.

frequency The rate of a sound wave's vibration.

fuging tune A song in two sections, the first homophonic and the second polyphonic in texture.

fugue A polyphonic composition, originally for keyboard instruments, in which the imitative entrances of the voices alternate between tonic and dominant.

funk A music style rooted in soul, with lyrics that often express interracial concerns.

fusion or **jazz rock** A blend of rock instrumentation with the improvisation and flexible rhythms of jazz.

G

gamelan An Indonesian percussion ensemble.

Geneva Psalter The first complete psalter. It was published in French by Calvinists in Geneva, Switzerland, in 1551.

Gilbert and Sullivan operettas Comic English musicals, with words by W. S. Gilbert and music by Arthur Sullivan.

glass harmonica or **armonica** A musical instrument invented by Benjamin Franklin.

glee A part-song with three or more lines of music, in chordal or homophonic texture, with the melody usually in the top voice.

glissando An expressive slide between pitches.

glockenspiel An instrument consisting of a series of steel bars struck with a mallet.

Great Awakening An eighteenth-century revival movement that sought to Christianize whites and blacks alike.

Great Revival or **Second Awakening** A continuation and intensification of the evangelistic movement begun in the eighteenth century.

Gregorian chant The collection of Roman Catholic chants organized by Pope Gregory in the sixth century.

H

half step The smallest interval on a keyboard, and the closest interval in traditional Western music.

Harlem A black neighborhood in uptown New York City that became an important center for jazz.

harmony The simultaneous sounding of two or more different tones.

heavy metal A music style with a loud, heavily electronic, and often distorted sound.

hillbilly music The term applied to early country music.

homophony The texture in which a melodic line is accompanied by chordal harmony.

honky-tonk A Texas vocal style with harsh, honest lyrics.

Hudson River School The first important school of American painters.

hymn A religious verse set to music suitable for congregational singing.

I

Impressionism A style of art, and later music, that avoids definite statement in favor of suggestion and atmosphere.

impromptu A piece that sounds spontaneous or improvisatory in character.

improvisation The simultaneous invention and performance of music.

incomplete repetition form A formal structure or pattern in which the first part of a song is not repeated in successive renditions. It may be illustrated graphically as **AABCD BCD.**

indeterminacy Another term for chance or aleatoric music.

interval The distance between two tones.

inversion The term for a twelve-tone row played in its inverted or upside-down version.

irregular meters Meters other than duple, triple, or quadruple.

J

jam To improvise together informally.

jazz A means of performing music. There are many moods and styles, but improvisation is an inherent characteristic of jazz.

jazz rock or **fusion** A blend of rock instrumentation with the improvisation, lighter beat, and flexible rhythms of jazz.

jew's harp A folk musical instrument consisting of a small metal frame, held between the teeth, with an elastic strip that is plucked by the fingers.

K

kabuki A highly stylized form of Japanese music drama.

key or **tonality** The name of the tonic upon which a tonal piece is based.

key signature The number of sharps and flats in a key.

K. numbers These refer to the **Koechel catalogue,** in which Mozart's works are organized in approximately chronological order.

L

leading tone The seventh note of a major or (often) minor scale; so called because it is a half step that implies resolution to the nearby tonic.

legato Smooth, uninterrupted.

Les Six Six French composers who shared a dislike for German Romanticism and often found popular music a source of inspiration for their works. They were Georges Auric, Louis Durey, Arthur Honegger, Darius Milhaud, Francis Poulenc, and Germaine Tailleferre.

libretto The words of an opera or other dramatic vocal work.

lifeways Term used by Native Americans for the cultural norms, values, and ceremonies by which mankind lives.

linear polyphony The texture in which two or more lines of music have independent melodic interest and should be heard in a linear fashion rather than as part of chords.

lining out The practice of having each line of a psalm tune sung by a leader and echoed by the congregation.

log drum A drum made from a hollowed-out log. It may have one or two heads, and may be either tall with a small diameter or short with a large diameter. The former is played by one or two people. The latter, called a **powwow drum,** is played by several people.

long meter Four-line verse with eight syllables per line.

M

MacDowell Colony An artists' colony established on the estate of Edward MacDowell in Peterboro, New Hampshire.

major and **minor scales** The tonal scales upon which most Western music has been based for nearly four centuries.

mandolin A pear-shaped plucked string instrument.

Mannheim School A group of composers of orchestral music in early eighteenth-century Mannheim, Germany.

marimba A musical instrument consisting of a series of wooden bars suspended over resonators and played with rubber- or felt-headed mallets.

Mass A musical setting for chorus, soloists, and orchestra of portions of the Roman Catholic church service.

mazurka A Polish folk dance of varying character, in triple meter.

measure A unit containing a number of beats.

melody A meaningful succession of pitches.

Mennonites A German Protestant sect.

metallophone A percussion instrument consisting of metal keys suspended over a bronze or wooded frame and struck with a mallet.

meter The organization of rhythm into patterns of strong and weak beats.

metric modulation Elliott Carter's term for changing from one metrical pattern to another by systematically lengthening or shortening the value of a basic note.

metronome An instrument to measure tempo.

Metropolitan Opera House An important opera house in New York City.

microtones Tones that lie somewhere between half steps.

minimalism A style of music based upon many repetitions, with gradual and slight variations, of simple melodic and rhythmic patterns.

minstrel show A performance in which white men perform music and comedy in imitation of stereotypical blacks.

modal Music based upon one of the modes.

mode A seven-note scale that may be played, beginning on any white key on a keyboard, using white keys only.

modern dance A contemporary American dance form, less stylized than classical ballet.

modulate To change keys systematically, usually by using a tone or tones common to both keys as a pivot.

monophony The musical texture consisting of one melodic line.

Moravians Europeans who settled in Pennsylvania and whose music compositions and performances were of highly professional quality.

motive A melodic fragment that is repeated and developed throughout a piece or section.

Motown A highly successful black company that recorded, published, and sponsored black popular music.

movement One section of a large composition, such as a symphony. Each movement has a formal design and a degree of independence.

multimedia shows
Performances including some combination of music, dance, film, slides, tape recordings, and other sound and visual techniques.

musical comedy A play with music, in which the elements of entertainment are connected by a plot.

musicianship A combination of qualities, including sensitivity to style, accuracy, originality, expressiveness, and virtuosity.

musique concrète See **concrete music.**

N

Nashville sound Country music's response to rock and roll, with country themes, pop instrumentation, and a heavy beat.

nationalism A nineteenth-century movement in which artists of many nationalities sought to express the particular characteristics of their own cultures.

Negro spiritual A traditional religious song of black Americans, with texts based upon the Bible and upon the black experience in America.

neoclassical music The twentieth-century approach to the classical style of music.

neoclassical style The eighteenth-century style of painting and architecture inspired by the arts of ancient Greece and Rome.

neoromantic music The twentieth-century approach to the romantic style of music.

new music The term used for music of an experimental nature.

New Orleans-style jazz Virtuosic improvisation by members of a jazz combo on a given melody.

new wave A term encompassing several music styles, all conceived within the context of modern studio and electronic techniques.

nocturne A piece about the moods of night.

notes The symbols by which music is written down.

O

octave The interval of an eighth.

octave displacement The choice of a note of the same letter name from a distant octave.

op art Combines lines and colors to create optical illusions.

opera A drama that is sung, usually with orchestral accompaniment.

opéra bouffe A French style of operetta, featuring satirical humor and visual spectacle.

operetta or **light opera** A form of music theater in which the music and dancing are closely integrated with the plot.

opus The opus number indicates the chronological order in which a music piece was written or, more often, published.

oral tradition The passing on of traditions (songs, dances, rituals, ceremonies) by word of mouth rather than by written documents.

oratorio A dramatic work based on a religious subject and performed by vocal soloists and chorus with orchestral accompaniment.

ostinato A repeated melodic and/or rhythmic pattern.

overture An instrumental introductory piece to a dramatic work. Also see **concert overture.**

P

pan-Indian styles Ideas, songs, and ceremonies used by Indian peoples of different cultures. For example, a pan-Indian powwow may include people from five or six tribes.

patter songs A feature of Gilbert and Sullivan operettas (and other forms of music theater) in which humorous words are sung very rapidly, with comic effect.

payola The acceptance by disc jockeys of money and gifts in return for plugging recordings.

pentatonic scale A five-note scale within the range of an octave.

pianissimo Very soft (**pp**).

pianississimo Extremely soft (**ppp** or **pppp**).

piano Soft (**p**).

pianoforte Early name for the modern piano; larger and stronger than the earlier fortepiano.

pitch The highness or lowness of a sound.

pizzicato The technique of plucking rather than bowing string instruments.

plainsong, plainchant, or **chant** Music to which portions of the Roman Catholic service are sung. Chant is sung in unison and in flexible, unmetered rhythm.

pointillism An art style related to Impressionism, in which tiny dots of pure color seem to blend when viewed from a distance.

polonaise A stately, festive Polish folk dance, in triple meter.

polymeters Two or more meters performed simultaneously.

polyphony The simultaneous combination of two or more melodic lines.

polyrhythms Two or more simultaneous rhythmic patterns.

polytonality Two or more keys at the same time.

pop art A style of painting that uses familiar, often commercial, subjects from everyday urban life.

post-Romanticism A general term for several romantic styles that succeeded the dominance of German Romanticism.

powwow A contemporary pan-Indian gathering for singing, dancing, rodeo, carnival, and other celebrations.

prepared piano A grand piano on which some or all of the strings have been "prepared" by placing foreign materials on them to alter pitch, timbre, and dynamic level.

Primitivism A style of art and music that emphasizes the relaxed, sometimes savage experience of life in uncivilized societies.

process music Steve Reich's term for music whose form can be heard to evolve from the repetition of patterns slightly out of synchronization with each other.

program music Instrumental music that describes a story, scene, idea, or event.

program symphony A symphony organized according to programmatic concepts, as opposed to principles of abstract or absolute music.

progressive jazz A symphonic approach to jazz, introduced by Stan Kenton.

Protestant Reformation A sixteenth-century movement of protest against certain procedures of the Catholic church.

psalms One-hundred-fifty inspirational verses in the Bible.

psalm tunes Tuneful settings of the psalms in versions suitable for congregational singing.

psalter A collection of the psalms in rhymed, metered verse.

pueblos Towns or cities built by Indians living in the America Southwest. The term also refers to the people.

punk A music style that expressed the British reaction to flagrantly commercial rock and roll.

Q

quarter tone The interval halfway between a half step.

quintuple meter Five beats per measure.

R

race records The term used before 1949 by the popular music industry for recordings intended for a black audience. Later called **rhythm and blues.**

ragtime A written piano music, duple in meter and moderate in tempo. The left hand generally marks the beat while the right hand plays a syncopated melody.

rap Rapid spoken patter accompanied by funk-style rhythms, derived from reggae performance practices.

rasp A sound instrument consisting of a stick with notches cut into one side. It is scraped by another stick or object.

recapitulation In sonata-allegro form, the revised restatement of material presented in the exposition.

recitative A declamatory setting of a text, with rhythms and inflections related to those of speech. Used in opera and other dramatic vocal works. May be accompanied by a keyboard instrument or continuo (**dry recitative** or **recitativo secco**) or by an orchestra (**accompanied recitative**).

reed organ (**parlor organ, cabinet organ, cottage organ, melodeon**) A keyboard instrument popular in the nineteenth century for its relatively small size and price, the variety of sound produced by adjusting its stops, and the small amount of maintenance it required.

reeds Wind instruments in which the player causes small, flexible pieces of material called reeds to vibrate. Clarinets and saxophones are single-reed instruments, and oboes and bassoons have double reeds.

reggae A blend of rock and African-Jamaican styles.

relative major and **minor** Keys that share the same key signature but have a different tonic.

reprise In music theater, the repetition of a song heard earlier in the show.

responsorial singing style A solo voice alternates with a chorus of singers.

rest The cessation of musical sound. Also the sign that notates silence.

revue Originally, a lavishly staged and costumed musical show with no integrated plot. Later, a series of scenes united by a theme but without a plot.

rhythm The arrangement of time in music.

rhythm and blues (**R and B**) Broadly, black popular music of the 1950s. More specifically, a black popular style in quadruple meter, with strong backbeats and a danceable tempo.

rhythmicon An instrument invented by Léon Thérémin and Henry Cowell for the purpose of reproducing rhythmic combinations beyond the capabilities of human performance.

riff A repeated rhythmic pattern that provides unity in a jazz composition.

rock A collective term encompassing many styles of popular music that evolved from and succeeded rock and roll.

rockabilly A close amalgamation of country music and rock and roll.

rock and roll A popular music of the mid-1950s to mid-1960s, combining characteristics of rhythm and blues and country-western music.

romantic style or **romanticism** Emotional, subjective style of art. The Romantic period of music was from about 1820 to 1900.

rondo An instrumental form consisting of three or more sections in which the first melodic material (**A**) alternates with other melodic sections (**B,** etc.), as for example, ABACA. The tempo is usually fast and the mood happy.

root position A chord sounded with the tone upon which it is based as the lowest pitch.

round A circular canon, or one that may be repeated indefinitely.

row A composer's arrangement of the twelve chromatic tones to organize a particular twelve-tone piece.

rubato Flexible rhythm and tempo. The word means "robbing" and refers to stealing from the tempo at some points and roughly repaying the lost time at others.

S

Sacred Harp, The A popular collection of hymns and spiritual songs, first published in 1844.

salsa A popular Cuban dance band music with rhythms derived from African-American dances.

scale A rising or descending pattern of pitches within the range of an octave.

scatting or **scat singing** Improvising on nonsense or neutral syllables.

score A notated composition.

Second New England School The first American composers to write significant works in all of the large concert forms. They lived in the late nineteenth and early twentieth centuries. Also called **Boston Classicists.**

sequence The repetition of a melodic pattern at different levels of pitch.

serialism (total serialism, serialization, serial technique) An extension of the twelve-tone technique, in which other aspects besides melody and harmony are arranged into series and systematically repeated throughout a composition.

shaped poems Poems that are conceived for the visual pattern they form on the page.

shape-note notation A method that assigns a shape to each of the syllables fa, sol, la, and mi, placing them on the staff in normal fashion.

shape of the sound wave As the shape of the sound wave is altered, the timbre of the sound changes.

sharp (#) Raises a tone one-half step.

shouts and **hollers** Simple but eloquent cries with which blacks communicated their joys and sorrows.

simple meter Each beat in a measure is divided in half.

singing school movement An effort begun by music amateurs in the early eighteenth century to teach New Englanders to read music and sing.

sitar A string instrument from India.

sonata A multimovement composition for one or two solo instruments.

sonata-allegro or **sonata form** A formal design including an exposition, development, and recapitulation, organized according to key relationships. Also called the "first-movement form."

song plugger A music store employee who played popular songs on the piano to demonstrate them for customers.

soprano The high female singing voice.

soul A fervent, emotional style of black music, rooted in gospel and the blues.

sound instruments Music instruments that hold up or support the songs in Indian cultures.

spiritual A traditional religious song with texts based upon the Bible. Spirituals (black or white) reflect the influence of African music customs and Protestant religious songs.

staccato Short, detached.

staff Five lines and four spaces upon which music is notated.

Sternhold and Hopkins The Puritans' psalter, published in England in 1562.

stops Levers or buttons that allow the player to adjust the timbres produced by certain keyboard instruments.

strain A melodic section in a rag, march, or other vernacular form of music.

stride piano A jazz piano style in which the left hand alternates low bass notes, on *one* and *three,* with mid-range chords, on *two* and *four.*

string bass or **double bass** A large string instrument, usually bowed in the symphony orchestra and plucked in a jazz combo, producing pitches an octave below those notated.

string quartet The most familiar chamber ensemble, consisting of two violins, a viola, and a cello.

string quintet A chamber ensemble of five string instruments, usually two violins, two violas, and a cello.

strophic form A song form with two or more verses set to the same music.

style The characteristic manner in which a composer uses the elements of music, formal design, and emotional expression.

subdominant triad The triad built upon the fourth note of the major or minor scale; the second most closely related chord to tonic.

subject The principal melodic theme of a fugue.

suite An instrumental work composed of several dances or other semi-independent pieces.

surfing songs Songs by the Beach Boys and other groups reflecting the easy California life-style.

suspension rattles Sound instruments consisting of a group of objects (shells, hooves) suspended from a stick that is shaken to produce the rattle sound.

sweet jazz Music with the sound and flavor of jazz, but arranged so that playing it requires little improvisation.

swing A term with many meanings, including (a) a mood of lilting spontaneity and (b) a danceable music played by big bands in the 1930s and 1940s.

swing eights A series of eighth notes played in uneven rhythm.

symphonic jazz Concert music with the sound and flavor of jazz, but without improvisation.

symphonic poem (See **tone poem.**)

symphony A multimovement orchestral composition.

syncopation The occurrence of accents in unexpected places.

T

tacet "Be silent." The word is used by composers to indicate that certain voices or instruments should not sound.

tambourine A small drum with metal disks that jingle when the instrument is struck or shaken.

tempo The rate of speed at which music is performed.

tenor The high male singing voice.

ternary form Three-part form (**ABA**).

terraced descending melody A melodic pattern that moves down in a stairstep-like pattern.

texture The manner in which melodic lines are used in music, whether or not accompanied by harmony.

theater scores Concert pieces that include visual and dramatic elements as well as music.

theme and variations An instrumental form in which a theme or melody recurs to provide unity, but in altered guises for variety.

theremin An early electronic instrument, invented about 1920 by Léon Thérémin.

third stream The combination, but not the blending, of jazz and classical music.

through composed A song form that contains new music throughout, such as **abcde.**

timbre The characteristic sound quality of a voice or instrument.

Tin Pan Alley The popular music publishing industry from the late nineteenth through the first half of the twentieth centuries.

tonality or **tonal system** The system of harmony based upon the major and minor scales, which has governed Western harmony since the seventeenth century.

tone A sound with a specific pitch.

tone cluster A chord, usually of several tones, built upon seconds.

tone poem or **symphonic poem** A one-movement orchestral piece whose form is based upon programmatic rather than abstract principles.

tonic The first and most important note of a tonal scale.

total serialism Also called **serialization** or **serial technique.** Application of the twelve-tone technique to other aspects of a composition, which may also be arranged into series and repeated systematically.

traditionalist A composer who makes no radical departures from the styles and conceptions of earlier music.

Transcendentalism A philosophy that relies upon intuition as the guide to truth.

transcription An arrangement of a piece so that it may be played by instruments other than those for which it was originally composed.

treble clef ($\flat$) Usually used to notate higher pitches.

Treemonisha An opera by Scott Joplin.

triad A chord formed of three alternate tones (as A-C-E).

trio A composition for three voices or instruments. Also, a section of a composition lighter in texture, softer in dynamic level, and sometimes more melodic than the rest of the piece.

tune A melody that is easily recognized, memorized, and sung.

twelve-bar blues The classic form of the blues, consisting of three-line stanzas with four bars or measures in each line.

twelve-tone technique A method of organizing music in which all twelve tones of the octave are of equal significance.

two-step or **fox-trot** An American dance derived from ragtime.

U

unison The same pitch, performed at the same or at different octaves.

urban blues Blues pieces written for publication and professional performance.

V

vaudeville A show with acts of every variety, including blackface, dogs, circus stunts, songs, and dance.

verismo Realism in opera.

vernacular The common language. In music, the term refers to popular music.

verse The section of a Tin Pan Alley song that tells the story.

vibrato A slight variation in pitch that adds warmth and intensity to vocal or instrumental sounds.

viol A bowed string instrument, precursor of the modern violin.

virginal A small keyboard instrument, similar to a harpsichord.

virtuoso A performer who has dazzling technical brilliance.

W

waila The contemporary dance genre of the Pimas and O'odham of southern Arizona, adopted from the Norteño style of Mexican music in the later nineteenth century.

walkaround A lively plantation song-and-dance routine that often formed the finale of a minstrel show.

walking bass A steadily moving pattern in the plucked string bass, with melodic as well as rhythmic implications.

waltz A ballroom dance in triple meter.

washboard Originally a laundry board scraped for its sound effects as a music "instrument." Modern imitations are strapped onto the player for easy access.

Wa-Wan Press A publishing company established by Arthur Farwell and dedicated to the publication of American music.

western swing The Texas swing band style, influenced by Mexican and Hawaiian sounds and jazz.

whistle A wind instrument that produces only a single pitch.

white spiritual A folklike religious song with a simple tune whose text often includes repeated phrases.

whole step The interval equal to two half steps.

Y

yodel A singing technique that involves changing rapidly back and forth between the normal and the falsetto voice.

Z

Ziegfeld Follies Elegant revues produced by Florenz Ziegfeld nearly every year from 1907 to 1932 to glorify the American girl.

zydeco A rock-flavored Cajun style of popular music.

INDEX